Public Support for Market Reforms
in New Democracies

Do people in new democracies that are undergoing market reforms turn against these reforms when the economic adjustment is painful? The conventional wisdom is that they do. According to economic voting models, citizens punish elected governments for bad economic performance. The contributors to this collection, in contrast, begin with the insight that citizens in new democracies may have good reasons to depart from the predictions of economic voting. If they believe the prediction that, with the transition to a market economy, economic conditions must deteriorate before they improve, they may interpret short-term deterioration as a signal that the transition is on course and things will improve in the future. If they perceive that not the government but forces from the past are responsible for economic deterioration, they may exonerate the government. With similar datasets from three new democracies in Europe (Spain, the former East Germany, and Poland) and three in Latin America (Mexico, Peru, and Argentina), the authors probe citizens' calculus of support for governments and economic reforms under changing economic conditions.

Susan C. Stokes is Professor of Political Science at the University of Chicago and Director of the Chicago Center on Democracy. Professor Stokes is the author of *Cultures in Conflict: Social Movements and the State in Peru* and *Mandates and Democracy: Neoliberalism by Surprise in Latin America* (2001, Cambridge University Press) and coeditor of *Democracy, Accountability, and Representation* (1999, Cambridge University Press). She has published articles in scholarly journals in the United States, Latin America, and Europe.

Cambridge Studies in Comparative Politics

General Editor
Margaret Levi *University of Washington, Seattle*

Associate Editors
Robert H. Bates *Harvard University*
Peter Hall *Harvard University*
Stephen Hanson *University of Washington, Seattle*
Peter Lange *Duke University*
Helen Milner *Columbia University*
Frances Rosenbluth, *Yale University*
Susan Stokes *University of Chicago*
Sidney Tarrow *Cornell University*

List continues on page following the Index.

Public Support for Market Reforms in New Democracies

Edited by

SUSAN C. STOKES
University of Chicago

CAMBRIDGE
UNIVERSITY PRESS

PUBLISHED BY THE PRESS SYNDICATE OF THE UNIVERSITY OF CAMBRIDGE
The Pitt Building, Trumpington Street, Cambridge, United Kingdom

CAMBRIDGE UNIVERSITY PRESS
The Edinburgh Building, Cambridge CB2 2RU, UK
40 West 20th Street, New York, NY 10011-4211, USA
10 Stamford Road, Oakleigh, VIC 3166, Australia
Ruiz de Alarcón 13, 28014 Madrid, Spain
Dock House, The Waterfront, Cape Town 8001, South Africa

http://www.cambridge.org

First published 2001

Printed in the United States of America

Typeface Janson Text 10/13 pt.   *System* QuarkXPress [BTS]

A catalog record for this book is available from the British Library.

Library of Congress Cataloging in Publication Data
Public support for market reforms in new democracies / edited by Susan C. Stokes.
     p.   cm. – (Cambridge studies in comparative politics)
     Includes bibliographical references and index.
     ISBN 0-521-66339-3 – ISBN 0-521-66341-5 (pbk.)
     1. Economic policy – Citizen participation – Case studies.   2. Democracy – Case
studies.   3. Latin America – Economic policy – Citizen participation – Case studies.
4. Germany – Economic policy – 1990 – Citizen participation.   5. Poland – Economic
policy – 1990 – Citizen participation.   6. Spain – Economic policy – Citizen
participation.   I. Stokes, Susan Carol.   II. Series.
HD87.P833   2001
338.9 – dc21

                                                                    00-065150

ISBN   0 521 66339 3   hardback
ISBN   0 521 66341 5   paperback

Contents

Contributors

Christopher J. Anderson
Department of Political Science
State University of New York at
  Binghamton
Binghamton, New York USA

Fabián Echegaray
Department of Psychology
Federal University of
  Florianopolis
Santa Catarina, Brazil

Carlos Elordi
Department of Political Science
University of Connecticut
Storrs, Connecticut USA

Jorge Buendía Laredo
Department of Political Science
Centro de Investigación y
  Docencia Económica
Mexico City, Mexico

José María Maravall
Juan March Institute
Madrid, Spain

Adam Przeworski
Department of Politics
New York University
New York, New York USA

Susan C. Stokes
Department of Political Science
University of Chicago
Chicago, Illinois USA

Yuliya V. Tverdova
Department of Political Science
State University of New York at
  Binghamton
Binghamton, New York USA

1

Introduction

PUBLIC OPINION OF MARKET
REFORMS: A FRAMEWORK

Susan C. Stokes

The debate about how the economy shapes people's views of governments
has been long and intense. Much, as we shall see, is at stake: whether citizens in democracies have the capacity to induce governments to act in
their interest. The spread of democracy and the dramatic conversion of
governments to pro-market economic policies offer new opportunities
for understanding the link between economic performance and popular
opinion. The authors of this book analyze the dynamics of public opinion
in new democracies because we believe these experiences can shed light
on enduring questions about how democracies work.

What we find in this study is the following. Governments that embark
on painful adjustment are not always opposed by the public that must
endure the pain. In the six new democracies pursuing market reforms that
we study, people sometimes rally in support of governments and reforms
when times are hard. Sometimes they do so because they believe that hard
times now foreshadow good times ahead. Conversely, they may observe
good times now but believe that good news is a prelude to disaster. Sometimes painful adjustment makes people pessimistic about the future but
they still rally in support of the government, reasoning that the bad times
they experience are not the government's fault. Rather, the government's
reform program may be an antidote against today's ills and the force
needed to counteract opposition to change. Some painful costs are just too

This book draws on some materials that first appeared in a special issue of *Comparative
Political Studies*, "Public Support for Market Reforms in Emerging Democracies,"
29(5):499–591. Thanks to John Baughman, Jorge Buendía, James Fearon, Gretchen Helmke,
Simon Jackman, David Laitin, Steve Pincus, and Adam Przeworski for comments. Todd
Benson and Gretchen Helmke provided excellent research assistance. Research supported by
Nation Science Foundation Grant SBR-9617796.

high, such as when many people are thrown out of work. But people are also surprisingly aware of trade-offs in the economy and the complexities of political responsibility.

The picture that emerges from our studies is important for democratic theory. Democracy is more than a mechanism by which people impose their immediate will on government. It can instead function to encourage governments to pursue the public good over the longer term, to hold governments accountable when they cause hardships that are unnecessary, and to hold them accountable when they avoid hardships that are necessary.

This introduction is organized as follows. In the first section I discuss the debate over how economic change influences citizens' support of governments and argue that the received wisdom, that support for governments rises and falls on the basis of economic performance, is too simple. Because our knowledge was basically restricted to the advanced industrial democracies where economies were relatively stable and governments were plausibly in control, retrospective economic voting came to be seen as an inherent feature of democracy. But in view of new experiences we see that economic voting is a variable and retrospective economic voting – turning against the government when current economic conditions deteriorate – just one of several possible values or categories of this variable. The claim that retrospective economic voting solves problems of democratic accountability should also be reconsidered.

In the second section I explain why people in new democracies pursuing deep pro-market transformations may be particularly prone to a logic of economic voting different from normal retrospective economic voting. In the third section I present alternatives to retrospective economic voting, alternatives that we might expect to encounter when people think that economic change may not be linear and when they think that the government is not responsible for the economic outcomes they observe. In the fourth section I place in a comparative perspective the new democracies dealt with in this book, outline the methods we have used to study public support of governments and reforms, and provide an overview of the chapters.

The Limits of Retrospective Economic Voting

I define retrospective economic voting as the linear extrapolation of past economic performance to the future and the use of these predictions in formulating postures of support or opposition toward the government. A voter who follows the predictions of normal retrospective economic voting observes past performance, assumes that past trends will persist into the future if the government remains in power (or if its policies do not change), and derives an opinion (or voting intention) about the government based on the expected trend. When a retrospective economic voter observes bad performance of the economy, she predicts continued bad performance under this government or these policies and turns against the government. When she observes good performance, she predicts continued good performance and supports the government.

Although there are dissidents, the majority view has favored the retrospective voting paradigm. Several factors explain its hegemony. First, considerable evidence from advanced industrial democracies has accumulated showing that past economic performance influences people's vote decisions and their support for governments, as measured in public opinion polls (Chapell and Keech, 1985; Hibbs, 1987; Kiewet and Rivers, 1984; Lewis-Beck, 1988; Markus, 1988; Nannestad and Paldam, 1994; Paldam, 1991; Tufte, 1978). The impact of economic performance on electoral outcomes and future economic performance is less robust (see Bartels, 1988a; Cheibub and Przeworski, 1998; Host and Paldam, 1990; Powell and Whitten, 1993; Remmer, 1991). Writers often assume that if past performance has a significant impact on support, then prospective considerations are irrelevant, although logically both may affect support. In contrast to the extensive literature on retrospective economic voting, less has been done to study the impact of predictions of the future on voting and support, the influence of past performance on predictions (Bartels, 1988a; Bratton, 1994; Johnston, Feldman, and Knight, 1987; Langue, 1994; Lewis-Beck, 1988; Lockerbie, 1992; Mackuen, Erickson, and Stimson, 1992), and the role of campaign messages and other sorts of campaign-generated information on support (see Alvarez, 1997; Sniderman, Glaser, and Griffin, 1990).

Retrospective voting also seemed appealing because it held out the promise that retrospectively oriented voters would induce governments to be responsive. Theories of democracy, such as Downs's *Economic Theory of Voting* (1957), involved voters who were prospective (in that they paid attention to campaign promises) and governments that were responsive, because governments would try to pursue policies that were popular and hence allow them to be reelected.

Yet this model came under attack. Empirical studies of elections and voting behavior in the United States in the 1950s and 1960s painted a picture of voters as lacking information about candidates and policies and lacking preferences about policies (the Michigan School) and of campaigns as devoid of policy information and persuasive power (the Columbia School; for an excellent review see Alvarez, 1997). Voters were driven by party attachments inherited from their parents and by symbols, emotions, and what we would now call *identities* (Edelman, 1964). Later scholars pointed out that if officeholders had interests at odds with those of voters and their actions were not fully observable by voters, then candidates' policy pronouncements were not credible (Alesina, 1988; Ferejohn, 1986; see also McKelvey, 1976). Furthermore, democracies lack institutions to enforce imperative mandates (Manin, 1997). Prospective voting – listening to campaign policy pronouncements and voting for the candidate whose pronouncements most closely approximated one's own – appeared to be not just an unrealistic description of how people vote but a feeble mechanism of representation.

The retrospective voting model claimed to solve these problems and thus held out again the possibility of representative government. Voters simply set a standard for economic performance (or, more generically, welfare), observe their welfare at the end of the term, and reelect governments when performance meets the standard or elect challengers when performance falls below the standard. No one need have policy preferences or know the position of candidates or the policies enacted by incumbents. The anticipation of this retrospective evaluation will induce governments to work as hard as they can to improve voters' welfare (Fiorina, 1981; Key, 1996; Manin, 1997; Mayhew, 1974). Hence retrospective voting induces representation.

But in the enthusiasm for retrospective voting the importance of messages conveyed in campaigns, through the press, and from the opposition has been sold short. As an empirical matter, people seem to listen to what politicians say and pay attention to other cues in campaigns (Bartels, 1988b; Graber, 1980; Iyengar and Kinder, 1987; Sniderman, Glaser, and Griffin, 1990; Zaller, 1989). McGraw, Best, and Trimpone (1995) find that experimental subjects support a hypothetical legislator when the legislator offers ex post justifications of measures that had harmed voters. Sniderman et al. (1990) show that better-educated voters drew from a whole range of sources, and only indirectly from the past performance of the national economy, in deciding whom to vote for in the 1980 presidential election in the United States. Alvarez (1997) shows that campaigns reduce the ambiguity of candidate positions and that voters punish ambiguous campaigns. Fearon (1999)

4

reasons that, in addition to providing information about the policy positions of candidates, campaigns can send signals to voters about the underlying characteristics of candidates, characteristics that have some bearing on how well they will perform. Arnold (1993:409) writes that activists and the opposition may inform inattentive voters "when things are seriously out of line," inducing "citizen control" over politicians.

Adherents of the retrospective voting paradigm doubt that voters *should* pay attention to what politicians say, as opposed to what they do: "Citizens are not fools. Having often observed political equivocation, if not outright lying, should they listen carefully to campaign promises?" (Fiorina, 1981:5). Yet we now know that voters have good reason to pay attention. In the advanced industrial democracies, party manifestos and campaign statements give reasonable predictions of what governments will do if they win the election (Budge, Robertson, and Hearl, 1987; Fishel, 1985; Klingemann, Hofferbert, and Budge, 1994; Krukones, 1984). And just as the desire for reelection may induce governments to behave in accord with citizens' interests, reelection pressures may also induce candidates to reveal in campaign messages their true intentions regarding policy (Harrington, 1993a, 1993b).

A certain revisionism also suggests that retrospective economic voting does not simplify the cognitive tasks facing voters as thoroughly as was once supposed. In the simple story, again, voters set a standard, observe their welfare at the end of the governmental term, and decide to reelect or reject the incumbent. But consider the following:

1. Empirical work in the United States and Europe shows that when people are retrospective, they pay attention not to their own welfare but to changes in the broader economy. In the terms coined by Meehl (1977), they are *sociotropic* and not *egocentric* (see Fiorina, 1981; Kinder and Kiewet, 1979; Lewis-Beck, 1988; Lockerbie, 1992). Sociotropism may enhance citizens' ability to control politicians (Ferejohn, 1986). And sociotropism may not be synonymous with altruism, as is typically supposed (see in particular Kramer, 1983). To see this, consider a person who thinks, not unreasonably, that the change in her family's income during a governmental term is jointly determined by idiosyncratic factors – the life cycle of the family's wage earners, the entry into or exit from the workforce of a family member – and overall trends in the economy. Overall economic performance, in turn, is jointly determined by the government's handling of economic policy and exogenous factors: a recession in a major trading power, the weather, and so on. Hence:

$$y_{it} = e_t + p_{it} \tag{1}$$

$$e_t = g_t + s_t \tag{2}$$

where y_{it} is the change in income to individual i during government term t, e_t is overall economic performance during the term, and p_{it} is the change in income of the individual during the term that is due to personal circumstances. In the second equation we treat overall economic change as due to government policy (g_t) and exogenous shocks (s_t).

If people are sociotropic – formulate opinions of the government based on overall economic performance, not their own – then they must know that general economic trends are only part of the story of their own fortunes, and that the government should be only partially exonerated or credited for economic performance. Yet even if people know this, they may not know what weights to attribute to each factor: Might I have gotten a bigger raise had the stock market performed better? Might the stock market have performed better had the government cut the deficit more quickly? Might I not have lost my job had my country not joined the European Economic Union? Our voter wants to use the vote to maximize her family income in the next governmental term: she is *ego-* or *family-centric*. Under full information she would simply reward a government that has maximized g_t (income due to government policy). But she does not observe g_t or know how it compares in magnitude to s_t (income due to external shocks). She observes her own income (y_{it}) but knows that it is a noisy signal of overall economic performance (e_t), let alone g_t. So she ignores it and instead uses e_t – itself a noisy signal of g_t but better than the change in her individual income during the term.

Hence if people are retrospective, sociotropic, and nonaltruistic but not fully informed, then they may (1) exonerate the government for changes in their private welfare over the past governmental term; (2) attribute general economic trends in the past to the government; but (3) forecast their private welfare in the future as a function of government policy. Such a thought process may not be unreasonable, but no formulation as simple as "observing one's welfare" captures these subtleties.

2. Sociotropism, as we have seen, means that people don't simply observe how their household income has changed, whether or not a family member has lost a job, or the height of their stack of unpaid bills. Instead they derive some notion of "the economy" (e_t in equation 2). Yet e_t itself is not an unambiguous fact that one simply observes, as any social scien-

tist who works with macroeconomic data knows. How do voters develop a notion of overall changes in the economy? Perhaps they focus on one variable, say the inflation rate, or unemployment, or the general trend in real wages, or some combination. Or perhaps they meld together these sorts of measures as well as other kinds of information to arrive at a general notion of economic performance. Which dimension of the economy they care about is politically consequential, because one party may be seen as good at controlling prices, its opponents at creating jobs. Ronald Reagan's *misery index* (inflation + unemployment) was one politician's effort to guide people in their retrospective estimations of the economy, but how in general such formulations work we do not know. Do people listen to political rhetoric? Observe prices at the grocery store? Listen to neighbors' stories of getting laid off? Or to news reports about "downsizing"? Again, nothing so simple as "observing one's welfare" is sufficient.[1]

3. Whether people are egocentric or sociotropic, it's hard to believe they attribute all economic change to actions of the government (see Harrington, 1993a, 1993b; Kramer, 1983). The Maastricht Treaty, a recession in Japan, conditions set by the International Monetary Funal (IMF), a fight with the boss – all these could reasonably enter a person's mind as causes of general or personal welfare. People may still rationally vote as though the government was to blame for everything as a way to invest in nonshirking by governments in the future (see Grossman and Noh, 1990; but see Przeworski, Manin, and Stokes, 1999). Yet under some conditions people may have compelling reasons to exonerate the government and cast blame elsewhere (see Anderson, 1995), and might reasonably support the government even when times are hard (see later).

---

[1] In his influential article defending the egocentric or nonsociotropic interpretation, Kramer (1983) usefully shows the advantages of aggregate time series over cross-sectional data in detecting the effects of general economic change as opposed to idiosyncratic factors (my e_t versus p_{it}) on the popularity of the incumbent. The authors of this volume for the most part follow this methodological lead. Yet Kramer is on shaky ground when he claims that sociotropism is merely a statistical artifact. Imagine a world, he suggests, in which people's perceptions of the economy are entirely shaped by partisan attachments. The hypothetical finding that, cross-sectionally, partisan attachments and not "actual, measurable economic events" explained all the variance in popularity for the incumbent would not be grounds for the inference that the economy had no impact on votes. This is because the relationship of interest, "how *real* economic outcomes affect *actual* voting decisions" and not "economic or perceptual imagery," is the phenomenon of interest (95; emphasis in the original). One wonders what mysterious mechanism would connect "actual economic events" to voting decisions if not individuals' perceptions of these events.

4. If people care about the future and use the past to make forecasts, we must wonder how this forecasting is carried out. The unstated assumption of the retrospective voting literature is that the process is one of simple extrapolation. But is it? People must assume that if they reelect the incumbent, policies will be stable or will only change appropriately as conditions change. Yet the government itself may tell people not to extrapolate; if the past has been bad, the government almost surely will make this claim. Governments frequently try to influence people's forecasts, usually so that they will be more optimistic but sometimes so that they will be more pessimistic. The Italian government of Romano Prodi tried to persuade voters that reducing the fiscal deficit would create not "paradise but a nice purgatory with air conditioning and decent toilets" (*New York Times*, May 5, 1998). And if people listen to the government's messages about the past and how to extrapolate to the future, then they may also listen to the messages of the opposition, the press, co-workers, and so on.

5. Let's assume, with the retrospective economic voting school, that people forecast the future from the past and that these forecasts generate the standard of retrospective performance for the next election. If these forecasts also are to induce good performance by the government, then they must be accurate. Yet evidence suggests that they are not so accurate. Jackman (1995), for example, shows that in the United States people consistently overestimate future unemployment and underestimate future inflation (see also Bartels, 1988a).

We have seen, then, that retrospective economic voting is neither simple nor always rational and does not necessarily imply citizen control over politicians. It is certainly conceivable, and seems to square with the facts in many countries, that "as the economy goes, so goes the election." But there are many steps between economic performance and people's postures toward their government, with many opportunities for popular opinion to turn in unexpected directions. The next section discusses how a context of recent transition to democracy and of pro-market reforms bring such opportunities to the fore.

Pro-Market Reforms, New Democracies, and Economic Voting

People in new democracies undergoing drastic pro-market transformations have especially good reasons to abstain sometimes from retrospective economic calculations. Oddly, however, the leading hypothesis in scholarship on the politics of reforms is that people are retrospective with regard to the economy. Because rising unemployment, falling wages, and higher prices of state-subsidized goods and services are the predictable short-term effects of fiscal adjustment and structural reforms, retrospective voters reject reforms. Yet over the long run, it is believed, reforms are good for most people: "From a long-term perspective, the social benefits of reform outweigh the costs" assert Haggard and Webb (1993:158). Hence the central paradox, as noted by Rodrik (1996), of the politics of reforms literature: those who contribute to this literature believe that under democracy, people reject reforms that are (in the long term) good for them.

Indeed, a common view is that it was a shortsighted economic vision that got the economy into trouble in the first place. In societies with maldistributed income and widespread poverty, the poor and working classes demand improvement in their material existence and ignore budget constraints (Berg and Sachs, 1988; Sachs, 1990). Citizens' myopia about the economy infects their voting behavior as well, producing the politics of populism (Dornbusch and Edwards, 1991; Sachs, 1990). Populist politicians spend public funds to mobilize votes and in so doing generate unsustainable budget deficits, inflation, and, in the end, the need for austerity. The populist "cycle" (Dornbusch and Edwards, 1991) is actually a downward spiral. And myopia is chronic: after the painful period of adjustment citizens will thirst for populist largesse, even though past largesse left them worse off than before the populist cycle started.

Faced with an economic crisis, the public, fixated on short-term pain and ignoring long-term benefits, wants to delay adjustment. People use whatever instruments of resistance are available: lobbying, strikes, looting, elections. Elected governments, with the time horizon of a single term, are as shortsighted as their constituents. Because elected officeholders are more vulnerable than dictators to populist pressures, in this view, macroeconomic instability is endemic to poor democracies. On a more optimistic note, myopia can also be turned to the advantage of reforms: politicians can manipulate a policy "business cycle," imposing painful reforms early in the term in anticipation of resumed growth in the period leading up to the next election. Hence the calls for swift, stealthy measures that will beat democracy to the punch.

The populist myopia explanation for resistance to purportedly beneficial reforms has been bolstered by some case studies (see Dornbusch and Edwards, 1991; Sachs, 1990; Skidmore, 1977). But skeptics abound. Two crossnational statistical studies find that democracies are not less likely than dictatorships to impose stabilization programs (Haggard and Kaufman, 1989; Remmer, 1990). And it is by no means inevitable that voters reject incumbents who have pursued reforms (Gervasoni, 1995; Nelson, 1992). In Latin America, voters reelected governments in Peru, Argentina, Bolivia, and Costa Rica that had pursued deep structural adjustment programs.

In addition to these empirical facts, scholars have raised a number of theoretical objections to the populist myopia view. One challenge derives from a special interest theory of democracy: elected governments in the developing world are sensitive not to "the whims of the voting majority" but to the military and business (Remmer, 1990:355). Sachs, writing about Venezuelan reforms, draws on a similar underlying theory of democracy, although the enemy of popular sovereignty in his case is not the military but parties and unions: "[T]he political parties and major corporatist interests in the society . . . had increasingly failed to 'aggregate' social interests in a truly pluralistic and democratic manner. Increasingly, they had become the leading participants in a feeding frenzy in which privileged groups plundered the dwindling resources of the ever-weakening state" (Sachs, 1993:3). For both Remmer and Sachs, if reforms are blocked it is not by the people but by special interests. A second objection is that voters may support governments that manage the economy well, even if good management means imposing austerity (Nelson, 1992). A sense of crisis may lead voters to favor reforms (Grindle and Thomas, 1991; Keeler, 1993; Nelson, 1992; Remmer, 1991). And in new democracies, the recent history of authoritarianism may lead people to cut elected governments some slack (Haggard and Kaufman, 1992; Powers and Cox, 1997; Remmer, 1991; Rose and Mishler, 1996a). Particular groups of citizens, moreover, may not know ex ante about how they will fare under reforms (Haggard and Kaufman, 1989; but see also Fernandez and Rodrik, 1991).

Another set of skeptics views reforms as imposing real, and not just short-term, costs on a large number of people. Hence resistance to reform reflects a conflict of interests, a conflict that is deeper and more legitimate than special interests in a feeding frenzy. The costs may be borne by the urban popular sectors (Walton and Ragin, 1989), the labor movement (Roxborough, 1989), the lower income strata (Berry, 1997; Cortes and Rubalcava, n.d.), all those who are uncertain ex ante whether they will be shielded from severe losses such as unemployment (Fernandez and Rodrik, 1991), or, more abstractly, those whose resources will be tapped for fiscal adjustment (Alesina and Drazen, 1991).

10

Explanations of economic crises that point to causes beyond the control of national governments also, by implication, challenge the populist myopia model. Changes in the lending behavior of foreign creditors or an unfavorable shift in the terms of trade, trade volumes, or world interest rates: all are exogenous shocks making adjustment necessary that have little to do with domestic policy in developing countries. Similarly, high inflation, a principal symptom of crisis, may reflect supply rigidities or inertial forces (for a review see Conway, 1992).

Writing about the politics of pro-market reforms, some scholars find reasons why myopic retrospective voting may be suspended in new democracies or, for that matter, in old ones. Elections give parties an opportunity to mobilize mandates for reform (Keeler, 1993; Waterbury, 1989). New governments can also blame outgoing incumbents and exonerate themselves for the crisis necessitating adjustment (Haggard and Webb, 1993).

The very notion that pro-market reforms generate resistance has been challenged. Gervasoni (1995) claims that reforms effectively reduced inflation in Latin America and that this success explains the electoral victories of liberalizing incumbents. "Stabilization and structural reforms preached by the 'Washington Consensus' can constitute not only an adequate economic model," he concludes, "they can also be a convenient political strategy" (1995:50).[2] And even if people want to recover their prior standard of living after a sharp economic decline, they may support risky reforms over less risky alternatives (Weyland, 1996).

Going a step further, Rodrik (1996) challenges the very notion that reforms impose even short-term costs. On the one hand, his claim is simply empirical. He contends that disinflation in countries suffering triple-digit inflation will be expansionary, not contractionary, and that the effect on aggregate demand of substituting regular taxes for the inflation tax will be neutral and good for many individuals.[3] More interesting for our purposes is his claim that, even if the economy fails to grow over the short run after

[2] Gervasoni's observations include only elections between 1982 and 1985, and he fails to consider the impact of other economic outcomes, such as unemployment, real wages, and production, where performance has been weaker. Gervasoni points to Carlos Menem of Argentina and Alberto Fujimori of Peru as examples of liberalizing governments that succeeded in bringing down inflation and subsequently won reelection. Yet in both countries, high unemployment rates and stagnating wages weakened support for both presidents in their second terms.

[3] The claim is tendentious. In all but a handful of countries the short-term effects of stabilization have been lower output and investment and higher unemployment.

11

stabilization, people might well think they are better off than they would have been were stabilization delayed. "[E]ven if the economy continues to decline, one has to ask whether the outcome would not have been worse in the absence of the program" (1994:21–22).

How *might* we expect people living through adjustment programs in new democracies to interpret the economic changes they see around them? Their reasoning might be like Rodrik's: they see the economy stagnating after stabilization but reason that, absent reforms, times would have been harder still. Therefore in relative terms there is no short-term downturn and no rationale for opposition.

But Rodrik's logic is not the only one they could adopt. They might simply compare their welfare after reforms begin to their welfare immediately beforehand, and infer, à la retrospective economic voting, that reforms are bad. Or, following Weyland, if they are risk-prone after suffering losses, they might infer from early deterioration that policies are appropriately risky and support the government. Or, even if they are wary of risk, they might believe politicians and experts who tell them that things have to get worse before they can get better and interpret decline as a source of optimism for the future. Politicians and experts also tell citizens that defenders of the old order will resist reforms. If politicians are believed, when things get bad the public may think that opponents are gaining the upper hand and rally around the government and its program. Or people may be concerned about the distributional aspects of reforms. They may observe a decline in their welfare, believe that things will get better, but think that they or others have been asked to sacrifice too much.

Rodrik's claims about the cognitive orientation of voters under reforms, whatever their specific merits, at least force us to ask, "How might people respond to economic changes during periods of pro-market reforms?" (see also Przeworski, 1991). The contributors to this volume hope to pry open the black box by analyzing the response of public opinion to economic reform programs in six new democracies. In the next section I derive propositions about the impact of economic changes on public support for governments.

Alternatives to Retrospective Economic Voting

Up to this point, we have seen that retrospective economic voting is not as simple or normatively appealing as is claimed even in advanced industrial democracies in normal economic times, and that it may be perverse in new democracies undergoing radical economic transformations. In this section I develop alternatives to retrospective economic voting (or support)[4] that may make sense in places where democracy is new and where stabilization and structural reform programs are underway. What I will call *normal retrospective economic voting* implies some assumptions in the minds of people as they observe the economy and formulate opinions of the government, assumptions that the economic voting literature often leaves unexplored. (1) Voters extrapolate from past economic performance to form predictions about future performance. (2) Voters view the government's policies as having caused past economic performance (Berle, 1963). And (3) in assessing past performance, voters make neither invidious nor solidaristic comparisons.

If voters do not hold these assumptions, we would not necessarily expect normal economic voting. If politicians offer rationalizations of past downturns or promises that the future will be different and people believe them, they will not necessarily punish poor past performance. Similarly, voters might reelect a government that presided over bad economic times if, in the voters' view, the government was not to blame. And if voters have distributional as well as individual-welfare concerns, they might, say, oust a government that they viewed as having improved their welfare but at too high a cost to themselves or others.

I turn now to a discussion of alternatives to normal economic voting and suggest empirically observable evidence of different individual calculi of support.

1. *Normal economic voting.* Voters use the past performance of the government to predict future performance and see the government as responsible for that performance.

Observational expectation: economic decline induces pessimism about the future and disapproval of the government.

2. *Intertemporal posture.* "Unless the unemployment rate grows to 8 to 10 per cent this year, we will not be doing our job," a Czechoslovak

---

[4] The chapters in this volume are concerned exclusively with public opinion. I know of no literature that discusses the differences between responding to polls and voting. Yet clearly they are different: poll respondents are merely expressing a view, whereas voters are deciding who will run the government. Furthermore the survey questions we look at simply ask whether the respondent approves or disapproves of the president and program, whereas elections confront voters with alternatives.

finance minister declares. "It will cost us, but together we will make the Great Change" runs a Peruvian presidential candidate's slogan. We need a "tough, costly, and severe adjustment, requiring major surgery, no anesthesia," warns an Argentine president-elect.

The message is that people must suffer hard times in the near future if they are to enjoy prosperity later. To return to the formulation of the Italian prime minister cited earlier, if paradise is to be regained and hell avoided, a period in purgatory is required. This is a common theme in societies undergoing stabilization and structural reforms because, contra Rodrik, when these programs bring down inflation, stabilize external accounts, and create conditions for future growth, these successes generally come at the cost of a period of declining output, falling income, and increased unemployment. Following Przeworski (1993) I call the belief that if things get worse they will later get better *intertemporal*.

Politicians who wish to generate a mandate for reforms before elections, and retain support despite the pain after elections, employ a rhetoric that anticipates the J-shaped curve of economic performance. To the extent that people believe these predictions, their responses to economic conditions may depart from normal economic voting in two ways. First, they are paying attention to what politicians say about the future rather than simply looking at economic performance on the incumbent's watch; they are thus prospective rather than retrospective. Second, rather than believing that past economic performance predicts future performance directly, the public views the past and the future as inversely related. Particularly if the economy goes down, the public becomes optimistic about the future. And if the economy improves early on, the public may believe that reforms are failing and turn against the government, contrary to the predictions of normal economic voting.

In countries where inflation has hit double-digit rates *per month*, and where changes in wages and output have also been catastrophic, the public may be more focused on economic trends and may gain more information about the economy from direct observation than in advanced industrial democracies, where economic changes tend to be less abrupt. And certain salient shifts in the economy may provoke an intertemporal mindset, even without the prompting of politicians. For example, the public may from its own experience sense that good economic outcomes sometimes need to be traded off against each other: price stability comes at the cost of low output and low wages. With these trade-offs in mind the public may

14

observe, say, increases in real wages and infer that the economy is heading into a cycle of overstimulation and inflation, one that will leave them worse off than at the outset. Quite apart from politicians' admonitions, the public may adopt an intertemporal posture.

Observational expectation: an intertemporal posture is consistent with the finding that economic decline makes the public optimistic about future economic performance and supportive of the government.

3. *Exonerating posture.* "Fiscal adjustment is made necessary by the errors and mismanagement of the prior government," a Peruvian finance minister claims. "The causes of the striking economic indolence rest deeply embedded in the previous economic system," the official document of the Polish economic program begins. Normal economic voting requires that people believe the government is responsible, in a causal sense, for the performance of the economy. We might not expect people to turn against a government that was seen as having adopted the best policies possible but had presided over an economy that, for reasons beyond its control, had performed badly. Moreover, if citizens see their government as locked in a struggle against hostile forces for control over the economy, and if they view the current government's reforms as not the cause of but an antidote to "economic indolence," they may respond to deterioration by supporting the government overseeing reforms.

There are compelling reasons to believe that people in developing and post-Communist countries view their economies as substantially out of the control of governments. Reforms cover a vast range, from trade liberalization, to fiscal reform, to privatization of state enterprises, to deregulation, and on and on. At any given point after the initiation of reforms, the public might well believe that the enduring features of the inherited economic model or agents of the old regime, rather than the new model that the current government is attempting to put in place, are responsible for declining incomes, resurgent inflation, or unemployment. And to the extent that market reforms do entail pain up front, the reformist government may attempt to exonerate itself and implicate ghosts of the past. The old model, the public will be told, has its defenders in the parliament, the courts, the state enterprises, labor unions, and business associations. These opponents of change, as well as the budget deficits run up by the former government, are responsible for the hardship. The economic reform program, far from being the cause of hardships, is an antidote to them.

15

As with intertemporal politics, we would expect the public to favor the antidote – the economic reform program – whenever the symptoms of the illness flare up. As in intertemporal politics and as opposed to normal economic voting, people should approve of the government when the economy gets worse. And to the extent that this, like other antidotes, has its own painful side effects, people may turn against the government's program once conditions improve.

Like intertemporal politics, this pattern reflects a basically prospective mindset: the public takes account of other information including the pronouncements of politicians, rather than just of past economic performance. Yet an exonerating posture toward the government and an antidotal posture toward reforms should be empirically distinguishable from intertemporal politics. In the former, economic decline generates public optimism. In the latter, economic decline should not be associated with optimism. Indeed, hardships may mean that the government is losing its battle against the old model, and the public may become pessimistic when it observes the economic downturn.

Observational expectation: under an exonerating posture, bad times fail to produce public optimism but do produce support for the government and reforms.

4. *Distributional or oppositionist postures.* Many people living under reforms may foresee an intertemporal structure of benefits – the downturn now foreshadows improvement in the future – but nevertheless oppose the government and its policies. Perhaps they believe that the downturn will hurt their family, neighborhood, or region more than those of others and was therefore unfair. Or perhaps they believe that the downturn was more severe than was necessary, or that although the government's program will stimulate growth in the future, under the opposition the future would be still brighter.

Another posture, perhaps observationally equivalent to the distributional one, is one that Maravall and Przeworski in this volume call *oppositionist*. People hold partisan attachments to the opposition and will support it no matter what their appraisal of past economic performance or optimism for the future. It may be that they support their opposition party come hell or high water; or it may be that, in a kind of resolution of cognitive dissonance, even when they think the future will be good under the incumbent, they always believe the opposition's claim that it will perform better; or perhaps they are prone to wishful thinking, believe that

Introduction

Table 1.1. *Alternative Patterns of Public Responses to Economic Deterioration*

	Support Reforms/ Government	Oppose Reforms/ Government
Optimistic about future of economy	Intertemporal	Distributional or oppositionist
Pessimistic about future of economy	Antidotal or exonerative	Normal retrospective economic voting

their party will win in the future, and associate their party's future rule with good times ahead.

Observational expectation: bad times induce optimism about the future general trends in the economy but fail to mobilize support for the government or reforms.

Table 1.1 illustrates contrasting empirical observations consistent with normal economic voting, intertemporal politics, an exonerating/ antidotal posture, and distributional or oppositionist ones. Assuming economic *decline*, the public's response may be one of *optimism or pessimism* about future economic performance and *support for or opposition to* the government and the economic program. Normal postures fall into the southeast cell: people interpret deterioration as forecasting more deterioration in the future and hence turn against the government. Intertemporal postures fall into the northwest cell: the public expects economic performance to follow a J-curve, and therefore deterioration makes them optimistic about the future and they support the program and the government. Exonerating or antidotal attitudes fall into the southwest cell: economic deterioration means that the well-intentioned government does not control the economy, perhaps because the enemies of change have gained ground. The public interprets deterioration now as signaling further deterioration in the future and yet rallies around the government and reforms. Distributional and oppositionist postures fall into the northeast cell: people believe the future will be better, but their optimism does not carry over into support for the government, because they think either that the distribution of costs was unfair or that under the opposition the future would be better still.

To summarize, I have outlined four ways in which people living through a process of pro-market reforms may respond to economic hardships. They may observe decline, infer that decline will continue in the future, and blame the government (normal). They may observe decline, infer that prosperity is around the corner, and credit the government (intertemporal). They may observe decline, infer that hardships will continue in the future, blame the government's opponents, and support the government (exonerating). Finally, they may observe decline, infer that the economy as a whole will improve, but see the costs as too high for themselves or others or think the opposition would do better and turn against the government (distributional/oppositionist).

Case Selection

The chapters in this volume analyze the dynamics of public opinion during periods of pro-market reforms in six new democracies in Europe and Latin America. We selected these countries because they were undergoing deep economic transitions, and we had access to roughly similar datasets tracking public opinion over the course of the reforms. It is worthwhile to emphasize the overarching task of this volume: to show that a phenomenon (retrospective economic voting) previously considered to be an inherent feature of democracy is in fact a variable. Our task is to convince, from both logical and empirical standpoints, that the public's calculi of support for governments in response to the economy do in fact vary. The causes of this variation are merely suggested by our collective project. From the perspective of explaining this variation, our case selection does not follow the strictures of the comparative method. In the following section I offer a first cut at specifying factors that may explain variation in calculi of support. I speculate that these factors include the majority status of governments, the age of the democracy, the nature of the opposition, partisanship, and income distribution. The analysis in each chapter permits fairly definitive coding on the dependent variable (calculi of support) and some hints as to which contextual factors might be explanatory factors. It falls to later research to address more systematically the causes of variation.

Under what conditions would one anticipate normal economic voting?

The ruling party is clearly in control (Powell, 1990). Older democracies and older governments can less credibly claim that when things go awry, someone else is to blame (exonerative). And people may have difficulty attributing responsibility under coalition, minority, or divided governments.

The opposition is not associated with the recently discarded regime. As long as the opposition is composed of discredited former Communists or backers of the military, self-exoneration is a viable strategy. But an opposition composed of parties with solid democratic credentials is less obviously to blame for all that goes wrong, and citizens have the option of supporting the opposition without simply hankering for the past.

Economic trends in the recent past have been nonlinear. A recent experience of nonlinear economic trajectories, such as vigorous growth followed by a crash or by high inflation, may make it natural for people to think of economic change as nonlinear and hence to have in mind intertemporal trade-offs.

The pro-market reform program is old. The exhortation to endure pain because prosperity will follow (intertemporal) is more palatable after 1 year of painful reforms than after 6 or 10.

Party identification among the citizenry is not widespread. Otherwise, support for the government or the opposition will be driven by party loyalties and not outcomes.

Differences in income and wealth are small. Otherwise, the view may be that although the future will be brighter, some have been made to suffer too much (distributional).

Where do the countries included in this volume fall in relation to these factors?

Spain

The period covered by José María Maravall and Adam Przeworski, 1980–1995, encompasses both majority governments and coalitional governments. The governing party in the early period was the center-right Unión del Centro Democrático (UCD, 1979–1982), led by Adolfo Suárez; the social democratic Partido Socialista Obrero de España (PSOE) under Felipe González led majority governments in 1982–1993 and a coalition from 1993 to 1995. Hence, for the most part, the majority status of the governments would not cloud questions of credit and blame. At the beginning of the period covered in their chapter, Spanish democracy was only three years old; yet after a coup attempt in 1981 its stability appeared increasingly secure. The opposition, dominated by

PSOE until 1982 and by the Partido Popular (PP) thereafter, had solid democratic credentials and was not implicated in the Franco regime. Spain is a relatively egalitarian society in which partisan or ideological divisions have long histories and run deep. In sum, our leading expectation should be one of normal economic voting, although the newness of economic reforms, the partisanship of many Spaniards, and the youth of the democracy are suggestive of intertemporal, exonerative, and oppositionist postures.

East Germany

The peculiarity of the former German Democratic Republic (GDR), as Christopher Anderson and Yuliya Tverdova make clear in their chapter, is that the fall of the Communist regime was followed almost immediately by absorption into a long-standing democracy, which projected its economy, party system, and political institutions onto the East. Furthermore the major opposition party, the Sozialdemokratische Partei Deutschland (SPD), was scarcely a ghost from the past regime. There were ghosts in the figure of former Communists (the Partei des Demokratischen Sozialismus [PDS]), but their role, as Anderson and Tverdova note, was that of a lightning rod for protest. Germany was ruled by a majority coalition of the Christlich Demokratische Union–Christlich Soziale Union (CDU-CSU). For these reasons, clarity of control over policy was not in question. The East Germans found themselves in the position of assimilating a newly transported party system, and hence partisan identities were up for grabs. All of this leads us to expect normal retrospective economic voting. The twist, however, was that the pain borne by citizens of the East during reunification and economic integration was much greater than in the West, a difference that could easily give rise to a distributional sense of unfairness. And the public in the former East Germany may have been persuaded by the claim that economic well-being would arrive only after a difficult period of adjustment and therefore may have adopted an intertemporal mindset.

Poland

Adam Przeworski examines the push for reforms under the first post-Communist government of Tadeusz Mazowiecki, known as the *Balcerow-*

icz plan (1989–1991) after the finance minister, Leszek Balcerowicz. Democracy was in its infancy; former Communists were everywhere. The government's discourse was one of intertemporal sacrifices ("there is no example in the economic history of the world of inflation being squelched without serious social difficulties" – Mazowiecki, cited in Przeworski, 1993) and self-exoneration ("The causes of the striking economic indolence of the economy rest deeply embedded in the previous economic system" – see Przeworski, this volume). In sum, the setting was ripe for exonerative and intertemporal postures. Only partisanship of the pro-Communist/anti-Communist sort and relatively egalitarian income distribution would lead us to anticipate normal economic voting.

Mexico

We expect retrospective economic postures in settings where the government is firmly in control and thus the public sees it as responsible for economic performance; where no major political transition has taken place and a stratagem of self-exoneration for poor performance is unavailable to the government; and where reforms have been in place for long enough that the public would be impatient with arguments that with a little more sacrifice, prosperity is around the corner. All of these conditions described Mexico during the government of Carlos Salinas (1988–1995) and the early years of the government of Ernesto Zedillo (1995–1997) that Jorge Buendía Laredo analyzes in this volume. The opposition played virtually no role in the policy process, and claims of opposition obstruction would have rung hollow. And despite a protracted liberalization, no political transition had occurred. Thus there could be little doubt that the Partido Revolucionario Institutcional (PRI), in power continuously for 60 years when Salinas took office, was firmly in control of policy making. Reforms began under the De la Madrid government, after Mexico defaulted in August 1982 on its foreign loans. Hence reforms under the Salinas government were a continuation of the process that began 6 years before Salinas's election, 13 years before Zedillo, and the public would have been restive with calls for patience through another downturn. Our expectations are of normal economic voting postures among the Mexican populace. Only the severe ups and downs of the Mexican economy in these years might have led Mexicans away from a normal retrospective calculus of support and toward an intertemporal calculus.

Peru

Alberto Fujimori came to power a decade after the return to democracy. Susan Stokes analyzes the impact of economic states on opinions of the president and the economic program during the period 1990–1997, which captures all of Fujimori's first term and the early stage of his second term (1995–2000). Fujimori faced an opposition majority in the legislature, but one that favored his neoliberal program. And as in Argentina, Fujimori had extensive decree powers should the legislature cause problems. If there was any doubt about institutional control, it would have been whether it was really in the hands of the military, especially after the 1992 coup d'etat, but the military played little role in economic policy. Partisanship before Fujimori came to power was intense, but had begun to dissolve in the late 1980s and dissolved completely during Fujimori's rule. These factors suggest that retrospective economic voting might have been the norm in Peru. Yet the prior economic crisis had come after a period of expansion, and Peruvians were likely to view current economic policy in light of this history. Perhaps they would be willing to accept intertemporal trade-offs to avoid its repetition.

Argentina

There could be little doubt that Carlos Menem's government, analyzed by Fabian Echegaray and Carlos Elordi, was in control: it was a majority government in a country in which even majority presidents often make laws by decree. Partisans of the previous military regime were political has-beens. These factors would encourage a normal economic calculus. Yet the government came to power amid hyperinflation and social unrest, and its discourse was strongly intertemporal. In one of Menem's first speeches as president, he stated that Argentina needed "major surgery, no anesthesia" if it was to return to good health (cited in Smith, 1991:53). As Echegaray and Elordi show, the government also tried to remind people of the bleak situation it inherited from the previous government, a strategy of self-exoneration.

One contextual feature that I have discussed up to now as a constant is that these were all new democracies. But is political regime held constant? Poland, Germany, Spain, and Argentina are democracies by commonly accepted criteria: elections in which most adult citizens can vote are held regularly and these elections can result in the ruling party's being turned out of office, freedoms of association and expression are generally upheld, and elected civilians have power over nonelected and military personnel (Dahl, 1971; Schmitter and Karl, 1991).

Peruvian democracy was murkier. During the early 1990s, some provinces were under states of emergency, which meant that civilian authorities were subject to the military command structure, and rights of association and expression were curtailed, although residents of emergency zones had the formal right to vote. In April 1992 Fujimori carried out a coup d'etat and suspended the constitution. Free association was curtailed for a period, but freedom of expression was not much affected. Unscheduled elections to form a constitutional assembly/national legislature were held in November 1992; local elections scheduled for that month under the pre-coup political calendar were delayed until January 1993. In November 1993 the government held a referendum and the public narrowly approved a new constitution. Presidential and parliamentary elections were held in April 1995, the same date they would have been held had the prior constitution been in force. In sum, democracy was suspended for a time in Peru in the early 1990s, from April 1992 until November 1993, or perhaps until April 1995.

Mexico in the period Buendía studies was not a competitive electoral democracy but a one-party hegemonic system. We do not believe that Mexicans feel more inhibited than, say, Peruvians or Spaniards in expressing their views to pollsters, but telling a pollster that you did not approve of the performance of the government could have a different meaning in a country that had not experienced other than a PRI president in 60 years.[5]

Data and Methods

The chapters in this book analyze the impact of aggregate economic conditions (or, in the Spanish case, perceptions of economic conditions) on opinions about the economic reform program and of the government or president. Economic data are from official sources. Opinion data are

---

[5] Polls did a good job of predicting the outcome of the 1994 presidential election. For example, an exit poll conducted by Mitofski International projected results very close to the official returns.

from monthly polls conducted by a government agency in Mexico, a government-sponsored institute in Poland, a social science research organization in Spain, and private polling firms in Germany, Argentina, and Peru. In addition to individual data (analyzed in the chapters on Spain and Mexico), all authors make use of pooled time-series data.

In contrast to most studies of presidential approval, we study not only expressions of approval and disapproval but also uncertainty or agnosticism ("no opinion," "don't know," etc.) We followed this course for theoretical reasons and because the nature of opinions in the countries we studied called for it. We expect changes in economic conditions in the context of major economic transitions to generate a good deal of uncertainty, even confusion, rather than clear-cut approval and disapproval. Moreover, in countries such as Poland, where the political institutions implementing reforms were novel, and in Argentina and Peru, where the government's program represented a startling reversal of campaign promises, confusion would hardly be surprising. Indeed, levels of uncertainty were high and widely varying: in Poland the proportion of respondents reporting "don't know" regarding the Balcerowicz plan ranged from 27% to 66%, Peruvian "don't knows" about the Fujimori economic program ranged between 4% and 24%, and between 5% and 13% of Mexicans didn't know whether to support or oppose President Salinas.

Our decision to pay attention to uncertainty had methodological consequences. In our datasets, each observation is the aggregate result of a public opinion poll conducted, in general, monthly. In our models the explanatory variables are the states of the economy, such as the level of real wages, the unemployment rate, inflation, or gross domestic product. Our dependent variables are public support. Each observation includes the proportion of survey respondents that approved, disapproved, or didn't know their opinion of the government's economic reform program (or government/president). Dependent variables with this structure are known as *compositional data*: the proportions (e.g., approve, disapprove, don't know) are positive and sum to 1. Katz and King (1999) developed a set of techniques that adequately account for the features of compositional data.[6]

---

[6] In their chapter on Poland, Maravall and Przeworski employ multinomial logit estimates (MLE). They analyze pooled time-series data from Spain by estimating autoregressive integrated moving average (ARIMA) models.

The Katz–King model works by transforming the restricted data to an unrestricted space, for which many distributions exist, via the additive logistic transformation. This transformation allows us to use standard regression methods, such as Seemingly Unrelated Regression Estimates (SURE), which we report. Because the quantities of interest, such as the marginal effects of the independent variables – for example, the impact of a 1% increase in inflation on support for the economic reform program – are on the original, untransformed proportions, we offer simulations to take parameter estimates from the transformed model to shares. The simulations and their graphical illustrations follow the CLARIFY techniques developed by King, Tomz, and Wittenberg (2000).[7]

A Summary of Results

Our most startling result is that in every country people sometimes reacted to economic deterioration by supporting the government and its economic program more strongly. Conversely, they sometimes reacted to economic improvement with pessimism and opposition. (See Table 1.2, which summarizes the impact of aggregate economic deterioration on public responses in the six countries.) In our three Latin American cases, economic expansion (wage growth or gross domestic product [GDP] growth) elicited an intertemporal response – pessimism about the future and opposition to the economic reform program. A milder version of this same response is visible in the Polish data: rising real wages sparked not support for reforms but agnosticism. (Maravall and Przeworski find all four calculi of support among Spaniards, with about a third of their samples, on average, falling into the normal pattern.) What explains the intertemporal effect? Przeworski emphasizes the intertemporal discourse of the new democratic leadership in Poland. In contrast, Buendía, Stokes, and Echegaray and Elordi emphasize the recent experience of expansion followed by high inflation that Mexicans, and to a greater extent Peruvians and Argentines, had observed in the recent past. These Latin Americans may have believed that they continued to face a trade-off between current growth and future price stability, a belief that caused an intertemporal posture toward the government.

---

[7] We are grateful to Michael Tomz for developing software that allowed us to carry out the data transformations and simulations.

Table 1.2. *Public Responses to Deterioration of the Economy in Six European and Latin American Countries*

	Support Reforms/ Government	Oppose Reforms/Government
	Intertemporal	Distributional/Oppositionist
Optimistic about future of economy	Spain Germany (inflation) Poland (wages) Mexico (wages) Peru (GDP) Argentina (wages)	Spain
	Exonerating	Normal
Pessimistic about future of economy	Spain Poland (inflation)	Spain Germany (unemployment) Poland (unemployment) Mexico (unemployment, inflation) Peru (unemployment, inflation) Argentina (unemployment, inflation)

Another finding at odds with normal economic voting is that sometimes people seemed to exonerate their government for bad performance. This was true of a small proportion of Spaniards, who tended to exonerate the government early in the term. It was also true of Poles in the face of high inflation: they became pessimistic about the future but still rallied to support of their government, as though they thought other forces were at fault and the government's program – though not yet working – was the antidote.

Almost across the board, people responded to unemployment as one would normally expect: they became pessimistic and turned against the government and its economic reform program. In all but the East German and Polish cases, this was the response to inflation as well. For reasons considered in Przeworski's chapter on Poland, people in these countries interpreted rising unemployment rates as foretelling future deterioration. Apparently, unemployment is such a catastrophic event that when people think the probability of losing their job is high, they interpret this unambiguously as bad news and hold the government responsible.

26

Introduction

Our finding that normal economic voting, though common, is not the only pattern is echoed in other studies as well. Other researchers have encountered evidence that economic voting may not be omnipresent. Yet, under the hegemony of the retrospective paradigm, they have simply ignored these anomalies or regarded them as showing that people have not properly "read" the economy. In an analysis of the political impact of economic crisis in Latin America, Remmer (1991) gets results that are anomalous given the predictions of normal economic voting. She estimates the impact of economic conditions on votes for incumbent parties in presidential elections in 12 countries between 1982 and 1990, and finds that incumbent parties suffered larger losses at the polls when inflation went *down* (significant) and when GDP *rose* (not significant). Tucker (1998) analyzes the impact of economic conditions on the vote share of the incumbent party at the regional level in five post-Communist countries. The coefficients on inflation are "wrong" (given normal economic voting expectations) in 60% of his cases; they are "wrong" on income in 58% of his cases. We hope that the reconceptualization offered here will encourage other scholars to reconsider evidence that runs against the grain of normal economic voting.

To summarize, although we find considerable evidence of a normal retrospective economic calculus of support in new democracies pursuing promarket reforms, we also find evidence of other postures: intertemporal, exonerative or antidotal, distributional, and oppositionist. We posit, but leave for future research to refute or confirm, that these distinctive calculi are caused by contextual features generally absent in advanced capitalist democracies, where no leap of economic models is in the works and where relatively stable economic conditions reign.

References

Alesina, A. 1988. "Credibility and Convergence in a Two-Party System with Rational Voters." *American Economic Review* 78: 796–805.
Alesina, A., and A. Drazen. 1991. "Why Are Stabilizations Delayed?" *American Economic Review* 81: 1170–1180.
Alvarez, M. 1997. *Information and Elections.* Ann Arbor: University of Michigan Press.
Anderson, C. 1995. *Blaming the Government: Citizens and the Economy in Five European Democracies.* Armonk, NY: M. E. Sharpe.
Arnold, D. 1993. "Can Inattentive Citizens Control Their Elected Representatives?" In L. C. Dodd and B. I. Oppenheimer (eds.), *Congress Reconsidered*, 5th ed. Washington, DC: CQ Press.

Bartels, L. 1988a. "The Economic Consequences of Retrospective Voting." Unpublished manuscript, Princeton University.

1988b. *Presidential Primaries and the Dynamics of Public Choice*. Princeton, NJ: Princeton University Press.

Berg, A., and J. Sachs. 1988. "The Debt Crisis: Structural Explanations of Country Performance." *Journal of Development Economics* 29: 271–306.

Berle, A. A. 1963. *The American Economic Republic*. New York: Harcourt, Brace, and World.

Berry, A. 1997. "The Income Distribution Threat in Latin America." *Latin American Research Review* 32(2): 3–40.

Bratton, K. A. 1994. "Retrospective Voting and Future Expectations: The Case of the Budget Deficit in the 1988 Elections." *American Politics Quarterly* 277–296.

Budge, I., D. Robertson, and D. Hearl (eds.). 1987. *Ideology, Strategy, and Party Change: Spatial Analysis of Post-War Programs in Nineteen Democracies*. London: Cambridge University Press.

Chapell, H. W., and W. R. Keech. 1985. "A New View of Political Accountability for Economic Performance." *American Political Science Review* 79(1): 10–27.

Cheibub, J. A., and Adam Przeworski. 1999. "Democracy, Elections, and Accountability for Economic Outcomes." In A. Przeworski, B. Manin, and S. C. Stokes (eds.), *Democracy, Representation, and Accountability*. Cambridge: Cambridge University Press.

Conway, P. 1992. "Debt and Adjustment." *Latin American Research Review* 27(2): 151–166.

Cortés, F., and R. M. Rubalcava. n.d. "Structural Change and Concentration: An Analysis of the Distribution of Household Income in Mexico, 1984–1989." Unpublished manuscript, Colegio de México.

Dahl, R. 1971. *Polyarchy: Participation and Opposition*. New Haven, CT: Yale University Press, 1971.

Dornbusch, R., and S. Edwards. 1991. "The Macroeconomics of Populism." In R. Dornbusch and S. Edwards (eds.), *The Macroeconomics of Populism in Latin America*. Chicago: University of Chicago Press.

Downs, A. 1957. *An Economic Theory of Voting*. New York: Harper and Row.

Edelman, M. 1964. *The Symbolic Uses of Politics*. Urbana: University of Illinois Press.

Fearon, J. 1999. "Electoral Accountability and the Control of Politicians: Selecting Good Types versus Sanctioning Poor Performance." In A. Przeworski, B. Manin, and S. C. Stokes (eds.), *Democracy, Accountability, and Representation*. Cambridge: Cambridge University Press.

Ferejohn, J. 1986. "Incumbent Performance and Electoral Control." *Public Choice* 50: 5–25.

Fernandez, R., and D. Rodrik. 1991. "Resistance to Reform: Status Quo Bias in the Presence of Individual-Specific Uncertainty." *American Economic Review* 81(5): 1146–1155.

Fiorina, M. 1981. *Retrospective Voting in American National Elections*. New Haven, CT: Yale University Press.

Fishel, J. 1985. *Platforms and Promises*. Washington, DC: CQ Press.

Gervasoni, C. H. 1995. "El impacto electoral de las políticas de estabilización y reforma estructural en América Latina." *Journal of Latin American Affairs* 3(1): 46–50.

Graber, D. A. 1980. *Mass Media and American Politics*. Washington, DC: Congressional Quarterly Press.

Grindle, M. S., and J. W. Thomas. 1991. *Public Choice and Policy Change: The Political Economy of Reform in Developing Countries*. Baltimore: Johns Hopkins University Press.

Grossman, H. I., and S. J. Noh. 1990. "A Theory of Kleptocracy with Probabilistic Survival and Reputation." *Economics and Politics* 2(2): 151–171.

Haggard, S., and R. Kaufman. 1989. "The Politics of Stabilization and Structural Adjustment." In J. Sachs and S. Collins (eds.), *Developing Country Debt and Economic Performance*. Chicago: University of Chicago Press.

1992. "Economic Adjustment and the Prospects for Democracy." In S. Haggard and R. Kaufman (eds.), *The Politics of Economic Adjustment*. Princeton, NJ: Princeton University Press.

Haggard, S., and S. Webb. 1993. "What Do We Know About the Political Economy of Reform?" *World Bank Research Observer* 8(2): 143–168.

Harrington, J. E., Jr. 1993a. "The Impact of Reelection Pressures on the Fulfillment of Campaign Promises." *Games and Economic Behavior* 5: 71–97.

1993b. "Economic Policy, Economic Performance, and Elections." *American Economic Review* 83: 27–42.

Hibbs, D. A., Jr. 1987. *The Political Economy of Industrial Democracies*. Cambridge, MA: Harvard University Press.

Host, V., and M. Paldam. 1990. "An International Element of the Vote?: A Comparative Study of Seventeen OECD Countries." *European Journal of Political Research* 18: 221–239.

Iyengar, S., and D. Kinder. 1987. *News That Matters*. Chicago: University of Chicago Press.

Jackman, S. 1995. "Perception and Reality in American Political Economy." Unpublished doctoral dissertation, University of Rochester.

Johnston, P. C., S. Feldman, and K. Knight. 1987. "The Personal and Political Underpinnings of Economic Forecasts." *American Journal of Political Science* 31: 559–583.

Katz, J., and G. King. 1999. "A Statistical Model for Multiparty Electoral Data." *American Political Science Review* 93(1): 15–32.

Keeler, J. T. S. 1993. "Opening the Window for Reform: Mandates, Crises, and Extraordinary Policy-making." *Comparative Political Studies* 25(4): 433–486.

Key, V. O. 1966. *The Responsible Electorate*. New York: Vintage.

Kiewit, D. R., and D. Rivers. 1984. "A Retrospective on Retrospective Voting." *Political Behavior* 6(4): 369–393.

Kinder, D., and D. R. Kiewet. 1979. "Economic Discontent and Political Behavior: The Role of Personal Grievances and Collective Economic Judgments in Congressional Voting." *American Journal of Political Science* 79: 10–27.

Kinder, D., G. Adams, and P. W. Gronke. 1989. "Economics and Politics in the 1984 American Presidential Elections." *American Journal of Political Science* 33(2): 419–515.

King, G., M. Tomz, and J. Wittenberg. 2000. "Making the Most of Statistical Analyses: Improving Interpretation and Presentation." *American Journal of Political Science* 44(2): 341–355.

Klingemann, H.-D., R. I. Hofferbert, and I. Budge. 1994. *Parties, Policies, and Democracy.* Boulder, CO: Westview Press.

Kramer, G. H. 1983. "The Ecological Fallacy Revisited: Aggregate versus Individual Level Findings on Economic and Elections, and Sociotropic Voting." *American Political Science Review* 77: 92–111.

Krukones, M. G. 1984. *Promises and Performance: Presidential Campaigns as Policy Predictors.* Lanham, MD: University Press of America.

Langue, D. J. 1994. "Retrospective and Prospective Voting in Presidential Year Elections." *Political Research Quarterly* 47: 193–206.

Lewis-Beck, M. S. 1988. *Economics and Elections.* Ann Arbor: University of Michigan Press.

Lockerbie, B. E. 1992. "Prospective Voting in Presidential Elections: 1956–1988." *American Political Quarterly* 20(3): 308–325.

Mackuen, M. B., R. S. Ericson, and J. A. Stimson. 1992. "Peasants or Bankers? The American Electorate and the U.S. Economy." *American Political Science Review* 86(3): 597–611.

Manin, B. 1997. *The Principles of Representative Government.* Cambridge: Cambridge University Press.

Markus, G. B. 1988. "The Impact of Personal and National Economic Conditions on the Presidential Vote." *American Journal of Political Science* 32: 137–154.

Mayhew, D. R. 1974. *Congress: The Electoral Connection.* New Haven: Yale University Press.

McKelvey, R. D. 1976. "Intransitivities in Multidimensional Voting Models and Some Implications for Agenda Control." *Journal of Economic Theory* 12: 472–482.

McGraw, K. M., S. Best, and R. Trimpone. 1995. "'What They Say or What They Do': The Impact of Elite Explanation and Policy Outcomes on Public Opinion." *American Journal of Political Science* 39(1): 53–74.

Meehl, P. E. 1977. "The Selfish Voter Paradox and the Thrown Away Vote Argument." *American Political Science Review* 71: 11–30.

Nannestad, P., and M. Paldam. 1994. "The VP-Function: A Survey of the Literature on Vote and Popularity Functions After 25 Years." *Public Choice* 79: 213–245.

Nelson, J. M. 1992. "Poverty, Equity, and the Politics of Adjustment." In S. Haggard and R. Kaufman (eds.), *The Politics of Economic Adjustment.* Princeton, NJ: Princeton University Press.

Paldam, M. 1991. "How Robust Is the Vote Function?: A Study of Seventeen Nations over Four Decades." In H. Northop, M. S. Lewis-Beck, and J. D.

Lafay (eds.), *Economics and Politics: The Calculus of Support.* Ann Arbor: University of Michigan Press.

Powell, G. B., and G. D. Whitten. 1993. "A Cross-National Analysis of Economic Voting: Taking Account of the Political Context." *American Journal of Political Science* 37: 391–414.

Powers, D. V., and J. H. Cox. 1997. "Echoes from the Past: The Relationship between Satisfaction with Economic Reforms and Voting Behavior in Poland." *American Political Science Review* 91(3): 617–633.

Przeworski, A. 1991. *Democracy and the Market.* Cambridge: Cambridge University Press.

1993. "Economic Reforms, Public Opinion, and Political Institutions: Poland in the Eastern European Perspective." In L. C. Bresser Pereira, J. M. Maravall, and A. Przeworski, *Economic Reform in New Democracies: A Social-Democratic Approach.* Cambridge: Cambridge University Press.

Przeworski, A., B. Manin, and S. C. Stokes. 1999. "Elections and Representation." In A. Przeworski, B. Manin, and S. C. Stokes (eds.), *Democracy, Accountability, and Representation.* Cambridge: Cambridge University Press.

Remmer, K. 1990. "Democracy and Economic Crisis: The Latin American Experience." *World Politics* 52(3): 315–355.

1991. "The Political Impact of the Economic Crisis in Latin America in the 1980s." *American Political Science Review* 5(3): 777–800.

Rodrik, D. 1996. "Understanding Economic Policy Reform." *Journal of Economic Literature* 34: 9–41.

Rose, R., and W. Mishler. 1996a. *Political Patience in Regime Transformation: A Comparative Analysis of Post-Communist Citizens.* Studies in Public Policy #274, University of Strathclyde.

Roxborough, I. 1989. "Organized Labor: A Major Victim of the Debt Crisis." In W. L. Canak (ed.), *Lost Promises: Austerity and Development in Latin America.* Boulder, CO: Westview.

Sachs, J. 1993. "Introduction." In M. Naim, *Paper Tigers and Minotaurs: The Politics of Venezuela's Economic Reforms.* Washington, DC: Carnegie.

1990. *Social Conflict and Populist Policies in Latin America.* San Francisco: ICS Press.

Schmitter, P., and T. Karl. 1991. "What Democracy Is . . . and What It Is Not." *Journal of Democracy* 2: 75–88.

Skidmore, T. E. 1977. "The Politics of Economic Stabilization in Postwar Latin America." In J. Malloy (ed.), *Authoritarianism and Corporatism in Latin America.* Pittsburgh: University of Pittsburgh Press.

Smith, W. C. 1991. "State, Market, and Neoliberalism in Post-Transition Argentina." *Journal of Interamerican Studies and World Affairs* 33(4): 45–82.

Sniderman, P. M., J. M. Glaser, and R. Griffin. 1990. "Information and Electoral Choice." In J. A. Ferejohn and J. H. Kuklinski (eds.), *Information and Democratic Processes.* Champaign-Urbana: University of Illinois.

Tucker, J. A. 1998. "It's the Economy, Comrade! Economic Conditions and Election Results in Russia, Poland, Hungary, the Czech Republic, and Slovakia."

Paper presented at the annual meeting of the Midwest Political Science Association, Chicago, April 23–25.

Tufte, E. R. 1978. *Political Control of the Economy*. Princeton, NJ: Princeton University Press.

Walton, J., and C. Ragin. 1989. "Austerity and Dissent: Social Bases of Popular Struggle in Latin America." In P. Canak (ed.), *Debt, Austerity, and Development in Latin America*. Boulder, CO: Westview.

Waterbury, J. 1989. "The Political Management of Economic Adjustment and Reform." In J. Nelson (ed.), *Fragile Coalitions: The Politics of Economic Adjustment*. New Brunswick, NJ: Transaction Books.

Weyland, K. 1996. "Risk Taking in Latin American Economic Restructuring: Lessons from Prospect Theory." *International Studies Quarterly* 40: 185–208.

Zaller, J. 1989. "Bringing Converse Back In: Modeling Information Flow in Political Campaigns." *Political Analysis* 1: 181–234.

PART I

Europe

2

Political Reactions to the Economy

THE SPANISH EXPERIENCE

José María Maravall and Adam Przeworski

Introduction

Common sense and abundant empirical evidence appear to indicate that voters respond to economic conditions. Ceteris paribus, when such conditions are good, people support governments; when the economy deteriorates, this support suffers. It has thus been claimed that "the proposition that voters will punish incumbents for poor performance should not be controversial" (Kiewiet and Rivers, 1985:225). If true, such a conclusion would provide empirical confirmation for standard conceptions of democratic accountability. Yet voters may accurately assess the economic situation and still find reasons not to act on these assessments. Indeed, they may decide how to vote first, and only then look for ways of rationalizing their decisions in the face of economic circumstances. We discuss the economic interpretation of voting using empirical evidence from Spanish politics between 1980 and 1995.

Models of economic voting postulate that voters base their decisions on the grounds of economic performance, either past or future.[1] According to one tradition of electoral research, the only information that enters into voters' decisions concerns their past experience.[2] Voters assess economic outcomes under the present government, ignore promises about the

We should like to thank Nieves Pombo and Mercedes Gabarro of Centro de Investigaciones Sociológicas (CIS) for their excellent work in preparing the data, which were purchased with the assistance of *the Comisión Interministerial de Ciencia y Tecnología*. Marta Fraile, Carles Boix, and José Ramón Montero provided helpful comments.
[1] See, for instance, Kramer (1971); Peffley (1985); Markus (1988); Bratton (1994).
[2] Examples of this tradition are Kramer (1971); Shaffer and Chressanthis (1991); Lanoue (1994); Monardi (1994); Svoda (1995).

future, and implement the reward-punishment mechanism. As Key (1966:61) put it, the voter is simply "an appraiser of past events, past performance, and past actions. It judges retrospectively; it commands prospectively only insofar as it expresses either approval or disapproval of that which has happened before. Voters may reject what they have known; or they may approve what they have known. They are not likely to be attracted in great numbers by promises of the novel or unknown."

A considerable number of studies have concluded, however, that political support is driven by expectations about the future performance of the economy[3]: "the past is surely past, so rational voters must be (directly or indirectly) prospectively oriented" (Bartels, 1988:2). Yet how do voters form expectations about future economic performance, whether under the continued tenure of the current incumbent or in the case of the victory of the opposition? Even if voters make decisions with an eye on the future, they may still base their forecasts exclusively on the past record(s) of the incumbent and the opposition by simply extrapolating from the past.[4] But such extrapolations are rational only if past and future economic performance are closely correlated when incumbents are reelected, and dissociated when they are replaced by the opposition. And individuals may think about the future without making inferences from the past, picking cues from the campaign or from other sources.[5] They may believe that the hardships of the past were necessary for a bright future (Przeworski, this volume). They may conclude that even if the future under the current incumbent is bleak, the opposition would only make things worse and, conversely, that even if the incumbent would perform well, the performance of the opposition would be superior.

Such interpretations may be based on the best evidence that voters can access. But they may also constitute ex-post rationalizations of voting decisions based on past political commitments or ideological stances. Hence, the direction of causality is not obvious.

The questions of whether people accurately perceive the economic situation, whether they extrapolate from the past to form forecasts, and whether they allow prior beliefs and commitments to shape their voting deci-

---

[3] These studies include Kuklinski and West (1981); Abramowitz (1985); Lewis-Beck and Skalaban (1989); Lockerbie (1992); MacKuen, Erikson, and Stimson (1992); Price and Sanders (1992).

[4] See, for instance, Fiorina (1981); Lewis-Beck (1988); Uslaner (1989); Bratton (1994); Lanoue (1994); Keech (1995).

[5] For instance, Kuklinski and West (1981); Abramowitz (1985); Conover, Feldman, and Knight (1987); Lockerbie (1992); MacKuen et al. (1992).

sions are empirical: they cannot be resolved by assumptions. Moreover, answers to these questions may be contingent on historical circumstances. In countries that newly emerge from an authoritarian past, governments are more likely to be exonerated for bad economic performance. In countries that face the necessity of restructuring the economy, governments are more believable when they present the current hardships as temporary, leading to a better future. Hence, it is possible that the calculus of economic voting is different in the new and in the well-established democracies – different under ordinary economic circumstances and in situations of economic crises.

Political reactions to the economy have a particular salience in new democracies that experience painful reforms. Do people have in mind the old regime and past economic conditions when they assess economic reforms? Is their reaction influenced by past and present hardships or by expectations about the future? Can citizens easily attribute responsibility or do they find it difficult to allocate the blame for hardships? Do they tend to exonerate their governments in the early years of the regime? Are they willing to accept intertemporal trade-offs?

If electoral punishment were the only answer to bad or deteriorating states of the economy, then governments interested in their own survival would avoid any policies that generate economic hardships, even if only in the short run. Facing hardships, citizens would extrapolate the future from the past and turn against the incumbents. Anticipating this reaction, governments would choose a populist path and short-term popularity. As the material costs of reforms fall mostly on the shoulders of workers, the policy constraints of leftist governments would be particularly strong. And because party identifications are often much weaker in new democracies, governments would be less able to rely on loyalties grounded in past political histories.

Yet we know that governments in new democracies do survive long and deep economic difficulties. Voters do not invariably reject reforms that bring temporary hardships. They are either sophisticated or gullible: they listen to explanations, consider constraints, scrutinize promises of the opposition, and search for clues to responsibility. They may conclude that the present policies are the least bad, that they will lead to a better future, or that they are not the cause of the poor performance of the economy: as a result, they back the government. If the regime or the government has changed, present difficulties may be blamed on the past. The political goods of democracy, in contrast to a recent experience of authoritarianism, may temporarily benefit an elected government. A deep economic crisis and a history of failed policies may both reduce risk aversion and increase the tolerance for painful reforms. If these are well timed and radical, resistance may be minimized, steps will be seen as irreversible, and growth may be resumed earlier (Przeworski, 1991:162–187). Broad mandates, combined with consultation, may also limit opposition to policies, generate the complicity of society, increase informational flows, and improve the technical quality of reforms (Maravall, 1997:32–37). By contrast, if a government cannot claim a mandate for reform, has reneged on electoral promises, delayed reforms, or been in power for a long time, it will be unable to avoid the blame or to enjoy the intertemporal patience of voters: as a consequence, it will face stronger social resistance and greater electoral punishment. These are familiar arguments that contradict the theses of voters' myopia, populist governments, and nonviable economic reforms in new democracies.

Economic Performance in a New Democracy: The Spanish Case

The Spanish experience serves as a means of examining the logic of economic voting in a new democracy facing economic difficulties. The first democratic elections were held in June 1977, on and a half years after Franco died and 41 years after the last election before the Civil War. Over the following two decades, conservative and social democratic governments alternated in office. These governments were both minoritarian (until 1982 and from 1993) and majoritarian (1982–1993). After a long period of growth, from the mid-1970s to the mid-1980s, the economy entered a crisis, which led to dramatic unemployment rates. When reforms were introduced during the two decades of democracy, they were always market-oriented; the state, however, played a much more active role in the provision of education and health, physical capital, and social policies than in economic protectionism. Once the crisis of the first democratic decade was over, successive cycles of expansion/recession/expansion followed. How did people react politically to these changing economic circumstances?

Our study spans the period from the beginning of 1980 to the summer of 1995. Thus the period starts two and a half years after the first democratic elections of June 1977, won by Adolfo Suárez and the Unión del Centro Democrático (UCD) with 34.6% of the vote. At that time, the performance of the economy was deteriorating rapidly. While the annual rate of gross national product (GNP) growth had stood on average at 6.5% between 1961 and 1976, in 1977, the year of the election, it had fallen to 2.8% and continued to decline in the following five years. The rate of unemployment, which had been on average 2.8% between 1961 and 1976, had risen to 5.3% in 1977 and reached 16.3% five years later. But the deterioration of the economy and a general feeling of crisis had started before Suárez became prime minister: this helped to exonerate him for several years. His leading role in reestablishing democracy was also widely acknowledged: this gave him a margin of maneuver regarding the economy. However, the delicate political transition and the initial fragility of the new democracy also greatly limited the ability of Suárez to undertake economic reforms. He initiated them only when all the parliamentary parties signed the Moncloa Pacts in the autumn of 1977. These pacts consisted of austerity policies and structural reforms: they brought inflation down from an annual rate of 23.4% to 16.9% in two years, but growth collapsed to 0.0% and unemployment rose by 3.5% (*Economie Européenne*, 1995:102–103, 116–117, 148–149). The Moncloa Pacts could not survive the effects of the oil shock of 1979 and the intensifying partisan competition after the new constitution was passed in December 1978. Suárez was still able to win the second democratic elections of 1979, with 34.9% of the vote, while support for the main party of the opposition, the Partido Socialista Obrero Español (PSOE), remained the same: 29.3% in 1977 and 30.5% in 1979. The strategy of Suárez was nevertheless much more defensive than in 1977: the slogan was retrospective ("UCD cumple"), while the opposition was presented as a threat to coexistence, tolerance, and Christian values, as a defender of abortion and of Marxist goals. The accomplishments emphasized were political rather than economic. The economy was in fact in a much worse condition. When our study starts, the second honeymoon of 1979 was over: since the elections, growth had fallen to 0.6% and unemployment had risen 2.8%. The explicit voting intention for the UCD stood at only 15.8%.[6]

Our study ends in the summer of 1995. The PSOE had won the general elections of October 1982, as well as those of June 1986, October 1989, and June 1993; it had formed majoritarian governments from 1982 to 1993 and a minoritarian government since then. The Partido Popular (PP) had been the main opposition party, winning 26.2%, 26.0%, 25.6%, and 34.8% of the vote, respectively, in the four elections. After 13 years in power, with Felipe González as prime minister, the socialists were now only 6 months away from losing the general elections of March 1996. They had already lost the elections to the European Parliament in June 1994,

[6] Survey of the *Centro de Investigaciones Sociológicas*, no. 1, 218 (February 1980).

Table 2.1. *Annual Economic Conditions*

	Growth	Unemployment	Inflation
1980	1.3	11.6	13.4
1981	−0.2	14.4	12.6
1982	1.6	16.3	13.9
1983	2.2	17.5	11.8
1984	1.5	20.3	11.6
1985	2.6	21.6	7.7
1986	3.2	21.2	11.1
1987	5.6	20.5	5.8
1988	5.2	19.5	5.7
1989	4.7	17.2	7.1
1990	3.7	16.2	7.3
1991	2.2	16.4	7.1
1992	0.7	18.5	6.7
1993	−1.1	22.8	4.4
1994	2.0	24.1	4.1
1995	3.1	23.7	4.2

Source: *Economie Européenne* (1995): Tables 3, 10, and 26.

as well as the local and regional elections of May 1995. Forecasts about the general elections were already assuming their defeat. The explicit voting intention for the PSOE had fallen from a record high of 40.1% in June 1986 to 21.9% in May 1995.[7] The only question was the size of their defeat. It turned out to be unexpectedly thin, with the PSOE getting 37.5% of the actual vote against 38.8% for the PP.

These were the circumstances at the beginning and the end of our study. What happened in between is summarized in Table 2.1, which shows the average annual rates of GNP growth, unemployment, and inflation.

This period of 16 years can be divided into five main phases that should be relevant for economic voting. Figures 2.1, 2.2, and 2.3 show the changing profiles of GNP growth, unemployment, and inflation over these five phases, using quarterly data.

1. The initial phase corresponds to UCD governments. It starts at the beginning of 1980 and concludes in October 1982. Suárez's government lasted until February 1981, when Leopoldo Calvo-Sotelo replaced him as

[7] Surveys of the *Centro de Investigaciones Sociológicas*, no. 1, 538 (June 1986), and no. 2, 154 (May 1995).

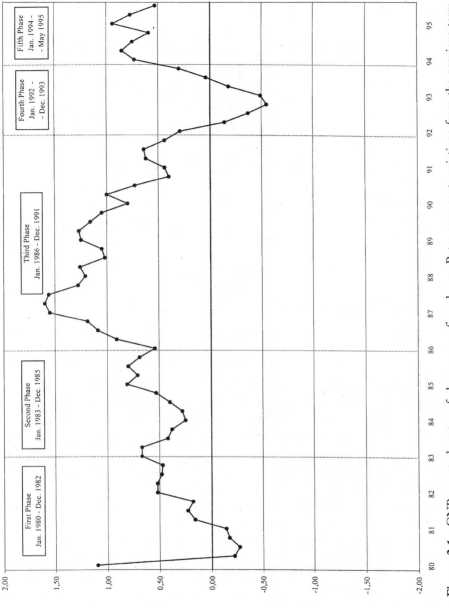

Figure 2.1 GNP: quarterly rates of change over five phases. Rates represent variations from the previous term. Source: Ministerio de Economía y Hacienda.

41

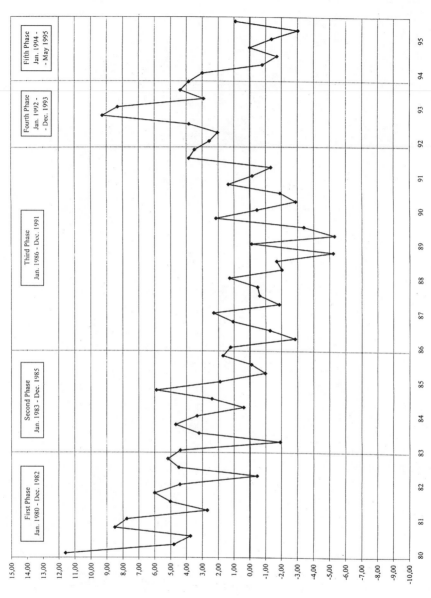

Figure 2.2 Unemployment: quarterly rates of change over five phases. Rates represent variations from the previous term. Source: Ministerio de Economía y Hacienda.

42

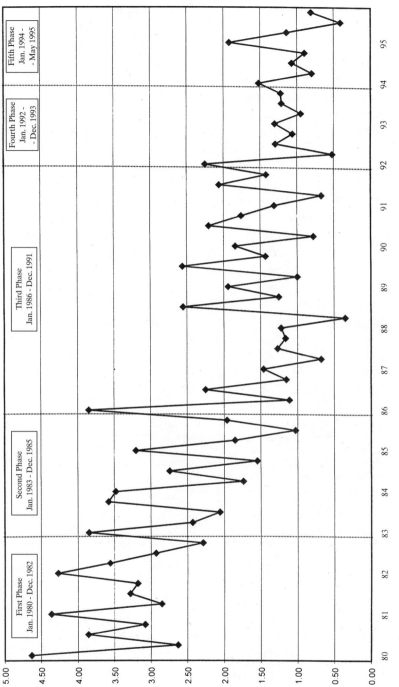

Figure 2.3 Inflation: quarterly rates of change over five phases. Rates represent variations from the previous term. Source: Ministerio de Economía y Hacienda.

prime minister, until the end of this period. Economic performance was always poor: the average annual rate of GNP growth was 0.9%, inflation remained close to 14%, and unemployment rose by 4.7%. Both UCD prime ministers framed their economic policies in exonerative terms: the blame was attributed, on the one hand, to legacies of the past and, on the other hand, to international economic circumstances, particularly the rise in oil prices. They demanded sacrifices of society but, after years of UCD government, found it difficult to offer intertemporal transactions.[8] The government was able, however, to reach agreements with the trade unions for wage moderation, particularly with the Acuerdo Nacional sobre el Empleo in 1981, supported also by the opposition. The crisis was also political: devolution to the new Autonomous Communities got out of control, right-wing subversive conspiracies and terrorist activities by ETA destabilized democracy, and internecine disputes within the UCD weakened the government. Support for the UCD declined under Suárez, rose for a couple of months after the attempted coup of February 1981 and with the new government of Calvo-Sotelo, and then continued to fall to its lowest level in October 1982, at the time of the general elections won by the PSOE with 48.4% of the vote. This loss of support was reflected in a string of defeats: in the referendum on political devolution to Andalusia (February 1980); regional elections in Catalonia, the Basque

---

[8] Examples may be found in two crucial parliamentary speeches of Adolfo Suárez: one when the PSOE presented a motion of no confidence in a debate on May 20–21, 1980, and another when he defended a motion of confidence in his government on September 16, 1980. He referred to the "disorderly and unbalanced development of the 60s and early 70s," to "the permanent incidence of continued increases in the price of oil," and to "the generalized recession of the world economy since mid-79"; he demanded a "spirit of saving and sacrifice, a collective effort to put a great country back on its feet," although such a "long and deep crisis could be stemmed, but not solved in the short-term because there are no rapid, free, and brilliant solutions." See *Primera Legislatura II (1980). Debates Políticos*, Madrid: Cortes Generales, 1980 (pp. 5.953, 5.956–5.957; 5.972, 7.072–7.073). Similar arguments may be found in the parliamentary speech of Leopoldo Calvo-Sotelo of February 19, 1981, when he was elected prime minister: "when democracy was established, Spain did not have efficient economic institutions"; "we must bring citizens to face this bitter and hard reality. This is the uncomfortable role that the government will assume. We shall avoid big promises made in exchange for small sacrifices." *Discurso de Investidura. Congreso de los Diputados. 19th February 1981*, Madrid: Presidencia del Gobierno, 1980 (pp. 16–17). The opposition, of course, rejected exonerative claims and criticized the absence of intertemporal perspectives. Thus, in the motion of no confidence of May 1980, Felipe González argued that "the oil crisis does not explain everything: there is an oil crisis in many countries," that "the government has failed in its socioeconomic policies," and that "there is resignation to the crisis. . . . No hopes are offered to the country" (speech of May 21, 1980). See *Primera legislatura II (1980). Debates Políticos* (pp. 6.006–6.011).

region, Galicia, and Andalusia (March 1980, October 1981, May 1982); and partial elections in Sevilla and Almería (November 1980).

2. The second phase corresponds to the tenure of the new PSOE government. It lasted from the end of 1982 to the end of 1985. This was a period of harsh adjustment policies, structural reforms, and bad economic conditions. The reforms were market-oriented, in contrast to the initial policies of the French Parti Socialiste (PS) in 1981–1982 and to those of the Greek Panellino Socialistiko Kinima (PASOK) from 1981 to 1989. This phase of austerity included a devaluation of the currency upon taking office, stricter limits on the money supply, limits on wage increases, a gradual reduction of the budget deficit, an orthodox payment of the public debt through state revenues, a reconversion of industrial sectors, and a reduction of labor market rigidities. The state, however, invested more in infrastructures and education: public expenditure in both areas increased by the equivalent of 1.7 points of GNP over this period (Boix, 1998:Table 5.1). Also, huge resources were drawn from the public budget in order to help financial institutions in crisis and the industrial reconversion.[9] Notwithstanding this adjustment, the rate of growth was higher than in the previous phase (2.1% on annual average), wages did not lose purchasing power (they grew on average by 1.5% in real terms), and inflation was lower (falling to 7.7%).[10] The major cost of the reforms was a sharp rise in unemployment, which grew by 5.3%. The arguments with which González framed his policies insisted on exoneration, the benefits of early timing, the need for a long-term horizon, and social compensations.[11] This period also included socioeconomic pacts with the unions (the Acuerdo Económico y Social of

[9] A total of $26.2 billion was spent on industrial reconversion, the economic recovery of the Rumasa group, and banks in crisis. See the statements of José Borrell, then secretary of state of finance, in *Diario 16*, August 2, 1988, and *La Vanguardia*, August 4, 1988.

[10] Data from *Economie Européenne* (1995).

[11] Thus, in his parliamentary speech when he was elected prime minister, Felipe González insisted on the long-term horizon of reforms. "To govern requires not only to be attentive to the curves of the road [but] to have a clear idea of the long-term. . . . The margin of manoeuvre of economic policy is limited in the immediate future, and only widens in the future. . . . We shall initiate reforms from this very moment, but their fruits will only be collected in the long-term." See *Diario de Sesiones*, Madrid: Congreso de los Diputados, November 30, 1982, no. 3 (pp. 29, 31). Three years later, at the end of this second phase, González argued that he had "tried to catch-up for a delay of several years. . . . Political priorities surely led in the past to the postponement of measures that countries of the European Community had taken in the 70s". He also defended the early timing of reforms, as painful decisions "have to be taken and the delay of decisions means greater harm, also for those people that one wants to protect"; and he insisted that economic

1985–1986), persistent conflict over industrial reconversion, reform of the public pension system, legislation on education and abortion, and successful negotiations over European Community (EC) membership. Support for the government, despite unemployment, remained high, with an explicit voting intention of 34.2% in September 1985.[12]

3. The third phase was one of rapid growth and intense job creation, also under the socialists. Economic performance benefited from a lower energy bill (due to the collapse of oil prices in 1986 and the fall of the dollar), the expansion of the European economies, and the previous adjustment. This phase lasted from the end of 1985 to the end of 1991. Spain joined the EC in January 1986 and entered the European Monetary System in June 1989. Over this period of six years, the average annual rate of GNP growth reached 4.1%, inflation was at 7.1% in the final year, and unemployment went down by 5.2%. Public expenditure on infrastructure and education expanded still further, by 3.8% of GNP. At the same time, the budget for social policies went up by 1.9% of GNP. Fiscal revenues also rose by 4.0% of GNP, particularly due to increases in direct taxation; together with changes in the internal structure of the budget, this allowed for a 1% reduction of the public deficit (Boix, 1998:Tables 5.1 and 5.2; Maravall, 1997:177–186). In this new phase of expansion and conflict, Felipe González framed his policies with references to past hardship, to the need to preserve progress achieved with great effort, and to the possibility of lowering unemployment and expanding social policies if stable growth was maintained.[13] But in these more favorable circumstances, the socialists were unable to reach socioeconomic agreements with the unions. Conflict spread over industrial reconversion, in different branches of transport, the textile industry, and the public systems of health and education and culminated in

reforms needed social protection: "these costs and traumas had to be attenuated with social policies." Speech on the State of the Nation, October 15, 1985, in *El Estado de la Nación*: Madrid, Oficina del Portavoz del Gobierno, 1985.

[12] Survey of the *Centro de Investigaciones Sociológicas*, no. 1.472 (September 1985).

[13] González insisted once and again on "not retreating from the advances we have made," "not going back in years," as economic expansion had "required painful adjustments." He strongly defended "a balanced and sustainable growth and social concertation as necessary for employment and further increments in social expenditure." See his parliamentary speeches on the State of the Nation of February 24, 1987, February 24, 1988, February 14, 1989, and March 20, 1991, in *El Estado de la Nación*, Madrid: Ministerio del Portavoz del Gobierno, 1987 (pp. 18–19), 1988 (pp. 30–35), 1989 (pp. 14–19, 25), and 1991 (pp. 17–26). Also, see his parliamentary speech when reelected as prime minister on December 4, 1989, in *Sesión de Investidura*, Madrid: Ministerio del Portavoz del Gobierno, 1989 (pp. 23–32).

a general strike in December 1988. Also, a string of scandals on insider-trading practices, illegal party funding, and corruption broke out at the beginning of 1990. The socialists won a very difficult referendum on North Atlantic Treaty Organization (NATO) membership in March 1986 and two general elections in this period, in June 1986 and October 1989, with 44.1% and 40.2% of the vote, respectively. But electoral support started to erode: the explicit intention of voting for the government in July 1991, as this phase was coming to an end, had fallen to 28.6%.[14]

4. The fourth phase was one of sharp economic deterioration and growing unemployment. It lasted for two years: 1992 and 1993. The effects of the European recession were reinforced by domestic factors: real wages had risen by 2.5% in 1990, 2.7% in 1991, and 3.4% in 1992; in this period, public expenditure went up by 4.1% of GNP and the fiscal deficit by 2.6% (*Economie Européenne*, 1995:Tables 61 and 72). The government combined this wage and fiscal laxity with tight monetary policies: it raised interest rates and devalued the currency. The result of this policy mix was a recession: the average annual rate of growth was: −0.2%. While inflation was reduced to 4.4%, largely due to the crisis, the rise in unemployment was brutal, reaching 22.8% (an increase of 6.4% in only two years). The economic record of the government was seen as bad by 70% of the people, while 86% considered its performance regarding unemployment a failure.[15] The government was again unable to reach socioeconomic pacts with unions, and labor strikes continued. Also, the scandals of corruption persisted and internal disputes within the PSOE became increasingly bitter. In November 1992, the explicit intention of voting for the socialists had fallen to 19.9%.[16] However, at election time, in June 1993, the PSOE achieved a new and unexpected victory, getting 38.8% of the vote. This capacity to survive was due, on the one hand, to very positive views of social policies (Maravall, 1997:91, 193–197) and, on the other hand, to skepticism about what an alternative government would deliver: 58% of voters thought that no other party would do better than the PSOE in reducing unemployment, and the percentages rose to 64% and 70% regarding management of the economy and education, respectively.[17]

---

[14] Survey of the *Centro de Investigaciones Sociológicas*, no. 1.972 (July 1991).
[15] Survey of DATA, S.A., in May 1993. This survey is part of the Spanish study for the Comparative National Election Project, carried out by a team including Richard Gunther and José Ramón Montero.
[16] Survey of the *Centro de Investigaciones Sociológicas*, no. 2.042 (November 1992).
[17] Survey of DATA, S.A., note 21.

But after the 1993 elections, the PSOE had to govern in a minority government, with the parliamentary support of Catalan nationalists. This government, however, introduced a fiscal adjustment and reformed the rigid and protected labor market.[18]

5. The final phase lasted from the end of 1993 to the spring of 1995. The economy again benefited from a new cycle of expansion in Europe and from the policies of economic adjustment. The EC as a whole moved from recession in 1993 (GNPs shrank on average by –0.6%) to growth in the following two years (2.6% in 1994 and 3.0% in 1995). In Spain, the fiscal deficit was trimmed by 1.5% of GNP over this period; the average annual rate of growth of real wages went down, from 1.9% in 1991–1993 to –0.4% in 1994–1995; the rate of inflation decreased from 6.7% in 1992 to 4.1% in 1995 (*Economie Européenne*, 1995:Tables 10, 26, 33, and 62). The economy resumed its growth, with a rate of 3.1% in 1995, and unemployment fell by 2%. But, after winning four successive elections, the socialists were now unable to survive. They were also deeply hurt by continuing scandals linked to the internal financing of the party, cases of personal corruption, and accusations of a dirty war against Basque terrorism.

Over our 16-year period, governments fell or survived when economic conditions were bad: these were the contrasting political outcomes of phases 1, 2, and 4. And governments could also do well or, on the contrary, be punished when economic conditions were good or at least improving: these were the opposite political outcomes of phases 3 and 5. On what grounds did voters make their electoral choices? To what extent were these choices influenced by sociodemographic conditions and ideological sympathies and to what extent by economic considerations? And did such considerations consist mostly of judgments about the past or expectations about the future?

Subjective Views of the Economy and Political Support

Our inferences about political reactions to the economy are based on individual data from 63 opinion polls carried out by the Centro de Investiga-

---

[18] Both had been political promises made by Felipe González in his parliamentary speech on taking over again as prime minister in 1993. In this speech González used intertemporal arguments, rather than exonerative or normal ones when framing his policies. He situated the Spanish crisis in a context of "international economic uncertainties" and referred to past economic achievements; he accepted, however, that domestic factors (particularly the public deficit and labor market rigidities) had aggravated the economic

ciones Sociológicas (CIS) covering the period from February 1980 to May 1995. The total number of respondents was 158,412 and the distribution by phases was as follows: 25,858 for the first, 12,106 for the second, 68,156 for the third, 20,734 for the fourth, and 31,558 for the fifth. We do not consider the actual vote at election time, but rather the vote intention declared by individuals when interviewed in such polls. We examine only sociotropic assessments, both retrospective and prospective: only a small number of surveys had "pocketbook" questions, and overwhelming empirical evidence has shown that political reactions are much more influenced by sociotropic assessments (Abramowitz, Lanoue, and Ramesh 1988; Feldman 1982, 1985; Kinder and Kiewiet 1979; Markus 1988, 1992).

Figures 2.4 and 2.5 indicate the incidence of retrospective and prospective judgments of the economy over time. Views of the economy, both retrospective and prospective, varied greatly over time. Bad retrospective views peaked at 75.1% under the UCD in January 1981, when the economy was in deep crisis and Suárez resigned as prime minister, and at 82.9% under the socialists in November 1993, in the depth of a new economic crisis and after the initial hopes generated by the elections in June of that year had been followed by frustration. The peaks of pessimistic expectations were 44.2% during the UCD period, in December 1980, and 55.0% during that of the PSOE, in November 1992: in both cases the economy had negative rates of growth and unemployment was increasing rapidly. But there was always less gloom about the future than about the past. Positive views about past economic performance were highest under the UCD in February 1980 (3.4%) and under the PSOE in July 1990 (12.1%); expectations about the future were much more optimistic, reaching 35.2% under the UCD in October 1982 and 50.6% under the PSOE in September 1987.

To determine whether subjective assessments accurately reflect the current economic situation, we need to revert to time-series analysis of aggregated individual responses. The basic answer is that they do. When income grows, people perceive the situation as good; when it declines, they see it as bad. Unemployment affects these perceptions independently of income: when unemployment is high, people see conditions as bad.

conditions. He then presented a program of fiscal adjustment, labor market reforms, social concertation, public investment in infrastructure, and education and training as policy priorities. See *Diario de Sesiones*, Madrid: Congreso de los Diputados, July 8, 1993, no. 2 (pp. 23–24, 26, 30).

50

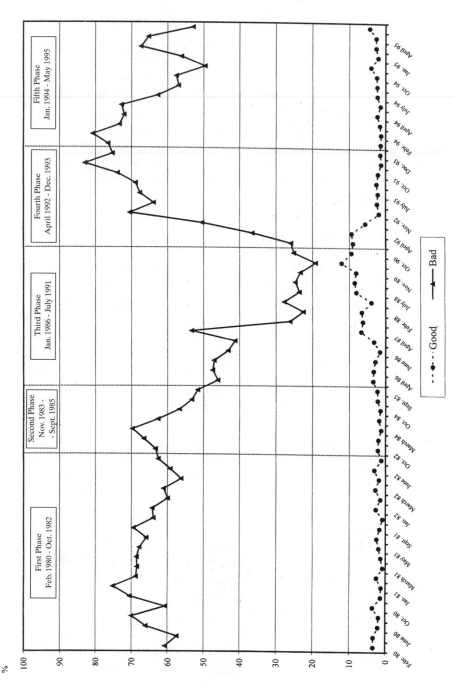

Figure 2.4 Retrospective views about the economy.

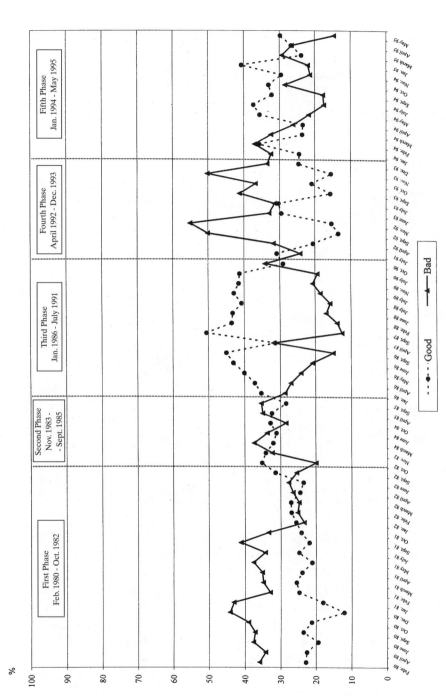

Figure 2.5 Prospective views about the economy.

51

Table 2.2. *Time Series (ARIMA) Analysis of the Relation between States of the Economy and Aggregate Assessments*

Model: $y(t) = \mu + \beta x + \phi(1)y(t-1) \ldots \phi(p)y(t-p)$
$\qquad + \in (t) + \Theta(1) \in (t-1) \ldots \Theta(q) \in (t-q)$
$\qquad y(t) = [(1-L) \wedge d]Y(t)$ (differences)
Dependent variable: mean retrospective economic assessments
Raw data were differenced $d = 0$ times.
Sum of squares at best estimates: 0.270129
Estimated standard deviation of $\in (t)$: 0.066546
Number of observations in the sample: 63

Variable	Coefficient	Standard Error	$Z = b$/s.e.	$P[\,\lvert Z \rvert \geq z]$
$\phi(1)$	0.8277420	0.07821	10.583	0.00000
μ	0.3266638	0.18454	1.770	0.07670
UNEM	0.00848	0.00501	1.695	0.09011
GNP	−0.1501050	0.03648	−4.114	0.00004
INF	0.00757	0.01299	0.583	0.56000
$\Theta(1)$	−0.3794359	0.13919	−2.726	0.00641
$\Theta(2)$	−0.4143131	0.12589	−3.291	0.00100

Box–Pierce statistic = 6.0263   Box–Ljung statistic = 6.5940
Degrees of freedom = 5   Degrees of freedom = 5
Significance level = 0.3037   Significance level = 0.2526

Lag	Autocorrelation Function	Box/Prc	Partial Autocorrelations
1	0.039	0.10	0.039
2	0.050	0.25	0.048
3	0.228	3.52	0.225
4	−.136	4.68	−.161
5	−.146	6.03	−.166

UNEM, unemployment; INF, inflation.

Inflation seems to play no role in shaping people's economic perceptions. Table 2.2 presents the results of what we think is the best estimate.[19]

The future was invariably seen as brighter than the past: in none of the 63 surveys did positive retrospective evaluations come close to positive prospective evaluations. Prospective views were influenced by both eco-

---

[19] Income is significant regardless of the model, but unemployment and inflation play a different role, depending whether or not the series is differenced: with $d = 0$, unemployment is always significant, with $d = 1$, it is always inflation, both with correct signs.

    The test for trend leads to the conclusion that there is none. The test if $\mu = 0$ when $d = 1$ borders on significance. Autocorrelations $r(t, t-s)$ are high and decline slowly.

nomic and political circumstances. Optimism grew with the economic expansion that started in the mid-1980s, although it began to fall from October 1990 on, well before the new economic downturn of phase 4: people seem to have detected the symptoms very rapidly. Optimism was also stimulated by new governments and elections: it went up in February 1981, with the election of Calvo-Sotelo as the new UCD prime minister and the failure of a coup against democracy, and particularly with the electoral victories of the socialists, overwhelming in 1982, expected in 1986, and surprising in 1993. The effect of the last election appears to have been both strong and short-lived: the percentage of optimists doubled and even past economic performance was seen in brighter terms, but three months later this surge of optimism had vanished. As Figure 2.4 shows, pessimism about the future declined at the end of both the UCD and PSOE governments: causation appears to have been reversed, as people were likely to be optimistic because they anticipated a victory of the opposition.[20]

Hence, while people accurately assess the state of the economy, they do not extrapolate from the past to form expectations about the future. Cross-tabulations of individual responses show that in no survey are the forecasts statistically related to current assessments. Contrary to the argument of Nannestad and Paldam (1994), expectations were not static: past experience was not taken as an indication of what could be expected about the future.

What then was the impact of economic considerations, either retrospective or prospective, on political support? Were political reactions grounded on judgments about past performance of the economy or on expectations about the future? And what was the relative influence of

---

But they depend only on s and they do decline to 0. Hence, the series appears to be stationary.

Testing for the structure p,q (corner method, based on the Box–Pierce statistic):

q	0	1	2	3
p				
0	38.80	50.13	explodes	explodes
1	34.89	13.08	6.03	explodes
2	26.63	10.67	5.64	explodes
3	26.51	8.51	2.56	3.48

The test for $\phi(2)$ shows that it is still somewhat significant, but the test for $\Theta(3)$ shows that it is not. The best model, therefore, appears to be ARIMA(1,0,2). None of the auto-correlations $r(t,t-s)$ for the residuals is significant. The expected value of error is -0.0024.

[20] On the possibility of this reverse causation see Nannestad and Paldam (1997); Lanoue (1994); Lockerbie (1991). This runs against the argument of Price and Sanders (1995) that no theoretically plausible hypothesis can explain why political preferences should determine economic optimism.

economic voting, compared to the effects of ideology? Did voting intentions vary across social groups? We examine the relative influence of retrospective and prospective views on the economy, of ideology, and of sociodemographic traits on voting intention over our 16-year period, under different governments and economic cycles.[21] Tables 2.3, 2.4, and 2.5 show the multinomial logit estimates of support for the government and the opposition and of indecision.[22]

If we look first at support for the government, the pattern of normal economic voting was consistent. Positive assessments, both retrospective and prospective, increased the probability of such support. There was no exception. If we compare the relative influence of retrospective and prospective views in the different phases, optimistic expectations about the economy had a much weaker effect on support when governments were old.[23] Under the socialists, the influence of the past became stronger as the government aged. (See the differences between the coefficients of phases 1 and 5 and those of phases 2, 3, and 4 regarding prospective views.) The change in the influence of retrospective assessments is shown in the coefficients of phase 2 and in those of phases 3, 4, and 5. This political effect of time operated whatever the conditions of the economy.

The surveys did not contain questions on ideology in the first phase of UCD governments. In the following periods of PSOE rule, leftism always increased support for the government. As for sociodemographic characteristics, the likelihood of backing the government, both in the UCD and the PSOE periods, was higher among women. As age went up, the probability of governmental support increased: young people only backed a government that was new and raised expectations (phase 2), but with the passing of time

---

[21] Very good and good assessments of the economy were coded as 1, neither bad nor good as 2, and bad and very bad as 3. Ideology was coded from 1 (left) to 10 (right). Men were coded as 1, women as 0. Education was coded on a 7-point scale (from "no studies" to "higher education completed"). Voting intention was coded from 0 to 2 (0 = incumbent; 1 = undecided; 2 = opposition).

[22] A word of caution is necessary here, since people who did not declare voting intentions may have been hiding them rather than being in fact undecided. Over the 16 years, this hidden vote changed. Until the end of the 1980s, many PP voters hid their support for the party whose democratic credentials were still suspect. From 1989 on, however, the political renovation of the PP and the growing unpopularity of the PSOE, largely due to economic scandals, caused the socialist electorate to conceal their voting intentions. To correct for the concealed vote, first for the PP and then for the PSOE, pollsters used answers about the vote in the previous election and the ideological proximity to the parties.

[23] Our data thus confirm the conclusion of Lancaster and Lewis-Beck (1986) that support for the PSOE in its initial period in government was mostly prospective.

Table 2.3. *Multinomial Logit Estimates of Support for the Government*[a]

Variable	Coefficient	SE	*t*-Ratio	Prob $|t| \geq x$
First phase				
Constant	0.01840	0.01007	1.827	0.06771
Gender	0.03651	0.00304	11.997	0.00000
Age	0.00215	0.00015	20.536	0.00000
Education	0.00306	0.00107	2.864	0.00418
Ideology	—	—	—	—
Retrospective	−0.05934	0.00226	−26.255	0.00000
Prospective	−0.03842	0.00207	−18.573	0.00000
Second phase				
Constant	1.18446	0.03262	36.306	0.00000
Gender	0.03719	0.00663	5.601	0.00000
Age	−0.00123	0.00022	−5.608	0.00000
Education	−0.03354	0.00254	−13.198	0.00000
Ideology	−0.10823	0.00326	−33.160	0.00000
Retrospective	−0.08164	0.00445	−18.358	0.00000
Prospective	−0.14914	0.00520	−28.665	0.00000
Third phase				
Constant	0.20998	0.01832	66.058	0.00000
Gender	−0.01429	0.00432	3.308	0.00000
Age	0.00068	0.00014	4.734	0.00000
Education	−0.05914	−0.00176	−33.611	0.00000
Ideology	−0.11212	−0.00174	−64.349	0.00000
Retrospective	−0.08266	−0.00283	−29.202	0.00000
Prospective	−0.16742	−0.00355	−47.176	0.00000
Fourth phase				
Constant	0.93180	0.02790	33.393	0.00000
Gender	0.01051	0.00482	2.184	0.02899
Age	0.00189	0.00016	11.486	0.00000
Education	−0.05112	0.00254	−20.135	0.00000
Ideology	−0.07160	0.00239	−29.976	0.00000
Retrospective	−0.10750	0.00396	−27.174	0.00000
Prospective	−0.11428	0.00408	−28.134	0.00000
Fifth phase				
Constant	0.69183	0.01799	38.453	0.00000
Gender	0.02782	0.00363	7.670	0.00000
Age	0.00206	0.00012	16.683	0.00000
Education	−0.05336	0.00189	−28.179	0.00000
Ideology	−0.06411	0.00177	−36.263	0.00000
Retrospective	−0.13541	0.00389	−34.784	0.00000
Prospective	−0.07613	0.00293	−25.999	0.00000

[a] Partial derivatives of probabilities computed at the means of the independent variables.

Table 2.4. *Multinomial Logit Estimates of Support for the Opposition[a]*

Variable	Coefficient	SE	*t*-Ratio	Prob $\lvert t \rvert \geq x$
First phase				
Constant	0.18689	0.04256	4.391	0.00001
Gender	−0.11730	0.01222	−9.596	0.00000
Age	−0.00402	0.00039	−10.399	0.00000
Education	0.01441	0.00453	3.178	0.00148
Ideology	—	—	—	—
Retrospective	0.06616	0.00765	8.649	0.00000
Prospective	−0.01284	0.00830	−1.548	0.12167
Second phase				
Constant	−0.94151	0.06483	−14.522	0.00000
Gender	−0.05680	0.01402	−4.052	0.00005
Age	0.00083	0.00046	1.796	0.07249
Education	0.03620	0.00527	6.863	0.00000
Ideology	0.08955	0.00551	16.249	0.00000
Retrospective	0.06087	0.00905	6.723	0.00000
Prospective	0.10638	0.00987	10.778	0.00000
Third phase				
Constant	−0.78521	0.02923	−26.868	0.00000
Gender	−0.04693	0.00725	−6.469	0.00000
Age	−0.00024	0.00024	−0.980	0.32720
Education	0.04293	0.00283	15.195	0.00000
Ideology	0.08627	0.00251	34.371	0.00000
Retrospective	0.05769	0.00453	12.738	0.00000
Prospective	0.10774	0.00543	19.826	0.00000
Fourth phase				
Constant	−0.88760	0.05613	−15.814	0.00000
Gender	−0.05151	0.01326	−3.884	0.00010
Age	−0.00037	0.00044	−2.180	0.02927
Education	0.04636	0.00613	7.565	0.00000
Ideology	0.08107	0.00431	18.828	0.00000
Retrospective	0.11745	0.00869	13.510	0.00000
Prospective	0.06550	0.00904	7.244	0.00000
Fifth phase				
Constant	−0.52584	0.03551	−14.807	0.00000
Gender	−0.07643	0.00951	−7.428	0.00000
Age	−0.00220	0.00031	−7.003	0.00000
Education	0.05000	0.00409	12.224	0.00000
Ideology	0.07777	0.00287	27.122	0.00000
Retrospective	0.12584	0.00812	15.489	0.00000
Prospective	0.04656	0.00666	6.988	0.00740

[a] Partial derivatives of probabilities computed at the means of the independent variables.

Table 2.5. *Multinomial Logit Estimates of Indecision*[a]

Variable	Coefficient	SE	t-Ratio	Prob $|t| \geq x$
First phase				
Constant	−0.20530	0.03272	−6.274	0.00000
Gender	0.08079	0.00964	8.384	0.00000
Age	0.00187	0.00031	6.025	0.00000
Education	−0.01747	0.00345	−5.064	0.00000
Ideology	—	—	—	—
Retrospective	−0.00682	0.00619	−1.101	0.27094
Prospective	0.05126	0.00620	8.268	0.00000
Second phase				
Constant	−0.24295	0.02862	−8.488	0.00000
Gender	0.01960	0.00737	2.661	0.00779
Age	0.00040	0.00024	1.660	0.09687
Education	−0.00266	0.00274	−0.970	0.33204
Ideology	0.01868	0.00278	6.720	0.00000
Retrospective	0.02077	0.00467	4.444	0.00001
Prospective	0.04277	0.00495	8.644	0.00000
Third phase				
Constant	−0.42477	0.00989	−42.945	0.00000
Gender	0.00326	0.00290	11.270	0.00000
Age	−0.00045	0.00010	−4.634	0.00000
Education	0.01621	0.00110	14.721	0.00000
Ideology	0.02585	0.00086	29.893	0.00000
Retrospective	0.02497	0.00179	13.937	0.00000
Prospective	0.05968	0.00208	28.752	0.00000
Fourth phase				
Constant	−0.04420	0.03612	−1.224	0.22108
Gender	0.04100	0.00846	4.846	0.00000
Age	−0.00092	0.00028	−3.261	0.00111
Education	0.00476	0.00398	1.193	0.23299
Ideology	−0.00947	0.00314	−3.013	0.00259
Retrospective	−0.00995	0.00571	−1.742	0.08154
Prospective	0.04878	0.00583	8.374	0.00000
Fifth phase				
Constant	−0.16599	0.02238	−7.417	0.00000
Gender	0.04282	0.00598	7.158	0.00000
Age	0.00014	0.00020	0.732	0.46442
Education	0.00336	0.00265	1.268	0.20467
Ideology	−0.01366	0.00215	−6.345	0.00000
Retrospective	0.00957	0.00515	1.859	0.06306
Prospective	0.02956	0.00420	7.031	0.00000

[a] Partial derivatives of probabilities computed at the means of the independent variables.

this same government was more likely to raise sympathies among old people. And while under the UCD governments higher levels of education had some effect on support for the incumbent, under the socialists the probability of such support increased when the level of education was low.

Support for the opposition increased in each of the five phases when views of past economic performance were negative. The effect was strongest in the last two phases of the PSOE government. The influence of prospective considerations changed over time: it was insignificant in phase 1, strongest in phases 2 and 3, and then declined in phases 4 and 5. Compare the coefficients of phases 2 and 5: under a new government, support for the opposition was more likely when future expectations about the economy were negative; under an old government, it increased when negative views referred to past performance. This is just equivalent to what happened with support for the government: sympathizers and opponents of a government looked at the future when it was a new one and to the past when it had aged.

Support for the opposition was more probable among right-wing voters under the socialist government, whatever the situation of the economy. It was higher among men and among young people, except in the first phase of the PSOE government. High education levels favored the opposition. There were therefore clear dividing lines between left and right and between low and high educational strata.

People tended to be undecided when views about the economy, either retrospective or prospective, were negative. These undecided respondents were unhappy about economic performance in the past and in the future, but they had not made up their minds about whom to vote for. There were exceptions, though: negative retrospective views had no statistically significant effect in the first, fourth, and fifth phases, when indecision was influenced only by pessimistic expectations. The influence of ideology varied: most of the time, indecision was more likely among right-wing voters, but in the last two phases, under the new economic crisis and increasingly a political one, its probability increased among leftist voters. A plausible interpretation is that in 1982 the collapse of the UCD left many conservative voters without a clear political option, while later on, leftists disenchanted with the socialist experience were uncertain about whether to punish the government to the benefit of the opposition. The effect of education also changed with time: under the UCD, political indecision was more probable when levels of education were low; under the socialists, when such levels were high, although the effect was significant only in phase 3.

The overall pattern of the effects of the independent variables on political support in the five different economic/political phases is summarized in Table 2.6. It is apparent that voters are not all the same: gender, education, and age all matter independently of the evaluations of the economy and of ideology. Both retrospective and prospective views of the economy shape voting intentions: people who have positive evaluations invariably support the incumbent, while people who see things as bleak either turn to the opposition or remain in doubt. Hence, it would appear that the model of economic voting, adjusted for individual differences, explains the behavior of the Spanish voters. But, then, what sense are we to make of the role of ideology, which is the most significant factor in explaining the voting intentions at every phase?

Ideological Interpretations and Vote Intentions: The Economic Model Revisited

The economic voting model supposes that people first form judgments about the current or future state of the economy and then decide how to vote. But the direction of causality is not obvious. For all we know, people may decide how to vote on some prior basis and then look for ways of rationalizing their decisions. Some people may consider the past to have been disastrous but persuade themselves, or can be persuaded, that the future bodes well. Others may even see both the past and the future as bleak, but still conclude that the incumbent government did all it could in the face of adverse circumstances and that the opposition would only do worse (Maravall, 1999:184–193). Conversely, some people may consider the past and the future to be good, but may feel that the government did not do what it should have and that the opposition would have acted better.

Such interpretations need not be unfounded. Under some conditions, there may be good reasons not to infer the future from the past. Under some circumstances, it is reasonable not to blame the incumbent for bad performance even if it is to continue in the future. Voting decisions inevitably entail counterfactual reasoning and, particularly if one party has been in office for a long time, expectations about how the opposition would have performed or will perform in its place must be based on guesswork. Thus, we do not know whether people who do not vote according to their perceptions or even their forecasts know something that others do not or are simply driven by stronger prior beliefs. For it is also possible that some people have such strong prior beliefs (Harrington, 1993) or such strong

Table 2.6. *Summary of Influences on Political Support by Phase*[a]

		1 Crisis/UCD	2 Crisis/New PSOE	3 Expansion/PSOE	4 Crisis/PSOE	5 Expansion/PSOE
Gender	Men	Opposition[b]	Opposition	Opposition/ undecided	Opposition	Opposition
	Women	Undecided/ government	Government/ undecided	Government	Undecided/ government	Undecided/ government
Age	−	Opposition	Government	Undecided/ opposition	Opposition/ undecided	Opposition/ undecided
	+	Government/ undecided	NS[c]	Government	Government	Government
Education	−	Undecided	Government	Government	Government	Government
	+	Opposition/ government	Opposition	Opposition/ undecided	Opposition/ undecided	Opposition/ undecided
Ideology	Left	—[d]	Government[b]	Government[b]	Government/ undecided	Government/ undecided
	Right	—	Opposition/ undecided	Opposition/ undecided	Opposition	Opposition
Retrospective	Bad	Opposition	Opposition/ undecided	Opposition/ undecided	Opposition[b]	Opposition[b]
	Good	Government	Government	Government	Government[b]	Government[b]
Prospective	Bad	Undecided	Opposition[b]/ undecided	Opposition[b]/ undecided	Opposition	Opposition/ undecided
	Good	Government	Government[b]	Government[b]	Government[b]	Government

[a] When an independent variable is related to more than one type of support, the order corresponds to the value of the coefficients.
[b] Highest values of coefficients for the independent variables in each phase.
[c] NS: Not significant.
[d] —: No data available.

commitments (Converse, 1969) that they decide first how to vote and then find reasons to do so. While we have cited evidence that people perceive the past accurately, ideology as well as past political behavior may shape the ways in which they use this information to form expectations and the ways in which they attribute responsibility, both for the past and for the future.

Thus, distinctions are necessary. Following Stokes (this volume), we can distinguish different interpretative mechanisms. We will refer to *types* of people who use distinct mechanisms to process and evaluate the information about the economy:

1. People may see the past economic performance as good, expect it to be good in the future, and reward the government. Alternatively, they may view the future as bad and support the opposition. Such postures are normal, or at least normally expected by the model of economic voting.[24]

2. People may see the past economic performance as bad but believe that it will improve if the incumbent is allowed to continue in office. So, even if retrospective assessments are negative, punishing the incumbent makes no sense: its policies, although painful, are the cause of the optimistic expectations. Such postures are intertemporal.[25]

3. People may expect the future to be bad, whatever their retrospective assessment of the past. That is, they may view economic performance, past and future, in consistently negative terms, or they may think that it will deteriorate. Yet they do not hold the government responsible for these gloomy prospects, which they see as caused by the economic mismanagement of previous governments

---

[24] Such combinations of normal economic voting are therefore the following:

Past	Future	Support
Good	Good	
Regular	Good	
Good	Regular	Government
Regular	Regular	
Bad	Bad	
Good	Bad	
Regular	Bad	Opposition
Good	Regular	
Regular	Regular	

[25] The combinations of intertemporal economic voting are:

Past	Future	Support
Bad	Good	
Bad	Regular	Government

or by forces beyond anyone's control. Voters are pessimistic, but they do not punish the incumbents. The opposition is not a better option. Such postures are exonerative.[26]

4. Whatever the past, many citizens think that the future of the economy will be good. But they do not reward the government for this optimism: if the economy is expected to perform well (and perhaps if it performed well in the past, too), either they do not relate this to the economic policies or they simply dislike the incumbents for whatever reason. Therefore they intend to vote for the opposition. Such postures are oppositionist.[27]

5. People look at the past, scrutinize the future, and, whatever their conclusions about the economy, extract none about political reward or punishment. Such hesitant (or undecided)[28] postures are then compatible with different retrospective and prospective diagnoses about the economy: citizens may be optimistic or pessimistic about the future but unclear about whether another option will improve this prospect of the economy.[29]

Table 2.7 shows the incidence of the five types in the five phases. Over the period of 16 years, indecision was predominant: it represented 45.1%

---

[26] Exonerative economic voting is expressed in the following combinations:

Past	Future	Support
Bad	Bad	
Regular	Bad	Government
Good	Bad	

[27] The following combinations show a pattern of oppositionist voting:

Past	Future	Support
Good	Good	
Regular	Good	Opposition
Bad	Good	
Bad	Regular	

[28] But remember the caveats in footnote 22.

[29] The combinations of undecided economic voting are thus:

Past	Future	Support
Good	Good	
Regular	Good	
Bad	Good	
Bad	Regular	
Good	Regular	Do not know
Regular	Regular	
Good	Bad	
Regular	Bad	
Bad	Bad	

Table 2.7. *Types of Economic Voting by Phases*

Economic Voting	1 Crisis/UCD		2 Crisis/New PSOE		3 Expansion/ PSOE		4 Crisis/PSOE		5 Expansion/ PSOE		Totals	
	(%)	(N)	(%)	(N)	(%)	(N)	(%)	(N)	(%)	(N)	(%)	(N)
Normal	23.7	2,756	24.9	1,867	43.0	13,139	24.0	2,705	33.8	4,632	33.6	25,099
Intertemporal	6.3	734	13.7	1,013	9.8	3,002	9.1	1,024	11.2	1,531	9.8	7,304
Exonerative	4.7	552	6.6	496	6.0	1,841	6.4	726	4.5	620	5.7	4,235
Oppositionist	6.9	803	2.9	219	6.2	1,888	2.3	261	8.5	1,168	5.8	4,339
Undecided	58.4	6,787	51.9	3,875	35.0	10,715	58.2	6,555	42.0	5,755	45.1	33,687
TOTALS		11,632		7,470		30,585		11,271		13,706		74,664

of the total number of respondents. Such people looked at past performance, imagined the future, and extracted conclusions about the economy but none about political reward or punishment. These conclusions could be pessimistic or optimistic: in neither case were they connected to attributions of responsibility. Over the whole period, 32.8% of undecided voters were pessimistic about the economy; 47.5% were optimistic; the remainder were just skeptical.

The rest were able to decide whom to support, but the reasons for such support were different. Most respondents were normal economic voters: they rewarded or punished politicians according to their views of economic conditions.

Intertemporal and exonerative types supported the government even though their views of the economy were negative. These reactions were less frequent: together, they amounted to 15.5% of the total over the five phases. Oppositionist postures were relatively infrequent: less than 6% on average over the 16-year period. Yet of those people who had clear voting intentions, between one-third and one-half did not make their decisions on the basis of the past: either they were convinced that the future would not follow the past, or they thought that the government was not responsible, or they were convinced that the opposition would do better.

Thus political parties receive support that is not motivated by their past performance. When the economy functions well, the government can rely on the support of people who adopt normal postures. But when the economic situation deteriorates, this support need not erode if people find alternative interpretations of this performance, adopting either intertemporal or exonerative postures. The political importance of these alternative mechanisms becomes apparent when we observe, in Figure 2.6, that there were moments when more than one-half of the support for the incumbent government, whether the UCD or the PSOE, was derived from people who did not reason like normal economic voters. And if governments can rely on people to find reasons to support them regardless of economic performance, having to confront voters does not work as a disciplining mechanism for governments. This is perhaps why Cheibub and Przeworski (1999) found that the survival of governments in office is unrelated to economic performance.

The question that is open is whether these alternative postures are based on rational beliefs, derived from the best information voters can get, or are

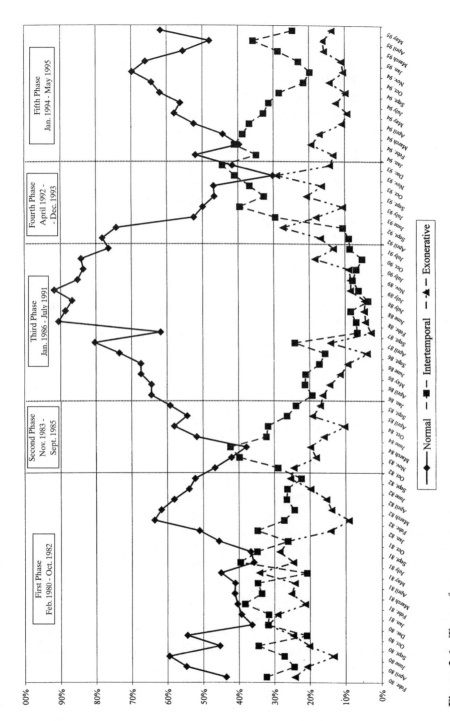

Figure 2.6 Types of government vote.

motivated by ideology or by past political commitments.[30] We have seen that ideology affects voting intentions independently of the way people see the economic past or the future. The reason may be that ideology shapes the way in which people interpret the state of the economy in political terms. Hence, to test the role of ideology, we need to see if the interpretive postures people adopt are driven only by their private information, which we assume to be related to sociodemographic characteristics, or also by their ideological positions or past commitments, independently of whatever information people may have. Thus, Tables 2.8 to 2.10 report the multinomial logit estimates of each of the types, with gender, age, educational level, ideology, and past vote as independent variables.

The intertemporal and exonerative types of voters support the government, even though they see present economic conditions as bad. The reasons for this apparent non sequitur are, however, different. Intertemporal voters attribute present hardship to the government but think that it leads to a better future, and their discount rate is low enough that expectations weigh more than present pains. By contrast, exonerative voters are pessimistic about the future: they think that the government bears no responsibility for the bad economic performance and/or that the opposition is a worse alternative. As we have shown, these two types were more frequent in phase 2, with an incoming socialist government and a continuing economic crisis. They were influenced, therefore, by political conditions; we also saw that the 1993 electoral victory of the PSOE led to a surge in both types. Reverse causation seems, therefore, to have existed in intertemporal and exonerative reactions: individuals first had political preferences; then they looked at the economy and reached an intertemporal or exonerative conclusion.

As Table 2.8 shows, intertemporal reactions were more likely among women. This fits with their tendency to support the government rather than the opposition, whichever party was in power or whatever the economic cycle. The influence of gender on exoneration, as can be seen in Table 2.9, was less clear: in phases 1 and 2, women tended not to blame the UCD and the PSOE; in phase 3, gender did not have a significant influence; eventually, in the last two socialist phases (one of crisis, the other of expansion), exoneration became more likely among men. Intertemporal reactions increased among younger voters in phases 2 and 3, with a

---

[30] The variable identifying past commitments is the recall of the vote in the previous election, coded in the same way as the voting intention, that is, 0 for the incumbent, 1 for no answers, and 2 for the opposition.

Spain

Table 2.8. *Multinomial Logit Estimates of Intertemporal Voting*[a]

Variable	Coefficient	SE	t-Ratio	Prob $|t| \geq x$
First phase				
Constant	−0.02552	0.00027	−94.935	0.00000
Gender	0.00069	0.00010	6.746	0.00000
Age	0.00006	0.00000	17.154	0.00000
Education	0.00261	0.00004	70.139	0.00000
Ideology	—	—	—	—
Past vote	−0.05846	0.00020	−288.926	0.00000
Second phase				
Constant	0.01494	0.00072	20.788	0.00000
Gender	0.01712	0.00024	71.907	0.00000
Age	−0.00086	0.00001	−117.342	0.00000
Education	−0.00403	0.00008	−51.266	0.00000
Ideology	−0.00087	0.00000	−215.685	0.00000
Past vote	−0.13305	0.00044	−301.782	0.00000
Third phase				
Constant	−0.04984	0.00048	−103.858	0.00000
Gender	0.01188	0.00019	63.967	0.00000
Age	−0.00029	0.00001	−48.925	0.00000
Education	−0.00500	0.00007	−76.320	0.00000
Ideology	−0.00072	0.00000	−210.529	0.00000
Past vote	−0.03925	0.00018	−212.238	0.00000
Fourth phase				
Constant	−0.01678	0.00019	−90.226	0.00000
Gender	0.00536	0.00006	95.625	0.00000
Age	0.00004	0.00000	20.154	0.00000
Education	−0.00099	0.00002	−44.810	0.00000
Ideology	−0.00038	0.00000	−388.332	0.00000
Past vote	−0.09022	0.00017	−523.514	0.00000
Fifth phase				
Constant	−0.01196	0.00043	−28.099	0.00000
Gender	0.00886	0.00012	74.528	0.00000
Age	0.00004	0.00000	10.429	0.00000
Education	−0.00068	0.00005	−14.883	0.00000
Ideology	−0.00473	0.00004	−131.271	0.00000
Past vote	−0.12252	0.00034	−365.464	0.00000

[a] Partial derivatives of probabilities computed at the means of the independent variables.

Table 2.9. *Multinomial Logit Estimates of Exonerative Voting*[a]

Variable	Coefficient	SE	t-Ratio	Prob $|t| \geq x$
First phase				
Constant	−0.01951	0.00022	−89.934	0.00000
Gender	0.00116	0.00008	14.018	0.00000
Age	−0.00003	0.00000	−12.949	0.00000
Education	0.00001	0.00003	0.493	0.62204
Ideology	—	—	—	—
Past vote	−0.04540	0.00016	−285.763	0.00000
Second phase				
Constant	−0.00593	0.00040	−14.809	0.00000
Gender	0.01418	0.00014	100.635	0.00000
Age	−0.00094	0.00000	−209.482	0.00000
Education	−0.01170	0.00005	−222.409	0.00000
Ideology	−0.00030	0.00000	−130.548	0.00000
Past vote	−0.05763	0.00022	−261.045	0.00000
Third phase				
Constant	−0.06638	0.00031	−210.781	0.00000
Gender	0.00016	0.00012	1.282	0.19993
Age	−0.00015	0.00000	−36.428	0.00000
Education	−0.00745	0.00005	−163.007	0.00000
Ideology	−0.00016	0.00000	−71.371	0.00000
Past vote	−0.00262	0.00010	−26.68	0.00000
Fourth phase				
Constant	0.01533	0.00018	87.266	0.00000
Gender	−0.00187	0.00004	−42.421	0.00000
Age	−0.00043	0.00000	−285.955	0.00000
Education	−0.00653	0.00002	−333.481	0.00000
Ideology	−0.00010	0.00000	−121.744	0.00000
Past vote	−0.07099	0.00014	−517.742	0.00000
Fifth phase				
Constant	0.02502	0.00034	73.624	0.00000
Gender	−0.00251	0.00008	−31.126	0.00000
Age	−0.00059	0.00000	−213.352	0.00000
Education	−0.00748	0.00004	−213.270	0.00000
Ideology	−0.00189	0.00002	−78.421	0.00000
Past vote	−0.08055	0.00023	−357.216	0.00000

[a] Partial derivatives of probabilities computed at the means of the independent variables.

Spain

Table 2.10. *Multinomial Logit Estimates of Oppositionist Voting*[a]

Variable	Coefficient	SE	t-Ratio	Prob $|t| \geq x$
First phase				
Constant	−0.10847	0.01342	−8.085	0.00000
Gender	−0.02045	0.00399	−5.120	0.00000
Age	−0.00033	0.00012	−2.676	0.00749
Education	−0.00041	0.00133	−0.310	0.75693
Ideology	—	—	—	—
Past vote	0.06127	0.00582	10.522	0.00000
Second phase				
Constant	−0.05003	0.00974	−5.136	0.00000
Gender	−0.00662	0.00253	−2.621	0.00876
Age	−0.00004	0.00007	−0.544	0.58661
Education	0.00130	0.00080	1.629	0.10339
Ideology	−0.00015	0.00005	−3.050	0.00229
Past vote	0.02429	0.00426	5.707	0.00000
Third phase				
Constant	−0.09095	0.00689	−13.191	0.00000
Gender	−0.00889	0.00186	−4.794	0.00000
Age	−0.00017	0.00006	−2.898	0.00376
Education	0.00203	0.00064	3.169	0.00153
Ideology	−0.00023	0.00004	−6.367	0.00000
Past vote	0.04877	0.00299	16.314	0.00000
Fourth phase				
Constant	−0.03670	0.00695	−5.281	0.00000
Gender	−0.00240	0.00142	−1.690	0.09096
Age	−0.00013	0.00005	−2.508	0.01215
Education	−0.00015	0.00056	−0.271	0.78677
Ideology	−0.00015	0.00004	−4.037	0.00005
Past vote	0.01753	0.00313	5.602	0.00000
Fifth phase				
Constant	−0.05509	0.01094	−5.037	0.00000
Gender	−0.00237	0.00190	−1.247	0.21235
Age	−0.00017	0.00007	−2.422	0.01545
Education	0.00016	0.00074	0.218	0.82761
Ideology	0.00135	0.00057	2.386	0.01702
Past vote	0.02334	0.00447	5.220	0.00000

[a] Partial derivatives of probabilities computed at the means of the independent variables.

new government and under an economic expansion; but as governments aged, optimism about the future was more probable among older voters. However, younger voters were more likely to exonerate incumbents in all the five politico-economic phases. The impact of education on both types of voting varied: intertemporal reactions were more likely among the higher educational groups under the conservative government (phase 1); they increased, by contrast, among the lower ones under the socialists (phases 2 to 5). As for exonerative reactions, no statistically significant relation existed in phase 1, but in the four socialist phases their probability increased in the lower educational groups.

Yet independently of the individual differences, ideology and vote in the past election were most important in shaping intertemporal and exonerative reactions to the economy. Some people looked at the economy with political blinkers. Such postures were higher among voters situated on the left in the four PSOE phases and also among individuals who had supported the incumbent governments in the past elections. The coefficients for ideology were higher for both intertemporal and exonerative reactions at the beginning and at the end of the socialist period; this was also the case for the past vote on intertemporal reactions. That a new government would raise expectations among its supporters and not be blamed for the bad performance of the economy is to be expected. But an old government seems also to have found support among people on the left and among loyal voters who still did not hold it responsible for their economic unhappiness or remained optimistic about the future.

These blinkers also influenced oppositionist voters, but they led in a different direction. These people thought that the evolution of the economy was good, but they supported the opposition. They either decoupled governmental policies and economic performance or were overwhelmingly influenced by noneconomic considerations. Having supported the opposition in the past increased the probability of oppositionist reactions to the economy. This is where we find again the strongest coefficients. This reaction was also more likely among leftist voters in three out of the four phases for which we have data on ideology. Only at the end of the socialist governments was oppositionist voting more likely within the right. The left seems to have been divided in its voting intention: it provided both support for the socialists (in the form of normal, intertemporal, and exonerative reactions) and unconditional opposition.

The effects of the independent variables on all the five types of interpretative postures in the five politico-economic phases are summarized in Table 2.11. Demographic characteristics do play a role in shaping the responses of individuals to economic conditions. Thus, people located in particular places in the social structure are affected differently by general economic conditions and/or have different information about them. Yet the interpretive postures are driven largely by past political commitments and by ideology. Left-wing voters found all kinds of reasons to support the PSOE government. When conditions were good, as they were in phase 3, they could support the government by reasoning normally. When the economy turned down, in periods of economic crisis, these loyal voters turned to intertemporal and exonerative interpretations and still supported the government. And, in accordance with Converse (1969), past voting behavior was a powerful force in shaping future voting intentions. Once someone had voted for the government, he or she intended to vote for it again, whether for normal, intertemporal, or exonerative reasons; once someone had voted for the opposition, he or she would not vote for the government regardless of economic circumstances.

These patterns show the limits of economic voting explanations. Causality seems to have been often reversed: partisan allegiances rooted in social and political conditions influenced the interpretations of the economy. Once class and ideology mediated, people interpreted the same economic conditions in different ways and could thus maintain their ideological and partisan loyalties in the face of changing economic circumstances.

Conclusion

Over a period of 16 years, interspersed with four elections and under different types of government, the Spanish economy experienced phases of expansion and recession, with oscillations of nearly 7% in the annual rate of GNP growth, 10% in the annual rate of inflation, and 13% in the unemployment rate. People accurately perceived these economic changes. Yet their voting intentions remained much more stable. Thus it is clear that the model of economic voting is not sufficient to tell the story of Spanish partisan attitudes.

Both retrospective and prospective views on the performance of the economy influenced voting intention. When such views, regarding either the past or the future, were positive, governments were rewarded; when they were negative, support for the opposition increased. In the expansive phases, the incidence of normal economic voting went up and electoral indecision declined. Thus, we have prima facie evidence of a pattern of economic voting. However, this pattern was far from simple. First,

Table 2.11. *Summary of Influences on Types of Voting*[a]

		1 Crisis/UCD	2 Crisis/New PSOE	3 Expansion/PSOE	4 Crisis/PSOE	5 Expansion/PSOE
Gender	Men	Oppositionist[b]/normal[b]	Normal[b]/oppositionist	Normal[b]/oppositionist	Normal[b]/oppositionist/exonerative	Normal[b]/exonerative/oppositionist
	Women	Undecided[b]/exonerative/intertemporal	Intertemporal[b]/undecided[b]/exonerative	Undecided[b]/intertemporal/oppositionist/exonerative	Undecided[b]/intertemporal	Undecided[b]/exonerative/oppositionist
Age	−	Oppositionist/normal/exonerative	Intertemporal/exonerative/oppositionist	Undecided/intertemporal/oppositionist/exonerative	Undecided/exonerative/oppositionist	Undecided/exonerative/oppositionist
	+	Intertemporal/undecided	Normal/undecided	Normal	Normal/intertemporal	Normal/intertemporal
Education	−	Undecided	Exonerative[b]/intertemporal	Exonerative/normal/intertemporal	Normal[b]/exonerative/intertemporal	Normal[b]/exonerative/intertemporal
	+	Intertemporal/normal/exonerative	Normal[b]	Undecided[b]/oppositionist	Undecided[b]	Undecided[b]

Ideology / Past vote						
Ideology	Left	—[c]	Normal/intertemporal/exonerative/oppositionist	Normal/intertemporal/oppositionist/exonerative	Normal/intertemporal/oppositionist/exonerative	Normal/intertemporal/exonerative
	Right	—	Undecided	Undecided	Undecided	Undecided[b]/oppositionist
Past vote	Opposition	Oppositionist[b]/normal[b]/undecided[b]	Undecided[b]/oppositionist[b]	Undecided[b]/oppositionist[b]	Undecided[b]/oppositionist[b]	Undecided[b]/oppositionist[b]
	Government	Intertemporal[b]/exonerative[b]	Intertemporal[b]/exonerative[b]/normal[b]	Normal[b]/intertemporal[b]/exonerative	Intertemporal[b]/exonerative[b]/normal[b]	Intertemporal[b]/exonerative[b]/normal[b]

[a] When an independent variable is related to more than one type of support, the order corresponds to the value of the coefficients.
[b] Highest values of coefficients for the independent variables in each phase.
[c] —: No data available.

retrospective and prospective evaluations were unrelated: individuals did not infer the future from the past, being much more optimistic about the future than satisfied with the past. Second, the relative importance of retrospective and prospective evaluations changed according to the age of the governments: new ones were supported or rejected on prospective grounds, old ones on retrospective grounds.

The role of economic conditions in shaping partisan attitudes is limited because political reactions to the economy are mediated by political loyalties and by ideology. This did not prevent political choices: for instance, women were more likely to be undecided or to support the government; leftists, to vote for the PSOE or to be undecided in its last period in office; young voters, to opt for the opposition or for indecision. But, in general, partisan attitudes were considerably stable, whatever the conditions of the economy.

The social and ideological roots of party preferences were probably more consistent in Spain than in other new democracies: the PSOE had more than 100 years of history and could appeal to ideological and class loyalties embedded in the memory of "past political battles that had shaped the ways in which voters thought about politics and government" (Popkin, 1994:50). This historical memory perhaps explains why the influence of cleavages of class and ideology on voting intentions remained largely stable in the face of sharply changing economic conditions, the introduction of market reforms, or the vast increase in unemployment. Thus, economic voting may be limited when the roots of partisanship are strong; by contrast, its incidence may be greater in those democracies where such roots are weak.

Our evidence suggests that political reactions to the economy often did not correspond to a logic of economic voting. Although views about the economy may have produced political reactions, such views also seem to have been the result of previous political considerations. Voters often appear to have decided, for whatever reasons, to support the government or the opposition, and only then to have chosen arguments to sustain their decision. Thus, rather than views of the economy deciding the vote, the causation was often the reverse.

References

Abramowitz, A. 1985. "Economic Conditions, Presidential Popularity, and Voting Behavior in Mid-Term Congressional Elections." *Journal of Politics* 47: 31–43.
Abramowitz, A., D. J. Lanoue, and S. Ramesh. 1988. "Economic Conditions, Causal Attributions, and Political Evaluations in the 1984 Presidential Election." *Journal of Politics* 50: 839–862.

Bartels, L. M. 1988. "The Economic Consequences of Retrospective Voting." Unpublished manuscript, University of Rochester.

Boix, C. 1998. *Political Parties, Growth and Equality*. New York: Cambridge University Press.

Bratton, K. A. 1994. "Retrospective Voting and Future Expectations. The Case of the Budget Deficit in the 1988 Election." *American Politics Quarterly* 22: 277–296.

Cheibub, J. A., and A. Przeworski. 1999. "Democracy, Elections, and Accountability for Economic Outcomes." In A. Przeworski, S. Stokes, and B. Manin (eds.), *Democracy, Accountability, and Representation*. New York: Cambridge University Press.

Conover, P. J., S. Feldman, and K. Knight. 1987. "The Personal and Political Underpinnings of Economic Forecasts." *American Journal of Political Science* 31: 559–583.

Converse, P. E. 1969. "Of Time and Partisan Stability." *Comparative Political Studies* 2: 139–171.

Economie Européenne. 1995. Brussels: European Commission.

Feldman, S. 1982. "Economic Self-Interest and Political Behavior." *American Journal of Political Science* 26: 446–466.

1985. "Economic Self-Interest and the Vote: Evidence and Meaning." In H. Eulau and M. S. Lewis-Beck (eds.), *Economic Conditions and Electoral Outcomes: The United States and Western Europe*. New York: Agathon Press.

Fiorina, M. 1981. *Retrospective Voting in American National Elections*. New Haven: Yale University Press.

Harrington, J. E., Jr. 1993. "Economic Policy, Economic Performance, and Elections." *American Economic Review* 83: 27–42.

Keech, W. R. 1995. *Economic Politics*. New York: Cambridge University Press.

Key, V. O. 1966. *The Responsible Electorate*. New York: Vintage Books.

Kiewiet, D. R., and D. Rivers. 1985. "A Retrospective on Retrospective Voting." In H. Eulau and M. S. Lewis-Beck (eds.), *Economic Conditions and Electoral Outcomes: The United States and Western Europe*. New York: Agathon Press.

Kinder, D. R., and D. R. Kiewiet. 1979. "Economic Discontent and Political Behavior: The Role of Personal Grievances and Collective Economic Judgements in Congressional Voting." *American Journal of Political Science* 23: 495–517.

Kramer, G. H. 1971. "Short-Term Fluctuations in U.S. Voting Behavior, 1896–1964." *American Political Science Review* 65: 131–143.

Kuklinski, J. H., and D. M. West. 1981. "Economic Expectations and Voting Behavior in United States Senate and House Elections." *American Political Science Review* 75: 436–447.

Lancaster, T., and M. S. Lewis-Beck. 1986. "The Spanish Voter: Tradition, Economics, Ideology." *Journal of Politics* 48: 648–674.

Lanoue, D. J. 1994. "Retrospective and Prospective Voting in Presidential-Year Elections." *Political Research Quarterly* 14: 193–205.

Lewis-Beck, M. S. 1988. *Economics and Elections. The Major Western Democracies*. Ann Arbor: University of Michigan Press.

Lewis-Beck, M. S., and A. Skalaban. 1989. "Citizen Forecasting: Can Voters See Into the Future?" *British Journal of Political Science* 19: 46–53.

Lockerbie, B. 1991. "Prospective Economic Voting in U.S. House Elections, 1956–88." *Legislative Studies Quarterly* 16: 239–261.

1992. "Prospective Voting in Presidential Elections: 1956–88." *American Political Quarterly* 20: 308–325.

MacKuen, M. B., R. S. Erikson, and J. A. Stimson. 1992. "Peasants or Bankers. The American Electorate and the US Economy." *American Political Science Review* 86: 597–611.

Maravall, J. M. 1997. *Regimes, Politics, and Markets.* Oxford: Oxford University Press.

1999. "Accountability and Manipulation." In A. Przeworski, S. C. Stokes, and B. Manin (eds.), *Democracy, Accountability, and Representation.* New York: Cambridge University Press.

Markus, G. B. 1988. "The Impact of Personal and National Economic Conditions on the Presidential Vote: A Pooled Cross-Sectional Analysis." *American Journal of Political Science* 32: 137–154.

1992. "The Impact of Personal and National Economic Conditions on Presidential Voting, 1956–88." *American Journal of Political Science* 36: 829–834.

Monardi, F. M. 1994. "Primary Voters as Retrospective Voters." *American Political Quarterly* 1: 88–103.

Nannestad, P., and M. Paldam. 1994. "The VP-Function: A Survey of the Literature on Vote and Popularity Functions after 25 Years." *Public Choice* 79: 213–245.

1997. "From the Pocketbook of the Welfare Man: A Pooled Cross-Section Study of Economic Voting in Denmark, 1986–92." *British Journal of Political Science* 27: 119–137.

Peffley, M. 1985. "The Voter as a Juror: Attributing Responsibility for Economic Conditions." In H. Eulau and M. S. Lewis-Beck (eds.), *Economic Conditions and Electoral Outcomes: The United States and Western Europe.* New York: Agathon Press.

Popkin, S. L. 1994. *The Reasoning Voter.* Chicago: University of Chicago Press.

Price, S., and D. Sanders. 1995. "Economic Expectations and Voting Intentions in the U.K., 1979–87: A Pooled Cross-Section Approach." *Political Studies* 43: 451–471.

Przeworski, A. 1991. *Democracy and the Market.* New York: Cambridge University Press.

Shaffer, S. D., and G. A. Chressanthis. 1991. "Accountability and U.S. Senate Elections: A Multivariate Analysis." *Western Political Quarterly* 44: 625–639.

Svoda, C. J. 1995. "Retrospective Voting in Gubernatorial Elections: 1982–1986." *Political Research Quarterly* 48: 117–134.

Uslaner, E. M. 1989. "Looking Forward and Looking Backward: Prospective and Retrospective Voting in the 1980 Federal Elections in Canada." *British Journal of Political Science* 19: 495–513.

3

The Economy and Public Opinion in East Germany after the Wall

Christopher J. Anderson and Yuliya V. Tverdova

The fall of the Berlin Wall and the unification of East and West Germany have been at the heart of the wave of democratization that swept East Central Europe in the 1990s. They also marked the beginning of a new and difficult era of postwar German politics. Policy makers were suddenly charged with building a new political system and a viable economy in the eastern part of the newly united country, while East Germans instantly became citizens of a stable, well-functioning democracy and market economy. This chapter examines citizens' responses to these events. Specifically, we focus on economic conditions in East Germany after unification and how these affected popular support for the government. Based on monthly data for the period from 1991 to 1995, we trace the dynamics of public support for governing parties and their handling of the economy in East Germany. We seek to account for these dynamics with the help of theories developed in the research on economic voting and democratic transitions.

We first take a look back at the events leading up to and surrounding unification, as well as the economic and political situation in East and West Germany that resulted from it. These events provide the context in which we examine the relationship between economic conditions and government support and in which East Germans expressed opinions about the transition and the federal government. In particular, the history of East Germany and the way in which unification took place set the stage for the political socialization process of East Germans before and after the fall of

This research was supported by NSF Grant SBR-9818525 to the first author. We would like to thank Ilya Gofman, Michael McDonald, Kathleen O'Connor, and Susan Stokes for their help and advice.

the Wall and thus shaped how they responded to the economic hardship produced by the transition. The subsequent data analysis examines the relationship among objective economic conditions, people's perceptions of the economy, and support for the federal government among the citizens of the former East Germany. The concluding section discusses the findings and spells out further implications.

System Change in East Germany

To understand the radical transition that occurred in East Germany in 1989–1990 and how it may have affected people's responses to the government and the economy, a look back may be helpful.[1] The Federal Republic of Germany (FRG) and the German Democratic Republic (GDR) were founded as separate states in 1949 and subsequently developed along radically different political and economic trajectories (Childs, 1988; Dalton, 1993). While the FRG evolved into a liberal democracy whose citizens were among the most supportive of democratic principles in the Western world, the GDR became one of the most authoritarian Communist systems of Eastern Europe, whose legitimacy was perennially undermined by citizens' attempts to flee to the West. In fact, the inability of East German political elites to convince people that the GDR was a legitimate and viable counterpart to the FRG only accelerated the rapid collapse of the GDR in 1989.

After the Wall came down on November 9, 1989, the political hierarchy in the GDR crumbled fairly quickly. In rapid succession, the East German parliament elected a new prime minister and repealed the section of the Constitution that provided for the "leadership role" of the Communist Party, and the entire Communist Party leadership resigned. As the power apparatus of the Communist Party started to disintegrate even further, the government agreed to roundtable negotiations with the most prominent dissident groups and political parties. These negotiations led to the scheduling of free elections for a new East German parliament, which were subsequently held in March 1990.

The elections were dominated by a single overarching issue: the pace of German unification. The resounding winner turned out to be the Alliance for Germany – a collection of parties that included the Christian

---

[1] Parts of this section were modified and updated from Kaltenthaler and Anderson (1993).

Democrats (CDU, the major governing party in West Germany) and other, smaller political groups in the political center and on the right. The Alliance had run on a platform of free market economic reforms and, most important, German unification as quickly as possible. The clear win by the CDU and their allies, as well as the unmistakable mandate it carried, had important implications for the dynamics of the unification process and postunification politics.

In the short run, the express desire of East German citizens to speed up the process of unification moved the debate about the process of formal political unification to the forefront, prompting political decision makers in Bonn and East Berlin to choose the quickest possible route to unification. On August 31, 1990, the two German states signed a treaty, called the Unification Treaty, which outlined the terms under which unification would take place. Subsequently, on October 3, the GDR acceded to the FRG, formally completing the unification of Germany less than 11 months after the fall of the Berlin Wall.

During this time, it also became apparent that the West German (federal) elections, which had initially been planned as the regular national elections for the old (West German) FRG for December 2, would be the first free all-German elections to be held in both parts of the united Germany. To no one's surprise, these elections were dominated by the issue of unification and turned into a referendum on the performance of the government of Chancellor Helmut Kohl, consisting of Christian Democrats (CDU/CSU) and Liberals (FDP) during 1989–1990. Kohl's challenger for the chancellorship, the Social Democrats' (SPD) Oskar Lafontaine, argued that the unification process was proceeding too rapidly, that it was fundamentally flawed economically and unjust socially, and that a socially and economically just unification process was being sacrificed for the sake of short-term political gain. Even though Lafontaine's point was probably well taken as it turned out after the fact, it did not seem to matter to the German electorate: winning handily, the Kohl government had many of its unification policies thus ratified by way of a national election.

Unification and the East German Economy

During the GDR's existence, the glaring discrepancies in living standards between the two Germanies were perhaps the most crucial factor eroding the legitimacy of the East German state. Because they had access to West German television, East Germans for many years were keenly aware of how well off their West German neighbors were. And although East Germans enjoyed a better standard of living than virtually any other social-ist country in the world, the Communist regime was never quite able to quell people's desire to achieve the lifestyle in the West that was beamed to them nightly by West German television.

More than a month before the East German parliamentary (Volks-kammer) election in March 1990, the West German government had offered the East German leadership immediate negotiations toward the creation of a monetary union and an economic community. This proposal was quickly taken up by the two German governments after the election, in which East German voters had expressed their desire for a quick conclusion of the unification process. A treaty that was subsequently signed by the two German states specified that the West German deutsche mark (D-mark) would be substituted for the East German currency, while the GDR created the conditions for the intro-duction of a market economy.

The introduction of "good money" and the treaty in general had, and continue to have, significant implications for all aspects of economic, social, and political life in both East and West Germany. They affected such factors as wages, salaries, prices of goods, inflation and credit, welfare benefits and pensions, economic cooperation in the European Union, tax-ation and public debts, and the structure of the respective economies, among others. In hindsight, however, monetary union turned out to be a disaster for the East German economy. East Germans exchanged their worthless ost marks for the valuable D-mark at a one-to-one rate and then proceeded to buy mostly Western products. The East German economy collapsed and ever since has been kept alive by a steady stream of cash transfusions from the West, as well as by continuous crisis management by policy makers in Bonn (and now Berlin).

Economic Institutions after Unification

On a practical level, the task of dealing with the accumulated problems of 40 years of *real-socialist* economic management turned out to pose an enormous challenge. The reconstruction of the East German economy foundered mainly because of a lack of private investment for the modern-ization of East German firms. The structural similarities of the East and West German economies meant that the technologically outdated and unproductive East German firms were at a serious disadvantage vis-à-vis

West German businesses. In fact, West German firms were able to claim the East German market without investing in new production facilities there.

This lack of investment made it difficult to create a competitive productive base for the East German economy and achieve sustained economic growth. The primary reason for this lay in the way in which political and economic institutions were developed in East Germany. Instead of creating new institutions for the former GDR, the unified Germany merely transferred West German political and economic institutions to East Germany. Although this brought some semblance of political stability to the East, it also saddled firms there with regulations and laws designed for a highly developed modern economy.

Within a few years of unification, it was difficult to imagine that East Germany once had been considered a socialist version of the German economic miracle. Economic and environmental regulations in particular saddled East German firms. Rules such as standards for safety, working hours, and product specifications dissuaded potential investors from entering East Germany because they did not want to incur the costs of raising East German firms to West German standards. Many East German firms had seen only minor improvements since they had been inherited from the Nazis in 1945. The most cost-imposing set of institutions transferred from the West to the East, however, were environmental regulations. When West German investors bought an East German firm, they had to take on its usually considerable environmental liabilities resulting from antiquated technology and a lack of environmental measures. The cost of modernizing firms that employed technology from the turn of the century was enormous and not at all cost-effective.

Developing private property rights in East Germany also proved to be an immensely complicated task. Three sets of property rights issues had to be dealt with: (1) claims from those who had their property confiscated by the Nazis; (2) property confiscated by the Soviets during the early period of the occupation; and (3) property expropriated by the East German state. While the first two sets of issues were quickly settled by disallowing claims against properties confiscated by the Nazis or the Soviets, the issue of restoring private property rights from what had been East German state property became a major problem. Instead of compensating the former owners of confiscated property monetarily, the German government decided to restore the property to their owners. This decision to find the original owners of properties created an atmosphere of great economic uncertainty that became a major source of investors' unwillingness to underwrite firms in East Germany. More than a million claims were filed for property in the GDR in 1990 alone, many of them conflicting and exceedingly difficult to verify. By 1993, one out of every four properties in the former GDR was the subject of a claim.

Aside from issues of property rights and regulation, the German government had to decide what to do with the state-owned enterprises that had made up much of East Germany's economic capacity during the Communist era. It decided to privatize them by selling them to the highest bidder. Toward this end, it used a government agency – the Treuhandanstalt (THA) – to privatize former East German state properties. Considering its enormous task, the THA turned out to be surprisingly successful. It privatized the whole subset of service and trade firms of the former GDR. Unfortunately, however, it had much less success with East German industry.

Frequently, firms were sold in pieces rather than as whole productive units (*Kombinate*). West German firms typically bought parts of East German firms to produce components or selected lines rather than the full range of goods. Thus, in the end, the THA was left with the unattractive parts of firms that were difficult to sell and ended up subsidizing those divisions of firms it had little hope of selling. This kept people in jobs at uncompetitive plants while still forcing layoffs in those that had a chance of being turned around.

While the institutions of economic and environmental regulation were transferred to the Eastern *Länder*, the institutions of West German corporatism were not completely re-created in East Germany. Although West German organizations of labor and capital replaced their Eastern counterparts, these organizations had very different resources in the East. The relative strength of East German trade unions vis-à-vis East German industry meant that East German wages soared after 1990 as unions became more aggressive in their attempts to achieve wages that matched those in the West. Encouraged by their West German union leaders, who were fighting for wage increases higher than the rate of inflation, East German workers showed little willingness to moderate wage demands to give East German industry a chance to build an economic base. The end result was that wages in East Germany rose significantly immediately after unification for those lucky enough to have a job while productivity fell and unemployment soared.

Financing the Cost of Unification

The government originally had assumed that the immense cost of reconstructing the East German economy would be self-financed by private investment and from the sale of East German firms by the THA (Seibel, 1993). In fact, when Chancellor Kohl ran for reelection in the fall of 1990, he promised that East Germany would become "blossoming landscapes" after a short period of adjustment without much economic hardship on the part of average citizens in the East and West. After all, the government's message was, East Germans were Germans first and foremost, and why could there not be another German economic miracle just like the one West Germany had experienced during the 1950s?

At the outset of the reform process, expectations were thus extremely high – much too high, as it turned out in retrospect. Over a short period of time, economic conditions worsened considerably, the expected private investment did not materialize, the THA started to run into difficulties, and the costs of German unification began to accumulate. As a result, the Kohl government was forced to pump an average of 160 billion D-marks (app. US$90–100 billion) a year into East Germany in the form of subsidies and unemployment compensation, producing a growing budget deficit as well as rapidly declining approval ratings for the government along the way.

The government eventually was forced to confront economic reality, especially in preparation for a single European currency, which had mandated strict fiscal discipline under the so-called Maastricht criteria. Simply put, this meant higher taxes and fewer benefits. The Kohl administration tried to avoid some of the harsher blame by claiming that the tax increases would be temporary. They included a one-year 7.5% income and corporation surcharge starting July 1, 1991, and a tax increase of 25 pfennig per liter of gasoline. There also were tax increases on tobacco and insurance premiums, and the federal government further decided in late 1991 that a 25% withholding tax on investment income (with exceptions for personal savings) would be necessary. In light of the growing budget deficit, however, another round of taxes was imposed in February 1992 to go into effect in January 1993 in order to make up for the loss of revenue after the termination of the temporary surcharge (also called the *solidarity contribution*) on incomes. The value-added tax (VAT) was also increased from 14% to 15%. By 1997, the solidarity contribution – the 7.5% surcharge on incomes – as well as the other taxes meant to be (or at least sold to the public as) temporary were still in effect. Moreover, despite the various creative ways of financing the East German reconstruction, the growth in the federal deficit was held to manageable levels only by cutting various entitlement and welfare programs, thereby hitting East Germans who were in economic distress the hardest. In the end, it was clear that the Kohl government had consistently and radically underestimated the cost of bailing out a collapsing East German economy without shouldering much of the political blame for the situation.

Elections and Public Opinion after Unification

Given these developments, it should not come as a surprise, then, that economic conditions and the economic reconstruction in the East played a major role in the electoral arena following unification. Almost immediately after the December 1990 election and the Kohl government's resounding defeat of the opposition, the euphoria of electoral victory and unification started to wear off and the unification hangover set in. Barely five months into the new year, protest rallies were held against rising unemployment and the economic crisis in the East, and the government's public approval ratings plummeted.

Figures 3.1 and 3.2 show objective economic conditions (inflation and unemployment) and government support in East Germany between 1991 and 1995. Aside from tracking the significant increase in unemployment and the decrease in inflation, they document the precipitous decline in approval of the Kohl government among East Germans. Moreover, they show that the government's fortunes did not improve for much of the time between 1991 and 1993. It appeared that the financial costs of unification as well as the frustration with the slowness of economic progress took their political toll; the East German public reacted negatively as the promise of prosperity appeared to be slipping away.

By the end of 1993, however, the public mood showed hesitant signs of improvement, and government approval recovered somewhat.[2] To a large extent, this cautious trend reversal resulted from new economic forecasts that predicted modest economic growth for 1994 and 1995. Yet, even as late as April 1994 – that is, six months before the next national election was scheduled to be held – a majority of Germans believed that Kohl and

---

[2] Parts of this section are based on Anderson and Zelle (1995).

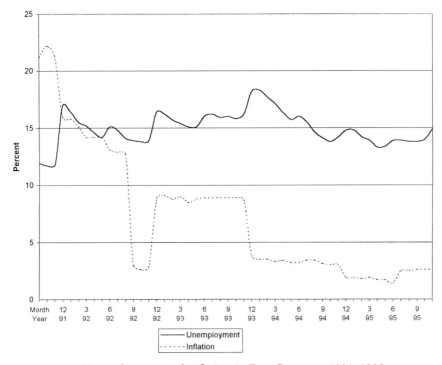

Figure 3.1 Unemployment and inflation in East Germany, 1991–1995.

the government were in trouble. A survey conducted by the polling institute Infas in April showed that only 31% of Germans expected the
CDU/CSU to win the federal election, while 65% saw the SPD ahead
(Infas, 1994). These numbers made the results of the June elections to the
European parliament all the more remarkable. While most polling insti-
tutes had predicted a head-to-head race only weeks before the elections,
the CDU/CSU came out 6.4% ahead of the SPD. The party, Helmut
Kohl, and the government as a whole gained significant momentum as a
result of this election, and by July Infas reported that 59% expected the
CDU/CSU to win the federal election – twice as many as in April.

The Economy and the 1994 Election

When the outline of the government's strategy for the 1994 election was
presented, economic policy was a central issue. To avoid being blamed for

85

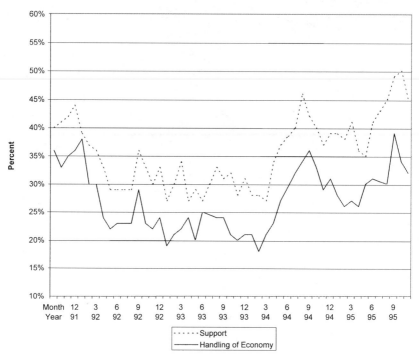

Figure 3.2 Government support and government handling of the economy, 1991–1995.

all the difficulties of the economic transition, the government tacitly acknowledged the economic problems that existed in the country. Moreover, it argued that even though things were looking grim, they would get better before too long, provided that the current parties remained in government. Thus, the government tried to produce or maintain a belief that economic performance in East Germany was following a J-curve, and that if things had gotten worse, it meant that they would get better later (Przeworski, 1993).

The tricky part of such a strategy was to avoid the conclusion that the CDU/CSU and FDP, which had led the country through the process of unification, were to blame for the difficulties and hardships suffered by parts of the population. This was particularly true in the eastern part of the country. Thus, government leaders went on record and acknowledged mistakes that had been made in the recent past without questioning the general direction of their policies. At the same time, they argued that the opposition parties would hardly have done any better, and that sticking to the policies that had been initiated was the best course of action to ensure prosperity in the long run.

The campaign's focus on Germany's economic situation was designed to address indirectly the problem of unemployment as well, even though public opinion polls showed that voters drew a clear distinction between general economic performance and unemployment. A number of surveys taken at the beginning of the year indicated that the government was considered more competent when it came to solving economic problems in general, while the opposition was perceived to be better able to deal with the specific issue of unemployment. By concentrating on the economy in general and not specific issues, while the opposition SPD focused on their number one issue of unemployment, the government hoped to convince voters that the problem of joblessness could not be solved without a general economic recovery. Throughout the election year, the unemployment issue led the rankings of political priorities among the public in both East and West, thus seemingly setting the stage for a downhill race for the SPD.

As it turned out, however, there was a strong upward trends in voters' belief that the CDU was better able to handle the country's economic problems as the election year progressed (Anderson and Zelle, 1995). While the German public was split fairly evenly at the beginning of 1994 as to which party could best deal with the question of an economic upswing, the government made significant gains and beat out the SPD on economic growth by a two-to-one margin toward the end of the campaign. The story for the unemployment issue was the reverse. At the beginning of the year, voters thought that the SPD was more competent to deal with the high unemployment by roughly a two-to-one margin; during the course of the campaign, however, the CDU managed to close that gap.

In the end, the Kohl government won the national election in part because of its perceived competence to handle the economy. People trusted that the CDU/CSU and free market-oriented Liberals were more likely to bring about an economic upswing and deal with the problems associated with the unification of the two German states. After the election, however, the government's fortunes quickly started to decline again as the economic recovery turned out to be less robust than had been hoped, as East Germany still was unable to stand on its own, and as the Kohl government began in earnest to walk down the path of European monetary integration.

Christopher J. Anderson and Yuliya V. Tverdova

Public Opinion and Economic Reform in East Germany

To understand people's reactions to the political and economic transition and economic reform, Susan Stokes (1996, this volume) has sought to devise a conceptual map that allows us to trace the different conditions and reactions that may occur in a country undergoing radical change. Specifically, she has argued that citizens in countries undergoing system change may display variable patterns of responses to economic deterioration: normal economic voting, intertemporal voting, exonerating or antidotal voting, or distributional (envy or solidarity) responses.

Normal economic voting behavior is consistent with the voluminous literature on economic voting in established democracies, where citizens punish incumbents for bad economic performance and reward them during good economic times. *Intertemporal economic voting* implies that citizens understand that, under economic reform, the economy may have to get worse before it can get better. In this case, they react to bad economic times following reform efforts with increased support (at least in the beginning) in order to ensure that the country (and they) will reap the long-term economic benefits of reform. *Antidotal or exonerating economic voting* assumes that voters in transition economies understand that the government may be battling an overwhelmingly negative economic legacy. In this case, reform policies and bad economic times will be associated with support for the government and its policies. In contrast to intertemporal voting, however, economic decline should generate public optimism about the economy. Finally, *distributional responses* differ from the other response models in that voters assume that the economy will improve but that their own welfare has suffered more than others' during times of painful adjustment. As a consequence, voters will be optimistic about the future economy during bad economic times, yet oppose reforms and those who implement them.

We investigated the validity of these response models with the help of data collected in East Germany between 1991 and 1995. Because East Germany merged with the biggest country in its hemisphere, taking on its political and economic institutions, East Germany thus constitutes an atypical case compared to virtually all other East Central European countries undergoing political and economic transitions. Whether East Germans' reactions to system change differed from those of citizens in other countries experiencing economic and political reform, or whether the dynamics of East German public opinion were

88

similar to those of other countries, are questions underlying the present analysis.

We argue that, among the cases analyzed as part of the larger project, East Germany would be the most likely case of normal economic voting (cf. Rattinger and Krämer, 1998). Consistent with the expectations outlined by Susan Stokes in Chapter 1 of this volume, East Germany fulfilled a number of conditions for such behavior. The ruling parties (CDU/CSU and FDP), through their status as governing parties of the FRG, were clearly in control of economic management in the East, and the political opposition (SPD and Greens) were not associated with the recently discarded regime. Though the party of the old regime – the reformed Communist Party, renamed the Party of Democratic Socialism (PDS) – contested elections and won seats in the national legislature, they were mostly a vehicle for protest without a serious chance at governing nationally. In addition, party identification was not particularly strong in the East, and studies of East German voting behavior in the 1990 elections found that voters were predominantly oriented toward short-term factors such as the economy, candidates, and issues, and that social cleavages, especially in the beginning of the transition, played a smaller role (see, e.g., Roth, 1990; for a contrasting view, see Bluck and Kreikenbom, 1991). Seen from this perspective, East Germany offered fertile ground for normal economic voting.

East Germany also seems to provide the economic and social context for normal economic voting. After all, while the transition has been arduous and on occasion painful, East Germany never underwent shock therapy the way Poland did. Instead, the government sought to ensure that most of the blows of market reform were cushioned by the welfare state. And although the pro-market reform program was new, East Germans were familiar with West German economic thinking because of their exposure to Western media even under the old regime. Finally, as a result of social and economic policies under the old regime, social differences were actually quite small in East Germany, especially when compared to the West. Taken together, the political as well as the social and economic conditions prevailing in East Germany during the transition support the hypothesis that we should see normal retrospective economic voting there.

However, we also believe that the intertemporal and antidotal logics have some face validity given the events surrounding unification described earlier. After all, East German voters did reelect the Kohl government –

albeit by a reduced margin – to another term in 1994 despite economic troubles. This would speak in favor of the view that East Germans understood that bad economic times were a necessary outcome of the transition and that the Kohl government deserved the credit for tackling difficult economic problems.

Finally, distributional responses are a distinct, though somewhat less likely, possibility as well. In the East German case, this belief and associated opposition to the new regime may have arisen from the understanding that East Germany suffered more than was necessary. Coupled with the feelings of many Easterners that West Germans were treating them unfairly and judged their lack of quick economic progress too harshly, we might expect normal economic voting to coincide with distributional postures among East German voters. Which logic of economic voting East Germans actually followed will now be examined.

Data and Measures

To test these hypotheses about how East Germans reacted to economic and political change, we rely on economic and public opinion data collected at monthly intervals between October 1991 and December 1995 in the territory of the former GDR.[3] The objective economic data were taken from the monthly reports of the Deutsche Bundesbank (Germany's central bank), whereas the public opinion data are based on surveys conducted by the Forschungsgruppe Wahlen, Mannheim (a widely respected survey organization). In the context of the East German transition experience, inflation-related issues such as the introduction of the West German D-mark, and unemployment (because of the shutting down of many state-owned companies) are particularly relevant measures of economic performance. The economic data used here thus are the monthly unemployment and inflation rates.

The public opinion data measure citizens' evaluations of future economic performance (good, bad, don't know), the percentage of respondents who would vote for the incumbent CDU/FDP coalition, opposition parties, or fringe parties (including the former Communists) if an election were held on Sunday and the percentages of respondents saying that the government or the opposition was better able to handle the East German

---

[3] The time series is constrained on both ends by data availability.

economy (the third category was "not sure"). Thus, all three public opinion measures – government support, approval of the handling of the economy, and economic projections – have three response categories of positive response, negative response, and indifference, representing the percentages that fall into each (and sum to 100%).

Analysis

To estimate the effects of objective economic conditions on economic expectations and government approval, we estimated a series of models that regressed government support and economic optimism on the economic indicators and a trend variable. The trend variable was included to account for the time element of the data series; this variable was scored 1 for the first month of the data series and increased by 1 for each subsequent month. The models estimated the effects of unemployment and inflation rates on East German support for the governing coalition measured in vote intention for the governing parties, the traditional opposition parties, and others (smaller fringe parties and the former Communists), as well as support for the government's and opposition's ability to handle the East German economy. The results indicated that objective economic conditions were related consistently to government approval.

To estimate the impact of the objective economy on government approval, we followed the techniques developed by King and his collaborators for analyzing compositional data (Katz and King, 1999; King, Tomz, and Wittenberg, 2000). Using the software program CLARIFY, also developed by King et al., the analysis involved the following steps. First, we transformed the dependent variables into log ratios; second, we estimated seemingly unrelated regressions and simulated the parameters of the multiple-equation model; third, to interpret the substantive impact of the independent variables on our dependent variables, we calculated the level of public support for the government or economic optimism under different economic performance scenarios (that is, when unemployment and inflation were low, at their mean level, or high) using simulations with the levels of approval or optimism conditional on the simulated parameters. The basic idea underlying these analyses is that we can interpret the results of the regressions by choosing different values for each of the economic variables and then examining the expected outcomes conditional on the levels of unemployment and inflation.

The Objective Economy and Government Support

Turning first to the effects of objective economic conditions on government approval, we find a mixed picture of economic voting. Higher unemployment reduced public approval of the governing parties and their handling of the economy, while higher levels of inflation improved their standing with the public. Thus, the results show evidence of both normal economic voting and intertemporal or possibly exonerating/antidotal economic voting among the East German electorate. Specifically, when judging the government and its economic management competence, East German voters differentiated among different aspects of the transition and among different economic outcomes. The Kohl government was seen as competent in dealing with inflation; as a result, the decline in inflation after the initial phase of the transition – that is, the *successful* handling of rapid price increases – actually hurt the government as inflation disappeared from the public mind as an important economic problem. The results of the seemingly unrelated regressions are shown in the appendix to this chapter.

The Impact of Unemployment on Government Support To evaluate the substantive impact of the economic variables on government support, we calculated the effects of different levels of unemployment on the probability of government support and the government's handling of the economy; that is, we computed the levels of support with unemployment held at its minimum (11.7%), mean (15%), and maximum (18.3%). These effects, shown in Figures 3.3 and 3.4, unambiguously produced a pattern of normal economic voting. The higher the level of unemployment, the lower the level of support for the governing parties and the government's handling of the economy.

Although the proportions supporting the governing parties were systematically higher than the proportions approving of the government's handling of the economy – there was a difference of about 8–10% – the effects of different levels of unemployment were almost identical across the two. Moving from the lowest to the highest level of unemployment produces a decline of about 10% in public support. Given that government approval was, on average, in the 35–40% range, this means that the increase in unemployment resulting from the privatization program initiated by the government and executed by the THA systematically and

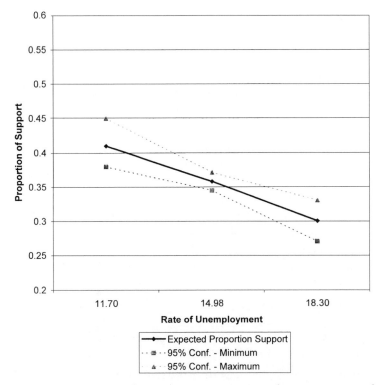

Figure 3.3 Expected proportion supporting the government, by rate of unemployment.

severely cut into the government's standing with the East German public. With unemployment at its peak of around 18% and inflation held at the mean, a mere 30% supported the governing parties and fewer than 25% approved of how the government was handling the economic situation in the country.

The Impact of Inflation on Government Support In contrast, the simulated effects of different levels of inflation on government support showed a pattern quite different from normal economic voting and consistent with either intertemporal or exonerating economic voting: higher levels of inflation went hand in hand with higher levels of government approval. Figures 3.5 and 3.6 show the substantive impact

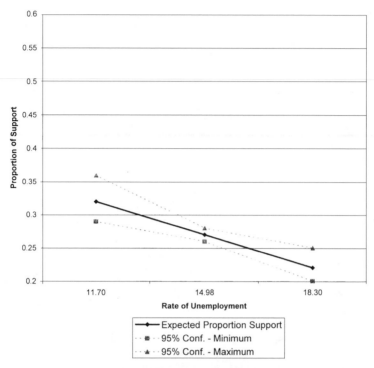

Figure 3.4 Expected proportion supporting the government's handling of the economy, by rate of unemployment.

of the effects of inflation on the probability of government support when inflation was at its minimum (1.4%), mean (7.3%), and maximum (22.2%) levels.

The estimated probabilities show that a move from the lowest to the highest level of inflation during the period examined here substantially improved governing parties' fortunes as well as people's perceptions of the government's handling of the economy. Especially when inflation was in excess of 10%, voters flocked to the governing parties and expressed faith in their economic management. What is more, these effects were so substantial that they were able to balance the negative effects of higher unemployment. However, and unfortunately for the Kohl government, low inflation did *not* coincide with low unemployment during the East German transition. Instead, periods of high inflation and lower unemployment during the early phase were followed by low inflation and higher

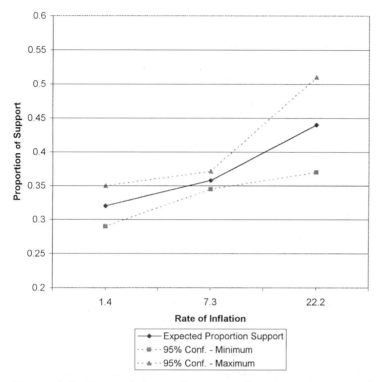

Figure 3.5 Expected proportion supporting the government, by rate of inflation.

unemployment, thus hitting the government particularly hard in terms of public approval.

Taken together, the effects reported so far paint a mixed picture of economic voting during the East German transition. East German voters reacted in ways that were consistent with both normal economic voting as well as intertemporal or possibly exonerating economic voting. While high unemployment was associated with lower approval of the government and its economic record, high inflation turned citizens into supporters. What is clear, however, is that East German reactions to economic conditions during the transition cannot be described as distributional or oppositionist postures. To determine whether East Germans' reactions were intertemporal or exonerating/antidotal, we subsequently examined the effects of economic outcomes during the transition on the public's willingness to express optimism about the future of the East German economy.

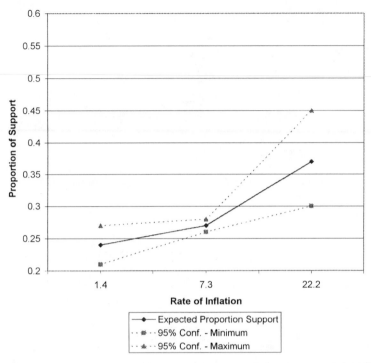

Figure 3.6 Expected proportion supporting the government's handling of the economy, by rate of inflation.

Economic Conditions and Economic Optimism

Normal economic voting and exonerating economic voting differ in their expectation of how economic deterioration affects government support, but both imply that bad economic times are correlated with pessimism about the country's economic future. In contrast, the notion of inter-temporal economic voting suggests that economic difficulty leads to an increase in optimism about the future performance of the nation's economy. Although we do not have data concerning citizens' attitudes about economic reform, we do have data on their prospective economic assessments – that is, on the proportions of people who say the economy will improve, stay the same, or get worse. Thus, we are able to differentiate among these competing perspectives empirically.

When we estimated the effects of objective economic conditions on sociotropic economic expectations (economic optimism, pessimism, no

East Germany

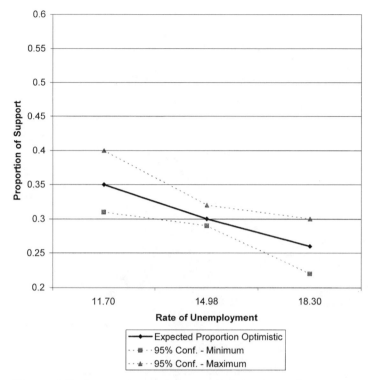

Figure 3.7 Expected proportion optimistic about the economy, by rate of unemployment.

opinion), we found a mixed picture of normal economic voting and intertemporal attitudes. As in the case of attitudes toward the government, higher East German unemployment was associated with lower levels of optimism about the economic situation. Similarly, rapid increases in prices were *positively* related to optimism about the economy. These results speak in favor of an intertemporal interpretation of the results, especially because high inflation rates were a fairly salient issue at the beginning of the East German transition experience. Thus, after having been promised "blossoming landscapes" by the Kohl government in the 1990 election, East German voters associated high inflation rates during the early stages with good times ahead. Later on in the transition, as inflation fell and unemployment rose, people became much less optimistic – and probably much more realistic – about the country's economic prospects. Figures 3.7 and 3.8 show the predicted proportions of optimism under different economic scenarios.

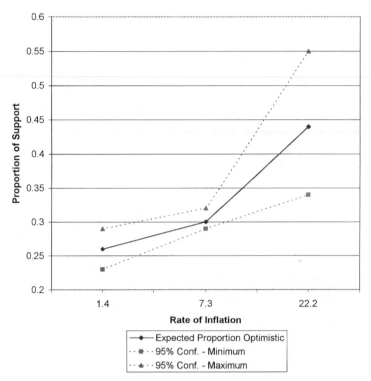

Figure 3.8 Expected proportion optimistic about the economy, by rate of inflation.

Ironically, this realism may have helped avoid the worst for the Kohl government. By the time the 1994 elections rolled around, the East German public was not particularly optimistic about the economic situation. As a result, the decline in unemployment from its highest point that started in late 1993 and lasted through 1994 may have led to a crucial boost for the Kohl government ahead of the federal elections.

Taken together, these results suggest that East German voters were of two minds during the transition. Massive job losses led to lower public approval of the government; however, East Germans did not appear completely retrospective in their evaluations of the economic situation and the government's role in it. Most East Germans were well aware that 40-plus years of Communist economic management could not be undone overnight or even over a few years. However, high levels of joblessness and the concomitant effects on the social fabric did not leave the government's

Table 3.1. *Patterns of Public Responses to Economic Deterioration in East Germany*

	Support Reforms/ Government	Oppose Reforms/ Government
Optimistic about future of economy	Intertemporal (inflation)	Distributional or oppositionist
Pessimistic about future of economy	Exonerating	Normal retrospective economic voting (unemployment)

fortunes and people's prospective evaluations untouched. Given the higher levels of inflation during the early period of the transition coupled with steadily rising unemployment rates up to the beginning of 1994, we thus conclude that East Germans adopted an intertemporal posture during the early phase of the transition. Eventually, however, East Germans came to grips with the harsh reality of the situation and became normal economic voters, but only after some time had passed.

Table 3.1 summarizes the contrasting empirical observations from the East German case. It shows that the East German reaction to economic reform was consistent with normal economic voting when it came to employment and intertemporal with regard to prices. Assuming economic decline, East Germans were optimistic about the economy and supportive of the government when prices were high but pessimistic and disapproving when unemployment was on the rise. Normal postures fall into the southeast cell, where deterioration was interpreted as forecasting more deterioration in the future and hence led to negative views about the economy and the government. Intertemporal postures fell into the northwest cell: East Germans' expectation that economic performance would follow a J-curve meant that high prices during the initial phase of the transition generated optimism about the future and support for the government.

Conclusion

This study sought to examine public responses to economic conditions in the old East Germany after unification. Based on monthly economic and public opinion data for the period 1991–1995, it examined public support for the governing parties and their handling of the economy, as well as people's expectations of future economic performance. Because East

Germany differs from other countries currently undergoing transitions, it is a particularly interesting example for an investigation into the relationships among economic reform and change, on the one hand, and public support for government, on the other. Unlike virtually all other transitioning states, East Germany merged with another state – in fact, it merged with the biggest democracy and economy in its hemisphere. How, then, did East Germans react to changing economic fortunes? And how did they translate their assessments about economic conditions into attitudes about the government and its handling of the economy?

The empirical analysis showed East Germans to be intertemporal as well as normal economic voters, given that unemployment and inflation did not have uniform effects on East German public opinion. In fact, it appears that East Germans evaluated inflation and unemployment differently. Rapid increases in prices, which were pervasive particularly during the early period of the transition, were greeted with optimism about the economic future and increased support for the Kohl government. In contrast, rising joblessness had significant and negative effects on the government's standing and people's economic expectations.

Overall, the East German case provided evidence for what Stokes has called intertemporal economic voting during the early years and normal economic voting a few years into the transition. However, it needs to be pointed out that these patterns were established on the basis of data for the entire period; it is possible, if not likely, that these results may change even more significantly when the period of transition is broken up into smaller segments or when different segments of the population are considered separately. In fact, Anderson and O'Connor (2000) have suggested that citizens in countries undergoing radical change may go through a period of learning before being able to reward and punish governments with some expertise. The results presented here are consistent with such an argument. Similarly, the results should be regarded with some caution because the dynamics of coalition government were not explored. Given that voters do not necessarily blame incumbent parties similarly, and sometimes blame one party but not the other, a more detailed analysis may find some shifting in vote intention among the parties of the governing coalition in addition to shifts from opposition to government and vice versa (Anderson, 1995).

Finding that East Germans a few years into the transition behaved as traditional theories of economic voting would predict also means that the government's fortunes in the 1998 elections in the East largely depended on how well the East German economy performed at that time. As the outcome suggested – the government was soundly rejected – the economic stagnation that had settled in, despite the continued massive investments by the federal government, ultimately led to the Kohl government's demise. It is unclear, however, what the long-run consequences of this situation are. There are signs of massive disaffection with the political process in East Germany; thus, instead of turning bad economic times into support for the opposition, the failure of market reforms to generate significant job growth may in fact translate into alienation from the political process altogether. During the 1993–1995 period, for example, 60% of West Germans said they were satisfied with the way democracy works in Germany, whereas only 40% of East Germans indicated the same (Anderson, 1998). Whether East Germans' understanding of the realities of a market economy and the consequences resulting from it will, in the medium to long term, translate simply into a loss of specific support for the incumbent regime or a decline in diffuse support (or both) are questions left to be answered in future analyses.

Appendix: The Effects of Economic Conditions on Public Opinion in East Germany, 1991–1995 (Seemingly Unrelated Regression Analyses)

Independent Variable	Effects of Economic Conditions on Government Support		Effects of Economic Conditions on Approval of Government Handling of the Economy		Effects of Economic Conditions on Economic Optimism	
	Support Government	Support Opposition	Approve	Disapprove	Optimistic	Pessimistic
Unemployment	−0.113***	−0.052**	−0.053*	0.063***	−0.054	0.065*
	(0.030)	(0.178)	(0.024)	(0.017)	(0.029)	(0.032)
Inflation	0.058***	0.042***	0.028*	−0.005	0.045**	0.011
	(0.015)	(0.009)	(0.011)	(0.008)	(0.014)	(0.015)
Trend	0.012*	−0.005	0.005	−0.020***	0.016**	−0.002
	(0.006)	(0.003)	(0.004)	(0.003)	(0.005)	(0.006)
Constant	1.680**	1.610***	−0.041	−0.806*	−0.475	−2.183***
	(0.586)	(0.346)	(0.456)	(0.330)	(0.537)	(0.591)
N	51		51		51	
R^2	0.5		0.28		0.27	
SEE	0.29		0.23		0.26	

* $p \leq 0.05$, ** $p \leq 0.01$, *** $p \leq 0.001$.

References

Anderson, Christopher J. 1995. "The Dynamics of Public Support for Coalition Governments." *Comparative Political Studies* 28(3): 350–383.

——— 1998. *Political Satisfaction in Old and New Democracies*. Ithaca, NY: Cornell University, Institute for European Studies Working Paper, No. 98.4.

Anderson, Christopher J., and Kathleen M. O'Connor. 2000. "System Change, Learning, and Public Opinion about the Economy." *British Journal of Political Science* 30(1): 147–172.

Anderson, Christopher J., and Carsten Zelle. 1995. "Helmut Kohl and the CDU Victory." *German Politics and Society* 13(1): 12–35.

Bluck, Carsten, and Henry Kreikenbom. 1991. "Die Wähler der DDR: Nur issue-orientiert oder auch parteigebunden?" *Zeitschrift für Parlamentsfragen* 22: 495–502.

Childs, David. 1988. *The GDR: Moscow's German Ally*. London: Hyman.

Dalton, Russell J. 1993. *Politics in Germany*. New York: HarperCollins.

Infas. 1994. *Politogramm Report Wahlen, Bundestagswahl 1994. Analysen und Dokumente*. Bonn: Infas.

Katz, Jonathan N., and Gary King. 1999. "A Statistical Model for Multiparty Electoral Data." *American Political Science Review* 93(1): 15–32.

King, Gary, Michael Tomz, and Jason Wittenberg. 2000. "Making the Most of Statistical Analyses: Improving Interpretation and Presentation." *American Journal of Political Science* 44(2): 341–355.

Przeworski, Adam. 1993. "Economic Reforms, Public Opinion, and Political Institutions: Poland in the Eastern European Perspective." In L. C. Bresser Pereira, J. M. Maravall, and A. Przeworski (eds.), *Economic Reform in New Democracies: A Social-Democratic Approach*. New York: Cambridge University Press.

Rattinger, Hans, and Jürgen Krämer. 1998. "Economic Conditions and Voting Preferences in East and West Germany, 1989–94." In Christopher J. Anderson and Carsten Zelle (eds.), *Stability and Change in German Elections: How Electorates Merge, Converge, or Collide*. Westport, CT: Praeger Publishers, 99–120.

Roth, Dieter. 1990. "Die Wahlen zur Volkskammer der DDR. Der Versuch einer Erklärung." *Politische Vierteljahresschrift* 31: 369–393.

Seibel, Wolfgang. 1993. "Necessary Illusions: The Transformation of Governance Structures in the New Germany." In Christopher Anderson, Karl Kaltenthaler, and Wolfgang Luthardt (eds.), *The Domestic Politics of German Unification*. Boulder, CO: Lynne Rienner, 117–134.

Stokes, Susan C. 1996. "Introduction. Public Opinion and Market Reforms: The Limits of Economic Voting." *Comparative Political Studies* 29: 499–519.

4

Public Support for Economic Reforms in Poland

Adam Przeworski

Introduction

Studies of voting and of public opinion are based on one assumption that appears obvious: citizens want governments to make them better off. And it is this norm that makes unambiguous interpretations of current performance when voters form retrospective judgments or when they assess the credibility of promises. Since things are supposed to improve, deterioration means that the government did not perform well or that the promises to improve things in the future are not credible. This is why studies of presidential popularity, voting behavior, and cabinet duration routinely assume that inflation and unemployment should work against the incumbents, while increases in real incomes should favor them.

But imagine that parties and politicians promise to make things worse off so that they could get better in the distant future. Union leaders "hope that there will be unemployment," finance ministers declare that "unless the unemployment rate grows to 8 to 10 percent this year, we will not be doing our job," and prime ministers proclaim that "there is no example in the economic history of the world of inflation being squelched without serious social difficulties, including bankruptcy of some enterprises and the unemployment associated with it." And suppose that these promises are fulfilled: unemployment mounts and real incomes tumble. How are people

This chapter first appeared in *Comparative Political Studies* 29(5): 520–543 (1996). I should like to thank Jorge Buendía, Jon Elster, Susan Stokes, and Jerzy J. Wiatr for their comments. Lena Kolarska-Bobinska generously shared the survey data on which this study is based.

to judge this performance: is the government leading them to a radiant future or are things simply getting worse?[1]

This is the central question concerning the dynamic of public opinion in the context of neoliberal economic reforms. Such reforms almost inevitably entail at least a transitory deterioration in the material welfare of large segments of the population (Blanchard, Dornbusch, Krugman, Layard, and Summers, 1991; Przeworski, 1991; Solimano, 1994). And while not all governments that launch such reform programs are forthcoming about these prospects – in many Latin American countries the aversion to recession tempted governments to hide them – Eastern European governments fell all over themselves in announcing how hard the "jump to the market" would be. Indeed, the first preceding quote comes from a Polish union leader and parliamentary deputy, the second from a Czechoslovak finance minister, and the third from the head of the first Polish post-Communist government.

Poland presents a clinical case: "Unless it tastes bad, it cannot be good for you" was the liberal doctors' message. "Horse therapy," "swallowing the bitter pill," "radical cure," and similar medical references proclaimed that the operation would be painful and dangerous. Specific predictions were announced: unemployment was to appear and to grow for some time, inflation was to jump in the first months of the program, additional increases in energy prices and charges for public services were to follow, real wages were to decline. Some sweeteners were promised in the form of minimal income assistance and unemployment compensation, but the general message was honest and grim. And these forecasts turned out to be true with a vengeance. Inflation jumped more than expected; over 26 months unemployment crept up from none to 14%; real wages fell;[2] and social services were deeply cut. The government's promises were being fulfilled: the great majority of the population were made worse off.

Economic conditions deteriorated: this much was clear. Yet the legacy of communism provided a powerful explanation for why this decline

---

[1] Here is an assessment by IMF (*Survey*, November 29, 1993, p. 357): "The Baltic countries made substantial progress toward establishing macroeconomic stability. Inflation decelerated rapidly, . . . and real incomes declined. . . . This process was associated with unavoidable losses in output and employment."

[2] Given that money was not a sufficient title to access goods and services under communism, real wages cannot be compared in monetary terms alone for the pre- and post-January 1990 periods. This point was made originally by Lipton and Sachs (1990).

would be inevitable. The opening statement of the Economic Program of the new government asserted that "The causes of the striking economic indolence of the economy rest deeply embedded in the previous economic system. Without their fundamental change we will continue to be stuck in an atmosphere of general indolence and a situation of a permanent crisis." Communist inefficiency was a vivid memory for everyone who lived under this system.[3] And the highly publicized activities of the remnants of the nomenklatura, some of whom conspicuously converted, to use Tarkowski's (1989) wonderful quip, from "apparatchiks" to "entrepreneutchiks," furnished a ready-made scapegoat for the obstacles the new government was encountering in its jump to the market. Indeed, Lech Walesa campaigned for the presidency not with an attack on the costs of reform but with a slogan of "acceleration": getting rid of the legacy of the Magdalenka agreement with Communists and purging the remnants of the nomenklatura.[4]

As Stokes indicates in Chapter 1, individuals can react to the material deprivation they experience and the economic deterioration they observe in four ways: (1) They may see it as an indication that things will continue to get worse and oppose the reform program as well as the government that pursued it. This is the *normal* pattern: if things get worse, people expect them to get worse and turn against the government. (2) They may infer that since things are deteriorating as forecast, they will soon get better and support the reforms and the government. This constitutes an *intertemporal* interpretation. (3) They may conclude that while the reform program is good, as is the government that put it forward, the economy is suffering from its legacy or from obstructionist behavior of some enemies of reform. Hence, they may be pessimistic about the future and yet eagerly support the program

---

[3] As Rychard (1991) emphasized, the disgust with the status quo need not translate into enthusiasm for reforms. One reason is that the term *reform* itself has been worn out by the entire history of the People's Republic. Reforms were endemic in all socialist economies. Moreover, the failure of the reform programs of 1982 and 1987 bred widespread skepticism about the success of any reforms. The "second stage" of Communist reforms, the 1987 package, was treated as at best the butt of innumerable jokes. Yet in spite of this "reform fatigue," even the last reforms by the Communist government did evoke a jump in the confidence in the government – from 33.6% in August to 72.4% in November 1988.

[4] Here is the *Financial Times* (March 4, 1993): "Russia's flirtation with hyperinflation and the continuing collapse in industrial output are not the fruit of 'shock therapy.' On the contrary, they reflect a failure to impose shock therapy."

and the government, seeing the reforms as an antidote. This is an *exonerating* or *antidotal* posture. (4) Finally, individuals may believe that the current difficulties forecast an economic improvement but may think that either they or others are being treated unfairly in the reform process, and still oppose the reforms and the government. This is a *distributional* pattern.

My purpose is to adjudicate empirically among these patterns using public opinion data. Given the high degree of consensus about the need to finish once and for all with the legacy of the Communist system, one would expect that Poles would exonerate the government for bad economic conditions even if they expected them to continue. Hence, there are grounds to expect an exonerating posture. Yet do they believe the government when it announces that bad economic performance indicates that reforms are working and an improvement is around the corner: do they think in intertemporal terms? And are they sensitive to distributional issues, comparing their own situation to that of those who are doing better or worse economically?

The reform program at issue, the Balcerowicz plan, was first announced on September 16, 1989. The principal legislation was passed by the Parliament at the end of December, and the plan was implemented as of January 1, 1990.[5] While the general policy orientation continued, the plan died in October 1991, when Balcerowicz left his post. The first survey when questions were asked about the Balcerowicz plan was done in November 1989. During the early months surveys were conducted twice, but none was conducted in July, August, and December 1990.[6] Altogether, we have 20 data points covering 22 months.

The support for the plan was very high when it was announced.[7] In November 1989, 90.3% of those who had an opinion expressed their support, although the proportion of respondents who thought they did not know enough to have an opinion was very large, 65.9%. Yet as time went

---

[5] The plan comprised price deregulation and a *tarifaso*, a stabilization plan (with foreign exchange as the anchor), incomes policy, a reduction of subsidies and price supports, and a variety of institutional legislation. For details, see Przeworski (1993).

[6] Aggregate public opinion data are derived from *Serwis Informacyjny*, a monthly publication of the Centrum Badania Opinii Spolecznej, Warsaw. The economic data are based on *Biuletyn Statystyczny* of the Glowny Urzad Statystyczny, Warsaw, various issues.

[7] The experience of hyperinflation must have affected these attitudes: in July 1989, nominal wages increased by 101.8% and by October the monthly inflation rate was still running at 54.8%.

on, the support among those who had an opinion declined. This decline was almost linear, except for sudden transitory dives in February and May 1991. By October 1991, only 31.8% of those who had an opinion supported the plan and 37.0% did not have an opinion. More dramatically, while in November 1989 3.1% of all respondents opposed the plan, by October 1991 43.0% did.

Which of the four patterns characterizes this dynamic of public opinion? Note that they are defined by answers to two questions: (1) Are people extrapolating from the past deterioration to the future or interpreting it prospectively as an indication of an impending improvement? (2) Are they supporting or opposing the reform program and/or the government? The normal pattern is characterized by extrapolation from the past and opposition to reforms or the government; the intertemporal interpretation is defined by a prospective reading of the past and support; the exonerating posture is distinguished by an extrapolative use of past experience accompanied by support; finally, the distributional pattern combines a prospective reading of the past with opposition.

To distinguish these interpretations, I proceed as follows. First, I examine the impact of aggregate economic conditions on the dynamic of support for the reform program and compare it with the support for the government. To highlight the ambiguity of the standard retrospective model, I then analyze the impact of subjective perceptions of economic conditions on postures toward the reform program. I ask if people were indeed extrapolating from the past when forming predictions about the future. After a partial conclusion, I examine the effect of these predictions on the postures toward reform. Finally, I focus on the distributional effects. I close by deriving substantive conclusions concerning the effect of economic conditions for the support of economic reform programs under democracy.[8]

The Impact of Economic Variables on the Postures Toward the Reform Program and the Government

How was the aggregate support for the reform program affected by the state of the economy? Specifically, do people tend to support the reform program when things are better or worse?

---

[8] To keep the discussion brisk, little context is provided throughout; it can be found in Przeworski (1993), OECD (1994), Ebrill (1994), and elsewhere.

Table 4.1. *Multinomial Logit Estimates of Attitudes Toward the Balcerowicz Plan as a Function of Economic Variables. Partial Effects Evaluated at the Means of the Independent Variables, with Standard Errors Corrected for Sample Size. Monthly Data*

Variable	Coefficient	Std. Error	t-Ratio	Prob $|t| \geq x$
		SUPPORT		
CONSTANT	0.33903E-01	0.4096E-02	8.277	0.00000
RWAGE	−0.21770E-03	0.1489E-03	−1.462	0.14385
INFL	0.86137E-03	0.2734E-04	31.501	0.00000
UN	−0.13541E-01	0.8489E-03	−15.951	0.00000
		NO VIEW		
CONSTANT	0.15433	0.9882E-02	15.618	0.00000
RWAGE	0.13442E-02	0.3332E-03	4.034	0.00005
INFL	0.17549E-2	0.3362E-03	5.220	0.00000
UN	−0.13843E-01	0.1233E-02	−11.230	0.00000
		OPPOSE		
CONSTANT	−0.18824	0.6670E-02	−28.222	0.00000
RWAGE	−0.11265E-02	0.2592E-03	−4.346	0.00001
INFL	−0.26163E-02	0.2643E-03	−9.897	0.00000
UN	0.27383E-01	0.1155E-02	23.702	0.00000

I first present results based on a multinomial logit analysis in which the dependent variable consists of monthly proportions of respondents who supported the Balcerowicz plan (SUPPORT), opposed it (OPPOSE), or had no opinion (NO VIEW),[9] while monthly changes in real wages (RWAGE), the monthly rate of inflation (INFL), and the current rate of unemployment (UN) are the independent variables.[10] As Table 4.1 shows,

[9] In fact, surveys allowed the respondents to answer "I do not know enough to have a view of the plan" or simply "No answer." These two categories of responses cannot be distinguished by any of the available variables; moreover, the relative proportions answering one way or the other fluctuate greatly across surveys. I ran all the analyses once only with those who said they did not know enough and then again with those who did not know and those who did not answer together. The results are almost identical and are somewhat stronger for the second case, which is reported subsequently.

[10] The issue of whether to use levels or first differences is the subject of an extensive debate (Ostrom and Smith, 1992; Paldam, 1991:11–12). Unfortunately, with 20 observations no fancy specifications can be entertained, and I decided to do what makes intuitive sense. However, I redid all the analyses presented later using the level of real wages, rather than the monthly change, and lagging the inflation rate by one month. No qualitative conclusions were affected.

when unemployment was high, people tended to have a clear view of the plan: they were against it. As unemployment increased marginally from its mean value during the period, support fell by 1.3%, the proportion of agnostics fell by 1.3%, and opposition increased by 2.7%. When real wages increased, people became agnostic about the plan: fewer supported it and fewer opposed it. And when prices increased, people either supported the plan or expressed no view.

Thus, while people turn against the reform program when unemployment is high, they become agnostic when wages increase and they support it when inflation is high. The finding concerning unemployment is normal, but the results concerning real wages and, in particular, inflation appear bewildering.

While these findings concern the economic program, that is, the plan, most studies of public opinion examine the support for governments rather than for policies. And one might conjecture that while people support the plan when inflation is high, they do not like the government that generates it.

A feasible generalized least squares (FGLS) analysis of the ratios of SUPPORT to OPPOSITION for the government and the plan shows that the joint structure of the coefficients is different (as indicated by the Wald test). When the coefficients are allowed to differ, the constant level of support for the government is almost twice that for the plan; real wages have no impact on government support and some impact on the support for the plan; unemployment affects negatively support both for the government and for the plan, about twice as strongly for the government; and inflation increases support for the government as well as for the plan almost identically (Table 4.2).

Hence, while the reactions to unemployment are those we are used to expect, people do not know what to think when wages rise, and they support both the economic program and the government when inflation mounts. The times of neoliberal reform are not normal times.

Predictions: Extrapolative of Intertemporal?

What would make people hesitate to oppose the reform program when their wages decline and to rush to support it when inflation mounts? In the standard model of retrospective voting, individuals set some standard of economic performance and compare current conditions to this standard, not paying attention to any promises (Ferejohn, 1986). As

Table 4.2. *Feasible Generalized Least Squares Estimates of the Ratio of SUPPORT to OPPOSE for the Government and the Plan. Monthly Data*

Estimates for equation: GOVERNMENT			Observations = 20	
$R^2 = 0.93$			Adjusted $R^2 = 0.92$	
Durbin–Watson stat. = 1.91			Autocorrelation = 0.05	
Rho used for GLS 0.35				

Variable	Coefficient	Std. Error	t-Ratio	Prob $|t| \geq x$
Constant	4.0223	0.3074	13.083	0.00000
RWAGE	0.37591E-02	0.8933E-02	0.421	0.67389
INFL	0.32958E-01	0.9276E-02	3.553	0.00038
UN	−0.31637	0.4247E-01	−7.450	0.00000

Estimates for equation: PLAN			Observations = 20	
$R^2 = 0.85$			Adjusted $R^2 = 0.82$	
Durbin–Watson stat. = 2.26			Autocorrelation = −0.13	
Rho used for GLS 0.18				

Variable	Coefficient	Std. Error	t-Ratio	Prob $|t| \geq x$
Constant	2.0363	0.2958	6.883	0.00000
RWAGE	0.15132E-01	0.9926E-02	1.524	0.12741
INFL	0.43691E-01	0.1004E-01	4.350	0.00001
UN	−0.16969	0.4042E-01	−4.198	0.00003

Wald test: $\text{Chi}^2(3) = 9.4721$, Prob = 0.02362

long as economic conditions are satisfactory, they support the policy or vote for the government; if they are not, they turn against it. So the retrospective model, at least this bare-bones version, cannot account for these findings.

Analyses that are not presented here indicate that people accurately perceive the actual economic conditions when they form evaluations of the policy: the assessments of the current general situation of the country, as well as of the material conditions of one's own family, do reflect the actual state of the economy. High unemployment causes people to conclude that the current state of the economy is bad, that material conditions of people are bad, and the situation of their own family is bad. Inflation and real wages play less of a role in shaping these assessments, but they have the expected sign.

When considered alone, subjective assessments of the general material conditions or of the general state of the economy have no impact on

Table 4.3. *Support for the Balcerowicz Plan as a Function of Assessments of the Current States of the Economy and Own Family Situation. Multinomial Logit. Partial Effects Evaluated at the Means of Independent Variables, with Standard Errors Corrected for Sample Size. Monthly Data*

Dependent Variable: support				
Variable	Partial Effect	Std. Error	t-Ratio	Prob $\lvert t \rvert \geq x$
CONSTANT	−0.22956E-01	0.1043E-01	−2.200	0.02780
ECONGOOD	−0.33661E-03	0.8311E-03	−0.405	0.68545
CONSTANT	−0.37721E-01	0.1138E-01	−3.314	0.00092
MATGOOD	0.18855E-02	0.1870E-02	1.008	0.31335
CONSTANT	−0.12339	0.1848E-01	−6.676	0.00000
OWNISGOOD	0.87789E-02	0.1533E-02	5.729	0.00000
CONSTANT	0.17680	0.2425E-01	7.291	0.00000
OWNISBAD	−0.49729E-02	0.6083E-03	−8.175	0.00000
CONSTANT	−0.11609	0.1869E-01	−6.212	0.00000
MATGOOD	−0.10555E-01	0.4135E-02	−2.553	0.01069
OWNISGOOD	0.13103E-01	0.2293E-02	5.715	0.00000
CONSTANT	0.35455	0.5006E-01	7.082	0.00000
MATGOOD	−0.15682E-01	0.3806E-02	−4.120	0.00004
OWNISBAD	−0.72819E-02	0.8408E-03	−8.661	0.00000

Variables
ECONGOOD: Proportion saying the general state of the economy is good.
MATGOOD: Proportion saying material conditions of the people are good.
OWNISGOOD: Proportion saying material conditions of their family are good.
OWNISBAD: Proportion saying material conditions of their family are bad.

attitudes toward the plan. In turn, as Table 4.3 shows, assessments of own situation do influence these attitudes in a predictable direction.[11]

Yet the mere fact that the reforms generate hardships should not affect attitudes if people had decided to support them knowing hard times would follow: if reforms follow the predicted path, then attitudes toward the reform program should not change as the costs are being experienced. And

---

[11] It thus seems that, in contrast to most findings concerning Europe and the United States, people are egocentric rather than sociotropic (Fiorina, 1981; Kinder and Kiewit, 1979; Lewis-Beck, 1988). Cowden and Hartley (1992) argue that people should be sociotropic about inflation and egocentric about wages (or incomes). Table 4.4 shows that inflation is important in shaping perceptions of the current states of the economy and general material conditions, but unemployment drives evaluations of one's own situation.

in Poland people did know that hardships would ensue: in March 1990, 53% of respondents agreed that "people think that it will be hard, but hardships are necessary so that things would get better." Hence, people knew that to evaluate the reform program, they should not extrapolate from past experience.[12]

The proportion willing to accept hardships declined over time, down to 23% by May 1991, as did support for the Balcerowicz plan itself. One reason may be that the time path of consumption under reforms was lower than expected. The surveys indicate that most people did find the costs of reforms to be greater than they had anticipated (and in fact, they were higher than forecast): this proportion reached 77.3% by July 1990 and declined only somewhat, to 68.7%, by October 1990. They also felt (again correctly; see Blanchard et al., 1991; Przeworski, 1993) that the costs were higher than necessary: 68.3% thought so in July 1990 and 61.4% in October of that year.

But most people were still willing to suffer hardships even as they responded that costs were higher than expected or too high, as long as reforms would eventually improve their material conditions. And the multivariate analysis again generates a puzzling finding: while people evaluated the reform program in accordance with their own conditions, when they perceived the general economic situation as good, they tended to oppose the plan. These are not retrospective judgments as we know them.

The Past and the Future

If individuals are prospectively oriented, they think about the future. The choice they face is between a pro-market policy, to which I will refer as *liberal*, and a *traditional* policy that represents the status quo until the liberal policy is implemented and some kind of a return afterward. People are not certain whether the liberal policy will succeed. Let $p(t)$ stand for the probability they attach at any time $t = 0, 1, \ldots$ to the success of the liberal reforms, where by *success* I mean that material conditions improve

And since unemployment dominates inflation and wages in shaping attitudes toward the plan, in Table 4.4 perceptions of one's own situation matter more than those of the economy.

[12] Note that in Brazil 71% of respondents thought that the Collor Plan was good one month after it was introduced even though 68% expected at that time that unemployment would increase. Either they did not care about unemployment, which is unlikely, or they too were willing to look beyond the immediate future.

after some period of hardship above the status quo level. The probability of failure is then $1 - p(t)$, where *failure* means that hardships continue indefinitely or at least sufficiently long that the eventual improvement no longer matters. Let S^* represent the present value of the stream of utility of consumption if the liberal policy is successful, let F^* stand for the present value of the stream of utility if it fails, and let T^* stand for the present value of the traditional policy, where all these present values are discounted for time and for risk aversion. Let the present value of future welfare under any of these outcomes be $W^* = \{S^*, F^*, T^*\}$.

Since $S^* > T^* > F^*$, under von Neuman–Morgenstern utilities an individual supports the liberal program at any time t if

$$L^*(t) = p(t)S^*(t) + [1 - p(t)]F^*(t) > T^*(t)$$

or

$$p(t) > \frac{T^* - F^*}{S^* - F^*} = V^*(t),$$

an individual is indifferent if $p(t) = V^*(t)$ and opposes it otherwise. Suppose that V^* is fixed over time. Then the postures toward the plan depend on the probabilities individuals attach to its success or failure.

The ambiguity comes from the fact that when things get worse, people can think either that reforms are working or that things are getting worse. Suppose people are told that prices must rise before inflation can be stopped (this is called *getting fundamentals right* by liberals; see di Tella, 1991) or that unemployment must rise before firms become competitive (so that some persons will lose their present jobs before they find new ones). Consumption must decline before it increases: this is the reform foretold. But what conclusions are people to derive from the fact that it does decline? Do they think that "the worse it is, the better it will be" or that "the worse it is, the worse it will be?"

Thus, what drives the attitudes toward reforms are the expectations that the plan will succeed. This is a conditional probability that

Pr {welfare will increase from $t > T$ on | decline to $W(T)$ until $t = T$} =
pr {welfare will increase from T on and decline to $W(T)$ until T}/
pr {welfare will decline to $W(T)$ until T} = $p(T, W(T))$

Assume that the distribution of the probability that things will improve at T is $F(T, W(T))$. Then the *conditional optimism*, that is, the likelihood that things will start improving at T, given that welfare is $W(T)$ and T has elapsed since the reforms were introduced, is given by the hazard rate

$$h(T, W(T)) = \lim p(T, W(T)) = f(T, W(T))/[1 - F(T, W(T))], \quad dt \to 0$$

where F is the cumulative distribution function of the normal distribution.

Since all we want to know is whether this probability increases or declines as the costs set in, I use the simplest distribution that admits changing hazard rates, the Weibull distribution, for which

$$h(T, W(T)) = \alpha T^{\alpha-1} \exp W(T), \quad \alpha \geq 0 \tag{1}$$

with

$$W(T) = \beta' X(T) \tag{2}$$

where β is a vector of coefficients and $X(T)$ = ONE, RWAGE, INFLATION, UNEMPLOYMENT.

Fortunately, the Polish survey data contain two variables that can be used as direct measures of this optimism. People were asked every month if they expected that the "economic situation of the country" and "material conditions of life" will improve in the near future. As one would expect, the answers are highly correlated, and not to clutter the exposition, I will use only the question about the general situation of the economy. The variable is IMPROVE: "the economic situation will improve." I estimate by ordinary least squares (OLS) a logarithmic version of (1) using (2):

$$\log(\text{IMPROVE}_t) = \beta' X_t = \log \alpha + (\alpha - 1)\log(t) + e_t \tag{3}$$

Bivariate regressions of the Weibull specification of the forecasts concerning the future show that changes in real wages do not affect future expectations. Yet high inflation is interpreted as grounds for pessimism: the coefficient on inflation is negative and significant. Unemployment increases pessimism even more. Thus, while changes in real wages are interpreted ambivalently, high inflation and unemployment are a source of pessimism (Table 4.4).

People thus were not thinking intertemporally about either inflation or unemployment. If they were, if they had believed the forecasts put forth by the architects of the reform program, they would have thought that if inflation was high, this was a sign that it would come down; that if unemployment reached a high level, it would soon start falling; in general,

114

Table 4.4. *Estimates of Conditional Optimism about the Future (Will Economy Improve?). WLS on Logarithmic Transformation. Monthly Data*[a]

Variable	Coefficient	Std. Error	t-Ratio	Prob $|t| \geq x$	R^2
Constant	4.1734	0.6130E-01	68.085	0.00000	0.65
RWAGE	0.11529E-02	0.1662E-02	0.694	0.49929	
LOGT	−0.16555	0.2971E-01	−5.571	0.00007	
Constant	4.3163	0.7455E-01	57.901	0.00000	0.76
INFL	−0.42925E-02	0.1574E-02	−2.727	0.01635	
LOGT	−0.21717	0.3150E-01	−6.894	0.00001	
Constant	4.0162	0.5496E-01	73.075	0.00000	0.83
UN	−0.71657E-01	0.1795E-01	−3.992	0.00134	
LOGT	0.94227E-01	0.6685E-01	1.410	0.18049	

[a] LOGT is the logarithm of the time index.

that once the predicted costs materialized, conditions would improve. Wages, in turn, appeared to be interpreted, albeit weakly, in intertemporal terms: people did not know what sense to make of the future when wages moved up or down.

We thus have the first conclusions: the Poles interpreted the rising unemployment rate as people do under normal times; they exonerated the government and the reform program for the intermittent bouts of inflation; and they were mildly intertemporal about wages, perhaps fearing that rising wages would cause a return of inflation.

Optimism, Risk Aversion, and Support for the Reform Program

We can now relate the conditional optimism about the future to attitudes toward the reform program.[13] These optimism variables should be interpreted as conditional forecasts that "things will get better in the near future, given the passage of time and the particular state of the economy," where the states are changes in real wages, the rate of inflation, and the rate of unemployment.

[13] This procedure is equivalent to a NL2SLS, with the states of the economy as exogenous variables. The structural model is

$$WEIMP = \exp(\beta'X) \, \alpha \, T^{\alpha-1} + e,$$
$$OPPOSE \ BP = \tau WEIMP + v$$

Table 4.5. *Optimism about the Future and Support for the Balcerowicz Plan. Multinomial Logit (Only SUPPORT Results). Partial Effects Evaluated at the Means of Independent Variables, with Standard Errors Corrected for Sample Size. Monthly Data*[a]

Variable	Partial Effect	Std. Error	t-Ratio	Prob $|t| \geq x$
CONSTANT	−0.41738	0.2986E-01	−13.978	0.00000
EXPWERW	0.90460E-02	0.2018E-02	4.482	0.00001
EXPWEIN	−0.83205E-02	0.2501E-02	−3.327	0.00088
EXPWEUN	0.75237E-02	0.1789E-02	4.206	0.00003
CONSTANT	−0.35245	0.2592E-01	−13.599	0.00000
EXPWEP	0.68694E-02	0.5320E-03	12.913	0.00000

[a] The EXPWEX variables are the predicted values of optimism conditioned on the particular economic variables and time. EXPWEP is the value of optimism about the future course of the economy predicted by the three economic variables jointly and by time.

The more optimistic people are that the economy will turn around, the more likely they are to support the plan: people think prospectively. The measure of optimism conditional on the three economic variables jointly (EXPWEP) is highly significant, and it has a positive sign in the SUPPORT equation. But it matters what this optimism is based on. Optimism based on wages leads people to support the plan, given optimism about other states of the economy. When people are optimistic based on unemployment, they support the plan. But optimism based on inflation leads people to oppose the reform program. Once again, reactions to inflation are not normal (Table 4.5).

This analysis, however, does not consider that the pace of reforms may matter independently of the experience of consumption (Kreps and Porteus, 1978). Suppose that consumption without reforms is T^* and that people know that at some time in the future, t, it will become clear if reforms are successful, which will cause consumption to equal S^*, or they will fail, with consumption equal to F^*. Let the probability that reforms are successful be p and, to keep matters simple, assume that the expected value of the reform lottery, $L^* = pS^* + (1 - p)F^* = T^*$. Weil (1990) has shown that risk-averse individuals will want an early resolution of uncertainty, regardless of their pure time preference. If individuals are intertemporally risk-averse, they turn against reforms because time passes and the uncertainty is not resolved.

Yet, while time enters with significant negative coefficients into explanations of optimism based on real wages and inflation, it is unemployment, rather than time, that makes people pessimistic: as Table 4.6 shows, in the presence of unemployment, time has no autonomous effect.[14] Thus, it appears that while people are eager to resolve uncertainty about real wages and inflation as soon as possible, they prefer to hold on to their jobs and prefer to put off the moment when uncertainty about employment may be resolved against them.

Suppose that 70% of the labor force is employed in the public sector at the onset of reforms and it is expected that 30% will be left in this sector once reforms are completed: 40% will lose their jobs at one time or another during the reform process and may experience a bout of unemployment. Then the fear of unemployment should be high at the beginning and decline as the proportion unemployed increases. Moreover, those who are currently unemployed should support the continuation of reforms, since presumably their faster rate should create new jobs at a more rapid pace.[15]

Yet the data show that in Poland the fear of unemployment did not decrease when the actual rate of unemployment grew. Moreover, those public employees who anticipated that they were likely to lose their jobs were less likely to support the reform program. A sample of employees in the public sector (about 80% of the nonagricultural sector) was interviewed at five occasions between February and November 1990 (Table 4.7):

The extent of fear of unemployment is striking: it certainly does not reflect individual experiences. In February 1990, when the actual rate of unemployment was 0.8%, 63% of respondents thought that unemployment would be widespread; by April 1990, when the actual rate was still 1.9%, 87% thought it would be. Again in February 1990, with a negligible incidence of actual unemployment, 36% felt the danger of losing their jobs, a proportion that stabilized around 55% by June 1991, when the official unemployment rate was 8.6%. In April 1990, when the unemployment rate was 1.9% and included people who never held a job (GUS, 1992), 20% said that a member of their family had been laid off, 33% reported

---

[14] Another piece of evidence against the Kreps–Porteus mechanism is that the proportions of respondents who did not know whether the economy or the material conditions would improve do not predict attitudes toward the plan.

[15] This paragraph is based on Rodrik (1994).

Table 4.6. *Multinomial Logit: OPPOSE the Balcerowicz Plan and NO VIEW Relative to SUPPORT. Monthly Cross Sections. (MLE estimates; t-scores in parentheses; sample sizes range from 994 to 1,502)[a]*

Date	OPPOSE			NO VIEW		
	Sex	Age	Education	Sex	Age	Education
11/89	0.4993	−0.0097	0.0423	0.7238	−0.0008	−0.2181
	(1.63)	(−1.31)	(0.64)	(6.09)	(−0.19)	(−8.18)
1/90	−0.0417	−0.0118	0.0125	0.3744	−0.0104	−0.1703
	(−0.21)	(−1.72)	(0.30)	(3.33)	(−2.69)	(−6.23)
2/90e	0.0770	0.0439	−0.1187	0.6021	0.0092	−0.2427
	(0.35)	(0.44)	(−2.56)	(4.18)	(1.36)	(−7.50)
2/90l	0.1703	0.0049	−0.1530	0.7914	0.0089	−0.3253
	(1.00)	(0.87)	(−4.08)	(6.61)	(2.23)	(−10.60)
3/90e	−0.0518	0.0083	−0.1855	0.5647	0.0127	−0.2234
	(−0.23)	(0.79)	(−4.17)	(3.85)	(1.81)	(−6.82)
3/90l	−0.0219	−0.0039	−0.1409	0.4947	−0.0006	−0.2242
	(−0.15)	(−0.82)	(−4.08)	(4.03)	(−0.15)	(−7.73)
4/90e	−0.0042	−0.0009	−0.1402	0.3910	0.0116	−0.2460
	(−0.02)	(0.11)	(−3.59)	(2.54)	(1.65)	(−7.36)
4/90l	0.1705	0.0052	−0.2306	0.5261	0.0094	−0.2743
	(1.08)	(0.90)	(−6.47)	(4.08)	(1.85)	(−9.27)
5/90	0.4432	−0.0012	−0.1931	0.8193	−0.0068	−0.2608
	(3.06)	(−0.22)	(−6.15)	(6.28)	(−1.37)	(−8.80)
6/90	0.2610	0.0150	−0.2499	0.5586	0.0149	−0.2546
	(1.80)	(2.80)	(−7.49)	(4.47)	(3.14)	(−8.70)
9/90	0.0847	0.0055	−0.2002	0.8147	0.0090	−0.3129
	(0.56)	(0.95)	(−6.04)	(6.31)	(1.78)	(−10.82)
10/90	0.3484	0.0015	−0.2745	0.8819	0.0078	−0.3261
	(2.26)	(0.27)	(−7.68)	(6.85)	(1.62)	(−10.81)
1/91	0.4169	0.0139	−0.3383	0.6776	0.0232	−0.3980
	(2.89)	(2.98)	(−9.99)	(4.87)	(4.75)	(−11.25)
2/91	−0.0075	−0.0042	−0.2329	0.1656	0.0101	−0.1877
	(−0.04)	(−0.78)	(−3.66)	(0.95)	(1.90)	(−3.19)
3/91	0.0775	0.0251	−0.3470	0.7237	0.0296	−0.3005
	(0.54)	(5.37)	(−9.63)	(5.41)	(6.39)	(−9.64)
4/91	0.1051	0.0048	−0.1669	0.9606	0.0087	−0.2718
	(0.63)	(0.86)	(−4.17)	(6.01)	(1.63)	(−6.89)
5/91	−0.3134	0.0085	−0.4746	0.5586	0.0151	−0.2814
	(−1.73)	(1.48)	(−7.58)	(3.15)	(2.56)	(−4.77)
6/91	0.0816	0.0026	−0.2917	0.6892	0.0004	−0.3163
	(0.48)	(0.43)	(−7.94)	(3.75)	(0.06)	(−7.18)
7/91	0.0679	0.0026	−0.2561	0.6217	0.0376	−0.2969
	(0.40)	(4.44)	(−6.82)	(3.21)	(5.32)	(−6.83)
8/91	0.3026	0.0146	−0.2529	0.8461	0.0041	−0.2852
	(1.77)	(2.55)	(−7.04)	(4.77)	(0.68)	(−6.69)
10/91	0.0938	0.0078	−0.2717	0.6158	0.0242	−0.3329
	(0.64)	(1.55)	(−8.62)	(3.98)	(4.46)	(−9.48)

[a] Coefficients rather than partial effects; e = early; l = late.

Table 4.7. *Proportion Supporting the Balcerowicz Plan*

	"Are You Facing a Danger of Losing Your Job?"				"Feel Danger"	Actual Rate
	Very	Great	Some	None		
February	29	37	44	42	42	0.8
March	27	32	38	42	39	1.5
April	21	25	33	34	41	1.9
June	15	24	38	44	49	3.1
November	20	20	22	36	48	5.9

"Feel danger" is the proportion in the national sample. Actual rate is the rate of unemployment.

that this had happened to a neighbor, and 50% reported that it had happened to a friend. Given that only 43,000 persons, about 0.2% of the labor force, were laid off by April 1990, these are not credible numbers. As the Polish expression has it, "fear has big eyes."

It is thus clear that people do not react to unemployment because it happened to them. They read the aggregate rate as a statistic from which to infer their own chances of losing their job: weighted aggregate elasticity of support with regard to unemployment is about −4.5, meaning that for every unemployed person, 3.5 others turn against the plan. Yet while the fear of losing employment turns people against the reform program, this is not an uncertainty that people want to see resolved. Perhaps they do not believe that unemployment will be simply frictional, fearing that once they lose their current job they will not find a new one.

There are good reasons why unemployment should turn people against reforms. Whatever else one may think about the Communist economy, it did provide full employment. Moreover, full employment was the principal mechanism of income insurance. Hence, when unemployment appeared and began to climb, people found themselves not only without jobs but also without incomes and other services that were traditionally provided by places of work. As of September 1993, there were 2,829,643 unemployed, 15.2% of the labor force. Of this number, 57% received no unemployment compensation, which covered in any case merely 80% of a minimum considered necessary to survive (*Zycie Warszawy*, September 14, 1993). Hence, the prospect of becoming unemployed was frightening.

119

Distributional Effects

All major economic transformations entail two redistributions of material welfare. The redistributions are across time and across social groups. How does social position affect attitudes toward the reform program?

The data indicating position in the social structure included Education, Age, and Sex. Unfortunately, no systematic data on incomes were available: prices changed so rapidly that no one seemed able to make sense of nominal incomes, survey researchers included.[16]

To assess the relative importance of sex, age, and education for attitudes toward the plan, one should note that many people – at the beginning most – did not have an opinion of the plan. Hence, we must again distinguish the determinants of having any position from the determinants of supporting or opposing.

Less educated people were much less likely at any moment to have an opinion of the plan. All the coefficients of NO VIEW on education are negative and significant. Women were also persistently less likely to have a view. Age was a volatile category: when the policy was announced, attitudes did not differ with age; in January 1990, younger people were more likely not to have a view, but during most of the period older people more frequently said that they had no position.

Whenever women did have a view, they tended to oppose the plan. They had reasons to do so: official unemployment was higher among women, who may also have been more affected by inflation, the decline of incomes, and the erosion of social services. Age was another volatile category: younger people tended to oppose the plan when it was announced, but older people stood in opposition as the costs set in. Note that policy toward the aged was one of the most erratic aspects of reform; hence, these results seem to reflect the reality.

While at the very beginning education had no impact on positions toward the reform program, as the costs set in the coefficients on education increased from about −0.12 in February 1990 to as much as −0.48 in May 1991.[17] Moreover, education dominates the explanation of the oppo-

---

[16] The data set includes some self-reported assessments of family situations, but these assessments are not sufficiently frequent to be considered. The occupational categories, in turn, differ from survey to survey. Hence, the only indication of class that is consistent throughout is education.

[17] I use coefficients since, in the case of individual data, the independent variables are not continuous.

sition toward the plan: t-values reached almost 10 by January 1991. The distribution of views toward the plan by income, available for some months, shows a linear relation: the lower the income, the higher the opposition to the plan. Occupational distributions show the same pattern: the plan was most opposed by unskilled workers and farmers; it was supported by the intelligentsia, private entrepreneurs, and executives. Hence, while education is not a perfect proxy for class, since the results with regard to education, income, and occupation are the same, we see a general class pattern. And the class basis of opposition to the plan is evident.

This class pattern of opposition may be due to three distinct reasons: (1) People who were less well educated (and poorer) when reforms were initiated expected throughout that they would lose more (or benefit less) from reforms in net terms, that is, that their welfare after the reforms were completed would be relatively lower in proportion to their transitional costs. If this is true, we should observe that the poor were more opposed to reforms at every moment but that the difference between their attitudes toward the plan and those of the rich remained the same. (2) The liberal program was little more than a veil over a major redistribution of income in favor of the rich: as the program was implemented, the poor become poorer and turned against it. We should then observe that the difference among classes increased over time. (3) Finally, even if the net benefits of reforms were the same for all the classes and if inequality did not increase, if the less well educated tended to think retrospectively, in the sense that they tended to rely on past experience in assessing the future prospects, while the better educated formed forecasts paying attention to promises (Sniderman, Glaser, and Griffin, 1990), then one will observe class patterns. The less educated extrapolated from the past, while the more educated looked toward the future, and since the past was full of hardships, a class pattern emerged. Thus, if this hypothesis is true, we would expect that the opposition to the plan would be shaped by current economic conditions among those with low education but not among the well educated.

It appears that while the general level of welfare declined precipitously after 1989 and the incidence of poverty skyrocketed,[18] neither the pre- nor the post-fisc inequality increased. According to UNICEF (1994:20), the

---

[18] The estimates vary somewhat, but the increase in poverty appears enormous. Schwartz (1994:82) cites numbers that vary between 16.7% and 21.8% for 1989 and between 38.7%

Gini index of income distribution was about the same in 1992 as in 1989. Moreover, subjective perceptions of the material conditions of one's family show little variation over the period of reform: while in November 1989 12% of respondents described their family's situation as good and 42% as bad, by October 1991 8% described it as good and 51% as bad. In general, these proportions tended to move up and down together: subjective assessments did not point to a growing disparity of incomes.

Nevertheless, the difference in the opposition to the reform program clearly increased over time: while in November 1989 the opposition among the least well educated was 6% lower than among the most highly educated (remember that many more among the less well educated did not have a view), by the end of the period the opposition among the least well educated was 14.5% higher. The correlation of this difference with time is 0.82. Hence, postures toward the plan crystallized along class lines (Table 4.8).

The least well educated were somewhat more sensitive to economic conditions than those with medium and high educational levels. They reacted more strongly to changes in real wages, to inflation, and, as one would expect, to unemployment. These patterns appear consistent with the hypothesis that the less well educated are more pessimistic about the future because they tend to extrapolate from the past, while those with more education form their expectations on other bases, a hypothesis we cannot test directly given the structure of the data. Yet it is again startling that those with low and medium education were more likely to support the plan when inflation was higher: they, too, were looking forward as far as inflation was concerned. And, in turn, their greater sensitivity to unemployment reflects the fact that they were the ones most likely to suffer from it. When unemployment mounts, it is the less well educated who turn against the program at the highest rate. Thus, while it appears that all groups made intertemporal judgments in a similar way, the less well educated, who suffered from higher unemployment rates, were more likely to oppose the plan. The attitudes toward the reform program followed class lines because the program had class effects.[19]

and 41.4% for 1992. UNICEF (1994:2) gives 22.9% in 1989 and 35.7% in 1992. It appears that farmers, single-person households, and children were particularly affected by the reforms.

[19] In February 1993 respondents were asked whether the standard of living of their family was lower or higher than it was five years earlier (that is, during the last full year

Table 4.8. *Multinomial Logit (MLE) Estimates of Opposition to the Balcerowicz Plan, as a Function of Economic Variables, by Education, Age, and Sex. Monthly Data*[a]

	Education		
	Low	Medium	High
RWAGE	−0.0158 (−4.48)	−0.0111 (−2.83)	−0.0189 (−2.83)
INFL	−0.0333 (−5.86)	−0.0332 (−5.21)	−0.0160 (−2.64)
UN	0.1629 (7.23)	0.0948 (4.27)	0.0886 (2.65)

	Age	
	>49	<50
RWAGE	−0.0121 (−2.90)	−0.0174 (−4.38)
INFL	−0.0326 (−4.29)	−0.0272 (−6.17)
UN	0.1538 (5.83)	0.1216 (5.99)

	Sex	
	Male	Female
RWAGE	−0.0149 (−3.54)	−0.0143 (−3.69)
INFL	−0.0319 (−5.54)	−0.0271 (−4.38)
UN	0.1318 (5.40)	0.1445 (6.99)

[a] Coefficients rather than partial effects.

Political Dynamics of Economic Reforms

The central finding that emerges from this analysis is that, in contrast to unemployment, with regard to inflation and, to a lesser extent, real wages, the politics of pro-market reforms are not the same as they are in normal times. Unemployment affects postures toward the reform program as one would normally expect: people do not tolerate it, and even if they are optimistic about it, they still react to current unemployment rates rather than future expectations and reject reforms. In turn, support for the plan declines when the actual rate of inflation is low and when optimism about inflation is high. Hence, with regard to inflation, people do not behave in the normal way. They exonerate the government and the program for the

under communism). The net differences between lower and higher living standards by occupational groups were −21% for managers and the intelligentsia, −53% for higher-level white-collar employees, −64% for lower-level white-collar workers, −70% for skilled workers, −72% for unskilled workers, and −80% for farmers. CBOS, *Opinia Publiczna*, Nr. 3(5), 1993.

bouts of inflation, seeing them as caused by forces independent of government control or by actors hostile to reforms. Once they are satisfied that prices are under control, people turn against the continuation of reforms. They seem to behave the way medical patients do when told to keep taking their medication even when the symptoms disappear: since the side effects are unpleasant, once the symptoms disappear, people throw the medicine away. Finally, people are hesitant about how to interpret increases in real wages. Such increases reduce opposition to the plan but do not generate support: people become agnostic. To the extent that people are uncertain if current wages increases can be sustained, rather than just cause inflation, they think intertemporally. Hence, to summarize these findings in terms of Stokes's distinctions, unemployment causes people to behave normally, inflation causes the exonerating pattern, and changes in real wages lead to some intertemporal thinking.

At the same time, support for the plan displays a class basis: people with lower education and lower incomes are much more likely to oppose the reform program. Moreover, while people with different educational levels react to the economic variables in a highly similar way, over time postures toward the plan become crystallized along class lines.

What are the implications of these patterns for the dynamic of support for pro-market reforms? First, it appears that people see the reform program as a remedy for, rather than a cause of, inflation. Note that Poland experienced hyperinflation in August 1989 and that, while prices soared during the first two months of 1990, except for January 1991, monthly inflation has remained in the single digits since then. Thus, there are good reasons to see the stabilization aspect of the Balcerowicz plan as a success. This is why people supported the plan when prices rose faster and saw its continuation an unnecessary when prices slowed down. The success of reforms with regard to inflation undermined political support for their continuation.

Second, while people reduced their opposition to the plan when wages increased, they remained agnostic about it: since they were told that wages would decline, they may simply have been disoriented by the sharp oscillations in real wages, which declined about 50% during the first two months of reforms, only to jump 31% in the subsequent month. Hence, increases in real wages reduced opposition but did not generate support either for the government or for its economic program.

Yet whatever the role inflation and wages played in shaping attitudes towards the Balcerowicz plan, they stand in sharp contrast to unemployment. People were not willing to believe that reform was a remedy for unemployment; they turned against the plan as unemployment mounted. We have seen repeatedly that the importance of unemployment far outweighed that of inflation, not to speak of wages. Even though unemployment grew almost linearly with time, future forecasts were based on the unemployment rate rather than simply on the duration of hardship. The actual rate of unemployment mattered more in shaping attitudes toward the Balcerowicz plan than future predictions based on it. While people wanted to resolve the uncertainty concerning inflation and income, they preferred to hold on to their jobs.

In conclusion, inflation and unemployment had different effects on the attitudes toward the reform program. People were willing to be persuaded that reforms were necessary to control inflation. They supported the reform program when prices flared but turned against it once inflation subsided. Hence, the success of reforms in controlling inflation undermined popular support for their continuation. In turn, the unemployment that these reforms generated was simply intolerable.[20] As it mounted, so did opposition to the reforms. Thus, when they succeeded in controlling inflation at the cost of unemployment, reforms lost support both because they were seen as no longer necessary to control inflation and because they caused unemployment. And since the poor were more affected by both inflation and unemployment, postures toward reforms crystallized along class lines.

References

Centrum Badan Opinii Spolecznej (CBOS). Various issues. Warsaw: Serwis Informacyjny.

Blanchard, O., R. Dornbusch, P. Krugman, R. Layard, and L. Summers. 1991. *Economic Reform in the East.* Cambridge, MA: MIT Press.

Cowden, J. A., and T. Hartley. 1992. "Complex Measures and Sociotropic Voting." *Political Analysis* 4: 75–95.

Di Tella, G. 1991. "Comment in the Panel Discussion." In M. Bruno, E. Fischer, N. Helpman, N. Livitan, and L. Meridor (eds.), *Lessons of Economic Stabilization and Its Aftermath.* Cambridge, MA: MIT Press.

---

[20] Indeed, by May 1991, only 26% of respondents agreed that unemployment was necessary for reforms to succeed, while upward of 80% found the very existence of unemployment "despicable."

Ebrill, L. P., A. Chopra, C. Christofides, P. Mylonas, I. Otkar, and G. Schwartz. 1994. *Poland: The Path to a Market Economy.* Occasional Paper #113. Washington, DC: International Monetary Fund.

Ferejohn, J. A. 1986. "Incumbent Performance and Electoral Control." *Public Choice* 50: 5–25.

Fiorina, M. P. 1981. *Retrospective Voting in American National Elections.* New Haven: Yale University Press.

Glowny Urzad Statystyczny (GUS). 1992. *Rocznik Statystyczny.* Warsaw: GUS.

International Monetary Fund. 1993. *Survey.* November 29. Washington, DC: International Monetary Fund.

Kinder, D. R., and D. R. Kiewit. 1979. "Economic Discontent and Political Behavior: The Role of Personal Grievances and Collective Economic Judgements in Congressional Voting." *American Journal of Political Science* 23: 495–517.

Kreps, D. M., and E. L. Porteus. 1978. "Temporal Resolution of Uncertainty and Dynamic Choice Theory." *Econometrica* 46: 185–200.

Lewis-Beck, M. S. 1988. *Economics and Elections: The Major Western Democracies.* Ann Arbor: University of Michigan Press.

Lipton, D., and J. Sachs. 1990. "Creating a Market Economy in Eastern Europe: The Case of Poland." *Brookings Papers on Economic Activity* 1: 75–145.

Organization for Economic Cooperation and Development (OECD). 1994. *Poland.* OECD Economic Surveys. Paris: OECD.

Ostrom, C. W., Jr., and R. M. Smith. 1992. "Error Correction, Attitude Persistence, and Executive Rewards and Punishments: A Behavioral Theory of Presidential Approval." *Political Analysis* 4: 127–183.

Paldam, M. 1991. "How Robust Is the Vote Function?: A Study of Seventeen Nations Over Four Decades." In H. Northop, M. S. Lewis-Beck, and J.-D. Lafay (eds.), *Economics and Politics: The Calculus of Support.* Ann Arbor: University of Michigan Press.

Przeworski, A. 1991. *Democracy and the Market: Political and Economic Reforms in Eastern Europe and Latin America.* New York: Cambridge University Press.

1993. "Economic Reforms, Public Opinion, and Political Institutions: Poland in Eastern European Perspective." In L. C. Bresser Pereira, J. M. Maravall, and A. Przeworski, *Economic Reforms in New Democracies: A Social-Democratic Approach.* New York: Cambridge University Press.

Rodrik, D. 1994. "The Dynamics of Political Support for Reform in Economies in Transition." Manuscript. Columbia University.

Rychard, Andrzej. 1991. "Limits to the Economic Changes in the Post-Communist Poland: Sociological Analysis." In S. Gomulka and C. Lin (eds.), *Limits to the Economic Transformation in the Post-Soviet Systems.* Oxford: Oxford University Press.

Schwartz, G. 1994. "Social Impact of the Transition." In L. P. Ebrill, A. Chopra, C. Charalambos, P. Mylonas, I. Otker, and G. Schwartz (eds.), *Poland:*

The Path to a Market Economy. Occasional Paper #113. Washington, DC: International Monetary Fund.

Sniderman, P. M., J. M. Glaser, and R. Griffin. 1990. "Information and Electoral Choice." In J. A. Ferejohn and J. H. Kuklinski (eds.), *Information and Democratic Process.* Urbana: University of Illinois Press.

Solimano, A. 1994. "Introduction and Synthesis." In A. Solimano, O. Sunkel, and M. I. Blejer (eds.), *Rebuilding Capitalism: Alternative Roads After Socialism and Dirigisme.* Ann Arbor: University of Michigan Press.

Tarkowski, J. 1989. "Old and New Patterns of Corruption in Poland and the U.S.S.R." *Telos* 80: 51–63.

United Nations International Children's Emergency Fund (UNICEF). 1994. *Crisis in Mortality, Health and Nutrition.* Regional Monitoring Report No. 2. Florence: UNICEF.

Weil, P. 1990. "Nonexpected Utility in Macroeconomics." *Quarterly Journal of Economics* 104: 29–42.

PART II

Latin America

5

Economic Reforms and Political Support in Mexico, 1988–1997

Jorge Buendía Laredo

Introduction

Good economic performance has traditionally been an asset for incumbent politicians. People support their government when the economy is doing well and oppose it when economic conditions decline. A healthy economy is good politics. In periods of economic reform, however, a healthy economy is out of the question. Economic policies usually produce a deterioration of welfare: inflation and unemployment rise and real wages decline. The purpose of this chapter is to explore the relationship between economics and presidential approval in Mexico during the years 1989–1997, when the Mexican economy experienced profound changes in its structure and Mexicans experienced hardships typical of pro-market reform processes. Did Mexicans' responses to these changes follow the pattern of normal economic voting, in which bad economic performance translates into opposition to the government and its policies? Or did intertemporal considerations lead them to accept pain and support the government in exchange for a brighter future? Or did Mexicans blame the previous government for the hard times and rally in support of the new government (exonerating posture)?

There are plausible reasons to expect exonerating, intertemporal, or normal economic voting patterns among the Mexican public (for more details see Chapter 1). Past memories, for instance, may lead the Mexican public to respond to self-exonerating arguments made by the

I would like to thank Patricio Navia, Adam Przeworski, Hector Santana, Susan Stokes, and an anonymous referee for helpful suggestions and comments. Rosario Aguilar and Carmina Borja provided invaluable research assistance.

government: three out of the four Mexican presidents in the last quarter of the twentieth century took power amid an economic crisis inherited from, or incubated by, the preceding government. In the public mind, the sixth and last year of any Mexican government is usually considered to be the "year we all live in danger," as economic but also political crises usually occur.[1] Because it is clear that the previous government is responsible for the economic crisis, there are some grounds to expect the Mexican public to be supportive of the new administration in spite of deteriorating economic conditions. If this is the case, support for the new government should not decline when the economy deteriorates. In this chapter I will assess whether exoneration was the prevailing posture people adopted toward the Zedillo government (1994–2000), which inherited precarious economic conditions from the Salinas government (1988–1994).

Normal economic voting patterns are also likely to occur in Mexico. The main assumption of normal economic voting – most people assigning responsibility to the government for the state of the economy – is fulfilled: seven out of 10 Mexicans consider the government responsible for the state of the national economy (Buendía, 1999; Nannestadt and Paldam, 1994). The same political party governed without interruption from 1929 until 2000, and until 1997 the ruling party had an absolute majority in Congress, giving the Mexican president extraordinary power to govern. Mexicans do know who is responsible for economic policy. Under these conditions, it is likely that the public will support the government when the economy grows, oppose it when the economy deteriorates. Did Mexicans behave according to normal economic voting rules in the period 1988–1997?

How likely are intertemporal considerations to occur in Mexico? By one account, intertemporal judgments are characterized by people's willingness to accept declining economic conditions in exchange for future benefits. In this scenario, bad times signal better times ahead and people support the government or the economic plan. Yet this mindset seems unlikely in Mexico in the period under study (1988–1997). The economic reform process had been underway since 1982; by 1988 the public had little patience with the government and was unlikely to interpret deteriorating economic conditions as a sign of the efficacy of the adjustment

---

[1] As there is no reelection in Mexico, the outgoing government has no incentives to perform efficiently, especially when its time is running out.

program. Rather, an increase in the unemployment or the inflation rate would mean that, once more, the stabilization program had failed. This type of intertemporal judgment is more plausible when a new government implements the economic plan and people have no prior information either about the economic program or about the government. In Mexico the time period most conducive to this type of calculus was 1982–1983, when a drastic adjustment program was introduced for the first time. However, there are no survey data available for this period.

A more compelling intertemporal story to apply in the Mexican case is told by Stokes in Chapter 6 of this volume. In Peru, wage growth was seen as a prelude to inflation and an economic slump. If people have memories of the expansionary policies pursued by a populist or manipulative government, they will remember that times of economic growth were followed by recessions. If the government manipulates the economy, individuals learn to discount positive economic information: they learn that good times now signal bad times ahead. In Mexico the last year of the Salinas government, an election year, was one of low inflation and a healthy rate of economic growth. The following year, the country experienced its worst economic recession since 1929. Do Mexicans interpret positive economic information as a signal that bad times are ahead?

This chapter is structured as follows. I first review some general features of the Mexican economy and the reform process, starting with the government of Miguel De la Madrid (1982–1988). Next, I discuss public support for the government of Carlos Salinas de Gortari (1988–1994), in particular how economic performance influenced presidential approval. In the following part, I analyze public opinion of the major stabilization program of the Salinas government, the Pact for Stability and Economic Growth. The last section deals with public support for the government and its economic policies during the first three years of Ernesto Zedillo's government (1994–1997).

Overview of the Mexican Economy (1982–1997)

By the time Carlos Salinas de Gortari took power in Mexico (December 1, 1988), economic adjustment had been underway for six years. From 1983 to 1985, the first two years of Miguel De la Madrid's government, economic policy was characterized by attempts to stabilize the economy, that is, correct the balance of payments problems and diminish inflation, while structural reform was postponed. It was not until mid-1985 that stabilization policies were accompanied by "an acceleration in trade liberalization signaling the beginning of the structural reform process"[2] (Lustig, 1992:39).

De la Madrid's efforts to curb inflation and to improve the efficiency of the economy produced disappointing results after five years. In 1987 gross domestic product (GDP) was at the same level as in 1982, per capita GDP had declined, annual inflation was at its highest level ever (159%), and real wages had fallen dramatically.

It was in this context that in December 1987 a heterodox stabilization program to curb inflation was announced: the Pact of Economic Solidarity (PES). The program had at its core sound public finances. Under the PES the government sought to increase its revenue and to reduce its expenditures. Prices and tariffs of goods and services provided by the state were increased and subsidies and programmable expenditures reduced. Programmable expenditures diminished 8.9% in real terms during the first year of the PES (Aspe, 1993:33). The adjustment focused mainly on lowering public expenditures (see Table 5.1).

One year after the PES was introduced, Carlos Salinas took power. Macroeconomic indicators for the first year of the PES show that inflation had fallen from the previous level of 159% to 51.7%, the GDP grew 1.3%, real wages in the manufacturing sector did not change,[3] and open urban unemployment declined. On the other hand, social spending fell, although by a mere 2% in 1988, a low figure given the magnitude of the fiscal adjustment. In per capita terms social spending was reduced 3.6% (Lustig, 1993:216).

One month after Carlos Salinas came to power, the PES underwent a change in name to the Pact for Stability and Economic Growth (PECE). In changing the name, the government sought to emphasize that restoring economic growth would now be a major governmental target. The PECE functioned from January 1, 1989, to October 1992, when its name was changed to Pact for Stability, Competitiveness, and Employment. With this change of name, the government emphasized the objectives of job creation and efficiency in anticipation of the competition of the United

---

[2] The opening of the Mexican economy is best symbolized by Mexico's signing of the General Agreement on Tariffs and Trade (GATT) in 1986.

[3] Using other sources, Lustig (1993:203–207) estimates that total income derived from wages and salaries declined 7.9% in 1988 and that the number of jobs created in 1988 increased 0.6% in comparison to the previous year. Success of the PES, then, was also based on a contraction of real wages.

States and Canada under the North American Free Trade Agreement (Pacto para la Estabilidad, Competitividad y el Empleo, 1992).

The main macroeconomic indicators during the years 1988–1994 show that the anti-inflationary strategy worked and that real wages in the manufacturing sector improved steadily.[4] In 1993 and 1994 annual inflation was below 10%. However, there were signs that one-digit inflation had been achieved at the cost of slowed growth and higher levels of unemployment, especially in 1993. If we consider GDP growth per capita, the picture is more somber still.

Ominous signs were also present in the external sector of the economy. From 1988 to 1994 the current account showed a deficit that increased year after year. In 1994 the current account deficit represented 7.7% of the GDP. This deficit could be sustained only by a constant influx of foreign investment: the 1993 current account deficit (US$23.4 billion) was financed by a surplus in the capital account of the balance of payments of US$32.6 billion (Bank of Mexico, 1995:250–251). This strategy could not be sustained for long. In 1994, the guerrilla uprising in Chiapas and in particular the murder of the ruling party's presidential candidate, Luis Donaldo Colosio, generated a great deal of uncertainty about Mexico's political stability. Foreign investors reacted immediately and took their money out of Mexico. The day Colosio was murdered (March 23, 1994), Mexico's international reserves amounted to US$28 billion. One month later, the reserves had diminished by more than US$10 billion (Bank of Mexico, 1995). The 1994 current account deficit (US$29.7 billion) could not be now financed through foreign investment, as the surplus in the capital account reached only US$14.6 billion, less than half of the 1993 capital account surplus (Bank of Mexico, 1997). These pressures meant that the anti-inflationary policy pursued until then had become unstable: if the peso was devalued to reduce the current account deficit, inflation would rise. The August 1994 presidential election was an additional reason not to devalue the peso.

Ernesto Zedillo took office as president of Mexico on December 1, 1994. By December 19 (the day the peso was finally devalued) the international reserves of the Bank of Mexico had dropped to a little more than US$10 billion from its highest level of US$29 billion in late February 1994

---

[4] Real wages outside of the manufacturing sector (contractual wages in the federal public sector and the minimum legal wage) do not seem to have improved as much as those in the manufacturing sector (Cortés and Rubalcava, n.d.:7).

Table 5.1. *Economic Indicators, 1986–1997*

	1986	1987	1988	1989	1990	1991	1992	1993	1994	1995	1996	1997
Basic Macroeconomic Indicators, 1986–1997												
GDP growth[a]	-3.6	1.8	1.3	3.3	5.1	4.2	3.6	2	4.4	-6.2	5.2	7.0
Interest rates[b]	n.a.	n.a.	69.5	45	34.8	19.3	15.6	15	14.1	48.44	31.39	19.8
Exchange rate[c]	n.a	n.a.	2.250	2.453	2.807	3.013	3.095	3.11	3.375	6.419	7.60	8.5
Annual inflation	105.7	159.2	51.7	19.7	29.9	18.8	11.9	8.01	7.05	51.97	27.70	15.72
Real wages[d]	93.8	91.5	91.4	99.7	102.5	109.3	119	127.6	132.3	114.4	101.7	
Unemployment[e]	4.3	3.9	3.5	2.9	2.7	2.7	2.8	3.4	3.7	6.2	5.4	3.7
Public Finances as a Percentage of GDP												
Economic balance[f]	-14.5	-14.4	-9.3	-4.6	-2.6	-0.5	1.5	0.7	-0.1	0.0	0.0	-0.8
Primary balance[g]	1.6	4.7	8	7.7	7.2	4.8	5.2	3.3	2.1	4.7	4.4	3.5
Public revenues[h]	29.7	27.8	27.7	25.8	25.3	23.5	23.7	23.1	22.8	22.8	22.8	22.9
Public expenditures[i]	26.5	22.4	20.3	18.4	18.5	18.8	18.6	19.8	20.8	18.4	18.7	19.5

Total net debt	80.7	76.6	61.9	55.1	45.8	35.8	26.7	21.9	21.9	31.3	28.6	22.3
Domestic debt	18.9	15.3	16	18.1	17.3	13.8	8	8.9	3.8	2.3	2.7	3
External debt	61.8	61.4	45.9	37	28.5	21.9	18.7	17	18.1	29	25.9	19.3
Number of public enterprises	737	617	412	379	280	239	217	210	215	204	185	n.a.

a GDP in thousands of millions of new pesos (1980 = 100) until 1994 (1993 = 100).
b CETES, 28 days.
c New pesos per dollar, average for period.
d Manufacturing sector, deflated by consumer price index.
e Open urban unemployment.
f Difference between revenues and expenditures of the nonfinancial public sector. (–) Deficit, (+) surplus. Data for 1991 and 1992 exclude nonre-current revenues derived from privatizations.
g Difference between revenues and expenditures other than interest payments of the nonfinantial public sector.
h Consolidated total revenues. Carpeta electrónica de Banco de México, April 1998.
i Budgetary primary expenditures. Carpeta electrónica de Banco de México, April 1998.

Sources: Banco de México: *Indicadores Económicos, Informe Anual*, various numbers.

(Bank of Mexico, 1995:222–223). The deterioration of Mexico's international reserves was counteracted by the issuing of Mexican government bonds denominated in U.S. dollars (called Tesobonos). In January 1994, Tesobonos constituted only 6% of all foreign investment in Mexican government securities. At the end of that year it represented 84%, signaling a shift in the portfolio of foreign investors from peso-denominated securities to dollar-indexed paper (Bank of Mexico, 1995:100, 261). The fact that a large amount of Tesobonos was short-term debt triggered the 1995 Mexican crisis.

To summarize, when Salinas came to power in December 1988, a good deal of the economic adjustment had already taken place. The period 1988–1994 then can be characterized as one in which stabilization policies continued (lowering inflation and cutting the budget deficit) and the structural reform of the economy was deepened (trade liberalization, fiscal reform, privatization, etc.). It is in this sense a period of consolidation of economic reforms (although the current account deficit and capital flight in 1994 would prove to be the Achilles heel of Salinas's economic policies). Ernesto Zedillo, on the other hand, had to implement in 1995 a drastic adjustment program in order to correct Mexico's huge current account deficit.

Economic Reform and Presidential Approval

Because they lie in the future, the benefits of economic reform are uncertain. Uncertainty allows a greater role for persuasion because people's beliefs about their economic interests can be influenced by political elites (Bates and Krueger, 1993:456; see also Zaller, 1992).[5] Furthermore, how issues are framed influences what people think about them (Quattrone and Tversky, 1993). As Kinder and Sanders put it, "By promoting a particular frame, political elites may alter how an issue is understood and, ultimately, what opinion turns out to be" (1990:74; Kinder, 1993:46). The Polish experience suggests that elite framing may forestall the normal economic voting response to inflation: if government officials are able to frame price increases in intertemporal terms, that is, that inflation must rise in the

---

[5] Due to the actions of "political activists," under conditions of uncertainty it is likely that "rather than shaping events, notions of self-interest are instead themselves shaped and formed" (Bates and Krueger, 1993:456).

short term if prices are to be stabilized in the medium term, it is possible that people will view rising inflation as a sign that the program is working and will support the government (see Chapters 1 and 4, this volume).

How did the Mexican authorities present the PES to the public in 1987? How did Salinas present the government's major economic objectives once he assumed office?

The timing of the implementation of the PES is singular for several reasons: unlike most economic reform programs (Bates and Krueger, 1993:457; Haggard and Kaufman, 1992:30–31), the PES was not carried out by a new government but by a government that had already been in power for five years. The De la Madrid government did not have the "political capital" derived from a recent electoral victory, as many Latin American countries did while pursuing economic reform (Remmer, 1993: 405). Governments may be able to mobilize support more readily if they pursue reforms early in their terms. The longer a government has been in power, the greater the chances that it will be blamed for the precarious economic conditions the reform seeks to address, making self-exonerating or antidotal rhetoric less credible in the public eye[6] (Alt, 1991:244–246; see also Chapter 1 of this volume).

For these reasons, it is not surprising that Mexicans did not have much confidence in the success of the PES. After five years of economic adjustment, people were skeptical of any economic reform package introduced by the De la Madrid government. In 1983 and 1986 two economic programs were introduced to stabilize the economy and to restore economic growth. But these programs failed to achieve their targets (in part due to the decline in the price of oil, Mexico's main export).[7]

It is highly unlikely, then, that Mexicans would evaluate the PES through the lens of intertemporal trade-offs. Mexicans perceived their current government as causally responsible for economic trends. In a survey conducted at the same time that the PES was introduced, 69% of the interviewees believed that the Mexican economic crisis was due to the

---

[6] The immediate impact on public opinion of governmental intervention in the economy, i.e., a reform program "depends on the balance between any positive effect on expectations (to the extent there is confidence in the effectiveness of the policy) and a negative effect on retrospective evaluations from increased awareness of economic problems" (Alt, 1991:240).

[7] The two programs were the Immediate Program of Economic Reorganization (PIRE) and the Program of Encouragement and Growth (Programa de Aliento y Crecimiento).

government's mismanagement (Alduncin, 1991:96–97).[8] Only if inflation slowed were Mexicans likely to infer that the program was working. Otherwise the PES would be another link in the chain of unsuccessful economic programs introduced by the De la Madrid government.

The De la Madrid government was probably aware of its constrained position vis-à-vis public opinion. It announced that after a temporary rise in inflation in the month following the implementation of the pact (January 1988) it expected inflation to go down. In its own words: "A major attempt will be made to bring inflation down *quickly* this year [1988], especially beginning the second quarter" (Text of the PES, 1987:68; italics mine). The main reason for the government's urgent need to curb inflation was that presidential elections were to be held on July 6, 1988, seven months after the introduction of the PES. Thus, the government could ask for little patience from the people.[9]

With these considerations in mind, we would expect Mexicans to evaluate their authorities and the economic reform program in the normal way: if economic conditions improved, they would be more likely to support the president and his policies; if they deteriorated, they would turn against him. In fact, the little data available on public opinion in this period suggest that overcoming public skepticism would require excellent economic performance. A Gallup poll taken in May 1988 (five months after the PES was introduced) shows that most people were skeptical about the future efficacy of the economic pact even though the monthly rate of inflation had gone down from 14.8% in December 1987 to 3% in April 1988 (Domínguez, 1993:205–206).

The government of Carlos Salinas also framed its economic policies in an orthodox way. In his inauguration address Salinas promised that the economic crisis would be left behind and that a "new age of growth" was coming, meaning more jobs and an increase in people's purchasing power. He was emphatic: "the priority will no longer be to pay [the external debt] but to resume economic growth" (Salinas, 1988:1140). Although he cautioned that 1989 would be a transition year to avoid overheating the economy, he expected to achieve GDP growth of 1.5% in real terms, to cut inflation to half of its 1988 level, and to protect people's

---

[8] Unfortunately, this survey does not include questions on the PES.

[9] The government also estimated a real GDP increase of 2% for 1988, although it cautioned that the anti-inflationary policies would have an "initial recessive impact" (Text of the Economic Solidarity pact, 1988:69).

purchasing power and their jobs (Presidencia de la República, 1989:68–71).[10] This would be the benchmark against which to judge the Salinas government.

Presidential Approval and Economic Performance

The analysis presented here is based on a statistical analysis of presidential approval for the years 1990–1994. The data analyzed here come from 42 polls sponsored by the Technical Advisory, Presidency of the Republic.[11] Thirty-six of the observations were derived from probabilistic samples taken in the six major cities of Mexico, which together comprise 67% of the urban population of the country. The cities included in the polls are Mexico City and its metropolitan area, Guadalajara, Monterrey, Tijuana, Mérida, and Tuxtla Gutiérrez (N = 3,500). Five other polls are representative of Mexico City, Guadalajara, Monterrey, and Tijuana (N = 2,500), and another one is representative of the latter cities excluding Tijuana (N = 2,000).

The question I use as the indicator of presidential approval is "Do you agree or disagree with the way the president is governing?" (¿Está usted de acuerdo o en desacuerdo con la manera como está gobernando el presidente?). The dependent variable has three choices, labeled SUPPORT, OPPOSE, and NO VIEW.[12] As stated in Chapter 1 of this volume, the

---

[10] The General Economic Policy Criteria for 1989 presented by President Salinas to the Congress on December 15, 1988, states the following: "We have to recover economic growth. During the 90s growth should be stable and permanent, at least twice the population growth" (Presidencia de la República, 1989:67).

[11] The data can be consulted at the Centro de Investigación y Docencia Económica (CIDE) in Mexico City or at the Roper Center for Public Opinion Research at the University of Connecticut. There is no significant difference between the aggregate results obtained from polls carried out either in three or four cities and the results of the polls carried out in all six cities because Mexico City, Guadalajara, Monterrey, and Tijuana have 96% of the population covered in the polls taken in the six cities. However, I isolated the latter four cities in the "six cities" polls, and the aggregate results obtained from this isolation did not differ by more than 1% from the overall results.

[12] I recoded "don't know" and "no answer" into a single item (NVIEW). It does not affect the results. Two other questions included in the polls related to presidential approval are: "On a scale of 0 to 10, which grade would you give to the President (GRADE)?" and "Of the 1988 presidential candidates, whom do you like most (con quién simpatiza más) (PREF)?". The correlation between these three questions is very high: 0.87 between AGREE and GRADE, 0.84 between AGREE and PREF, and 0.88 between GRADE and PREF. Hence, I am confident that I have measured presidential approval with the first question.

141

statistical model used treats the data as compositional where the sum of the choices adds to 1 and each proportion falls within the unit interval (for more details see Katz and King, 1999). The independent economic variables are monthly inflation rate, level of real wages per capita in the manufacturing sector (an index), and level of open urban unemployment.[13] A dummy variable named PRICE INCREASE was also used as an independent variable. It took on the value of 1 if a sudden price increase in fuel or basic goods occurred that month and 0 otherwise. Four such price increases occurred during the period I studied, May 1990 to November 1993. Political crises such as the guerrilla uprising in Chiapas and the Colosio murder were also included in the equation. This dummy variable for crises took the value of 1 in January and March 1994.

In order to account for autocorrelation in the data, this equation was run with and without lagged presidential approval as independent variable (models 1 and 2 in Tables 5.2 and 5.3, respectively).[14] The most substantive difference between models 1 and 2 is that in the former inflation does not influence support for the president. If no controls for past presidential approval are included in the model, then when inflation rises the president's approval rate diminishes.

In both models, unemployment and sharp price increases lead to a deterioration of approval rates, while the real wages variable does not have an impact on approval levels. Surprisingly, the dummy variable representing the political crises occurring in the last year of the Salinas government did not achieve statistical significance. In other words, neither the guerrilla uprising nor the Colosio murder reduced Salinas's support. What explains this finding? A likely explanation is that the Mexican public was divided regarding the responsibility of the president in these crises. For some people Salinas had some responsibility for each crisis, and they blamed him. Other people, in contrast, rallied around the president, as often happens when a political crisis erupts.

---

[13] The independent economic variables were lagged one month because in some cases my dependent variable was measured in the first two weeks of the month. My indicator of unemployment is the rate of open urban unemployment, a very restrictive definition of unemployment. It is defined as the proportion of the economically active population that works less than one hour per week. The level of open urban unemployment in the period under study ranges from 2% to 4%. This low variance is not statistically desirable, but this was the best measure on unemployment available on a monthly basis.

[14] In order to have an indicator of lagged presidential approval for some months where that information was unavailable, I used the coefficients obtained from model 2 to estimate the predicted presidential approval rate for the missing months.

Table 5.2. *Seemingly Unrelated Regression Equation: Model 1 (N = 41)*

Determinants of Presidential Approval, 1990–1994						
Oppose	Coef	Std. Err.	z	$P > \lvert z \rvert$	[95% Conf. Interval]	
Constant	.601569	1.353298	0.445	0.657	−2.050846	3.253984
Approval$_{t-1}$	−.0452381	.0079	−5.726	0.000	−.0607218	−.0297543
Inflation$_{t-1}$	.1286366	.1233845	1.043	0.297	−.1131927	.3704658
Real wages$_{t-1}$	.0053307	.0104643	0.509	0.610	−.015179	.0258404
Unemployment$_{t-1}$	.2196608	.1157424	1.898	0.058	−.0071901	.4465118
Price increase	.4417453.7	.1464221	3.017	0.003	.1547632	.287273
Political crisis	.169176	.2006731	0.843	0.399	−.224136	.5624881

$R^2 = 0.6297$

No View	Coef	Std. Err.	z	$P > \lvert z \rvert$	[95% Conf. Interval]	
Constant	−1.894287	1.259097	−1.504	0.132	−4.362071	.5734975
Approval$_{t-1}$	−.0053217	.0073501	−0.724	0.469	−.0197277	.0090843
Inflation$_{t-1}$	.0545188	.1147959	0.475	0.635	−.1704771	.2795147
Real wages$_{t-1}$	−.0070003	.0097359	−0.719	0.472	−.0260823	.0120818
Unemployment$_{t-1}$	.1771992	.1076858	1.646	0.100	−.033861	.3882595
Price increase	.3010872	.1362299	2.210	0.027	.0340815	.5680929
Political crisis	−.0139943	.1867045	−0.075	0.940	−.3799285	.3519399

$R^2 = 0.2141$

Note: Support is the base category.

The statistical models suggest that unemployment is the main economic determinant of presidential approval. The Mexican public behaved in a way consistent with normal economic voting: when unemployment rose, people were less likely to support Carlos Salinas and more likely to oppose him. Holding the other variables at their mean level, an increase of 1% in the rate of unemployment (from 3% to 4%, for instance) decreases the president's approval rate by 4% (see Figure 5.1). Regarding unemployment, there is no evidence supporting the existence of exonerating or intertemporal attitudes among the Mexican public.

Nor did changes in real wages or inflation rates seem to influence support for Salinas. Even when a different statistical model shows inflation to be a factor in accounting for support for the president (as in model 2, Table 5.3), Mexicans' behavior is consistent with normal economic voting patterns: when the economy deteriorates, presidential approval declines. No evidence of intertemporal or exonerating patterns emerges

Table 5.3. *Model 2: Seemingly Unrelated Regression Equation: Model 1 (N = 41)*

Determinants of Presidential Approval, 1990–1994						
Oppose	Coef	Std. Err.	z	$P > \mid z \mid$	[95% Conf. Interval]	
Constant	−4.764377	1.30987	−3.637	0.000	−7.331675	−2.197079
Inflation$_{t-1}$	.3808417	.1546224	2.463	0.014	.0777873	.6838961
Real wages$_{t-1}$	.0157422	.013825	1.139	0.255	−.0113542	.0428386
Unemployment$_{t-1}$	.493752	.1413751	3.492	0.000	.216662	.7708421
Price increase	.394126	.1961165	2.010	0.044	.0097448	.7785072
Political crisis	.2540563	.2684789	0.946	0.3440	−.2721526	.7802652
$R^2 = 0.3335$						
No View	Coef	Std. Err.	z	$P > \mid z \mid$	[95% Conf. Interval]	
Constant	−2.525525	.9142053	−2.763	0.006	−4.317334	−.7337151
Inflation$_{t-1}$	.0841877	.1079166	0.780	0.435	−.1273249	.2957003
Real wages$_{t-1}$	−.0057755	.0096489	−0.599	0.549	−.0246871	.0131361
Unemployment$_{t-1}$	.2094427	.0986708	2.123	0.034	.0160516	.4028338
Price increase	.2954853	.1368767	2.159	0.031	.0272118	.5637588
Political crisis	−.0040092	.1873811	−0.021	0.983	−.3712693	.363251
$R^2 = 0.2041$						

from the data. As mentioned, Salinas did not frame his political and economic discourse in an exonerating or intertemporal way. He had no reason to do so: the previous government left him an economy that, even if in bad shape, had started to grow, while inflation rates began a systematic decrease. Moreover, until becoming the ruling party's presidential candidate, Salinas was for five years the minister of budget and programming, the most important economic post in the cabinet. He had no one to blame but himself.

The closest evidence to an intertemporal pattern is the positive sign of the real wages variable in models 1 and 2, indicating that an increase in real wages leads to opposition to the government. Mexicans may have believed that current improvement in real wages would lead in the future to inflation, as producers would adjust the prices of goods in order to compensate for the increase in labor costs. However, in none of the statistical models presented here does the real wages variable achieve statistical significance.

The finding that unemployment is the most relevant variable in accounting for political support in Mexico is consistent with comparative

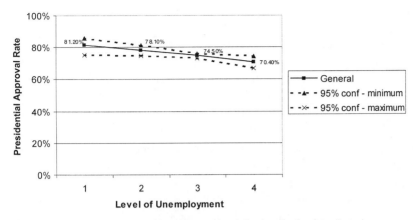

Figure 5.1 Expected presidential approval, by level of unemployment.

research. On the one hand, unemployment has a greater economic impact than inflation. As Douglas Hibbs pointed out, "movements in unemployment and real output (real income) are intimately connected," while "in principle, inflations do not adversely affect output and employment" (1987:136). Insofar as changes in welfare influence political support for the government or the incumbent party, the greater economic relevance of unemployment accounts for its larger impact on popularity levels.

Even if the rate of unemployment is low, its consequences may be felt by many. Exposure to unemployment is not confined to those without a job. The rate of unemployment includes only those who are currently out of work. In the United States, for instance, it has been estimated that the fraction of the labor force experiencing unemployment in a given year is two and a half to three times larger than the unemployment rate (Hibbs, 1987:49). Furthermore, exposure to job insecurity and unemployment is not limited to the unemployed themselves. As Schlozman and Verba put it (1979:43), "those who are fearful of losing their jobs, those who have been unemployed in the past, and those whose families or friends are out of work share in the experience of joblessness and unemployment insecurity." This may explain why anxiety about unemployment outstrips the unemployment rate.

We have some data with which to analyze public perceptions of unemployment. In a poll taken in July 1993,[15] when the open urban

---

[15] The survey ($N = 3,500$) is representative of the population living in Mexico City and its metropolitan area, Guadalajara, Monterrey, Tijuana, Mérida, and Tuxtla Gutiérrez.

unemployment rate was of 3.6%,[16] 59% of the interviewees declared that they knew somebody who had lost his or her job in the prior year. Among those who had jobs (62% of the total sample), 32% thought that they might lose them, whereas 46% thought their jobs were secure. Having met someone who has lost his or her job increases by 8% the likelihood that an employed person will fear losing his or her job (from 32% to 40%). By mid-1993, unemployment in Mexico was widespread in the eyes of most of the population. Although only a fraction of the interviewees feared they would lose their jobs, most of the population noticed that unemployment had been increasing, signaling that the state of the economy was not good. To the extent that unemployment lowered aggregate presidential popularity, this was not mainly through the unemployed or those who feared losing their jobs (a relatively small number of the population). Instead it was because many Mexicans regarded unemployment as an indicator of how well the economy was doing and as predicting the general future course of the economy, and held the president responsible for these trends.

Public Opinion and the PECE

My analysis turns now to people's attitudes toward the PECE, the main economic pact pursued by the Salinas administration.[17] Because monthly data are not available, the analysis is based on 10–12 polls carried out between 1989 and 1993. I have emphasized cross-sectional analysis while trying to distinguish, with the data at hand, temporal changes in public support for the PECE.[18]

Gaining the public's confidence was one of Salinas's major tasks. Economic stabilization and reactivation would enhance Salinas's standing

[16] From July 1992 to July 1993 the number of jobs created increased only 0.7% (Instituto Mexicano de Seguridad Social [IMSS] figures), a negative per capita growth. It must be stressed that because our definition of unemployment is a very restrictive one, it probably underestimates the number of people who do not have a job (it does not measure underemployment).

[17] In March 1995, the Zedillo government presented an economic program backed by all major economic actors. This economic pact was called the Agreement of Unity to Overcome the Economic Emergency (AUSEE). However, unlike the previous government, in the new administration economic pacts were not a central part of the government's economic policy.

[18] Unfortunately, public opinion data on other key components of the economic reform such as trade liberalization or privatization are scarce, forcing us to concentrate on the stabilization program.

Table 5.4. *Do You Think the Government Has Taken the Appropriate Economic Measures?*

Month	Net Scores			
	General	Low Income	Middle Income	High Income
Jun 89	−2	−3	−6	9
Jun 90	8	−1	10	8
Oct 90	17	8	18	24
Nov 90	5	−1	1	19
Apr 91	31	30	30	35
Nov 91	16	5	14	29
Jan 92	36	26	38	38
Feb 92	31	22	31	35
Aug 92	30	26	28	39
Oct 92	25	19	27	26
Jul 93	40	33	40	45
Oct 93	34	30	35	36

Net Score = Yes minus No.

and make it easier for him to embark on major reform initiatives, such as reform of the *ejido*, or cooperative farm sector, and the legal recognition of the Catholic Church. Salinas's approval rates were lower during his first two years in office than later. In March 1989, after four months in power, his approval was 57%. By 1993 his approval levels hovered between 75 and 80%.[19] As expected, the trend in approval rates followed changes in the citizens' judgment of the government's economic strategy. Support for the overall economic policies increased as time passed (Table 5.4). From a negative net approval score (yes minus no) it went to a positive net score of around 30%. At the beginning, people were divided on the wisdom of Salinas's economic policies. Later the number of people supporting them increased and the number of those opposed decreased. This trend was more accentuated among low- and middle-income people.[20]

Support for the overall economic policies was higher than support for the PECE. Many people did not believe the PECE was helping to reduce

---

[19] The same tendency, based on a different data base, is reported by Basáñez (1995).

[20] Low-income people are those whose income ranges between zero and less than one minimum wage. Middle-income people are those whose earnings range between one and less than three minimum wages, while high-income people receive three or more minimum wages. I took this classification from the Bank of Mexico (*estrato bajo, medio, alto*).

Table 5.5. *Do You Think the Economic Pact Has Helped to Reduce Inflation?*

Month	Net Scores			
	General	Low Income	Middle Income	High Income
Jun 89	3	−4	−1	20
Jan 90	−1	−36	1	22
Jun 90	−19	−24	−19	−14
Oct 90	−10	−24	−12	5
Nov 90	−15	−30	−16	0
Apr 91	7	4	5	13
Nov 91	−5	−17	−6	9
Feb 92	11	−8	10	27
Aug 92	−3	−6	−4	1
Oct 92	−18	−4	−22	−20
Jul 93	15	9	11	29
Oct 93	10	5	6	22

Net Score = Yes minus No.

inflation (Table 5.5). This is at first glance puzzling because inflation had fallen steadily after the introduction of the economic pact in 1987. The fact that all important price increases in this period were announced as part of the economic pact may help to explain people's skepticism about its effectiveness. Nor did it help that these price increases were on goods provided by the public sector such as fuel and electricity. Mexicans did not believe that to lower inflation it was necessary to increase prices (to correct relative prices). In this sense they did not make intertemporal judgments. As the previous statistical analysis showed (Tables 5.2 and 5.3), support for the president declined abruptly when a price increase was announced. A sudden jump in prices was associated with an increase of 7% in the probability of opposing the president and with a 2% increase in uncertainty. This is consistent with normal economic voting behavior.

Public confidence in the government's ability to control inflation also dropped significantly after a renewal of the PECE was accompanied by increases in energy prices. In June 1990, November 1990, and November 1991, after a price increase, most people were pessimistic about the ability of the government to keep inflation under control.[21]

[21] General net scores on the question "Do you think the government will be able to keep inflation under control?" were as follows: June 1990, −9.6; October 1990, 4.5; November

Lower levels of presidential approval and diminished confidence in the effectiveness of economic policies after a sudden price rise are understandable: people may see rising prices as a sign of the ineffectiveness of the anti-inflationary program or they may infer that economic conditions were not as good as they thought (Alt, 1991). Others might see price adjustments as a breach of the government's promise to fight inflation. Again we find evidence of normal economic voting.

The impact of inflation, then, was not only quantitative in nature but also had important qualitative features: price increases modified people's expectations about future economic conditions, led them to update their prior information on the state of the economy, and threatened the policy credibility of the government. Presidential approval rates fell sharply when price increases were announced. This negative impact did not last long. Usually approval rates rebounded after one month.

Another puzzle regarding the PECE is that polls show that most people wanted the program to continue, including many of those who thought the PECE was not helping to stabilize inflation (Table 5.6). In several polls taken between January 1990 and October 1993, the proportion of people who thought the PECE should be maintained varied from 48% in November 1990 to 71% in February 1992 and October 1993. There is no indication of any trend in the level of support for the PECE as time passed, although larger positive scores were registered in 1992 and 1993, years when inflation went down and price modifications due to the PECE were not substantial. Why did people want the PECE to continue even if many of them thought it did not work?

Although data are not available to sustain this hypothesis, Mexicans probably wanted the PECE to continue because it reduced economic uncertainty. People dislike inflation not only because of its negative real-income effects but also because of the uncertainty it creates regarding personal finances in the future (Peretz, 1983:93, 99). The PECE offered important clues about the future level of inflation because it fixed the prices of basic staples and the prices of goods produced by the state for a predetermined period. It also established the rate of devaluation of the peso

1990, −11.4; April 1991, 24.3; November 1991, 2.4; February 1992, 25.4; and July 1993, 28.6. After the price increase on energy announced in November 1990 and November 1991, general net scores dropped, in comparison with the previous measurements, 15% and 22%, respectively.

Table 5.6. *Do You Think the Government Should Keep the Pact?*

| Month | Net Scores | | | |
	General	Low Income	Middle Income	High Income
Jan 90	43	37	41	51
Jun 90	41	23	43	51
Oct 90	40	40	38	45
Nov 90	28	18	23	46
Apr 91	60	60	60	61
Nov 91	32	18	29	48
Feb 92	54	56	53	57
Aug 92	43	41	42	47
Jul 93	59	61	57	62
Oct 93	57	46	57	65

Net Score = Yes minus No.

vis-à-vis the U.S. dollar. Even if some Mexicans perceived the PECE as failing to reduce inflation, it helped to reduce the uncertainty that is inherent in inflation.[22]

Social Class and Support for the PECE

One would expect social class to affect significantly people's attitudes toward the government and toward the economic reform program. If the preference for present over future income is higher the lower the income (Hirschman, 1985:69–70), and insofar as success of economic reforms takes time, we would expect high-income people to be more supportive of the government and of economic reforms than low-income people. They have a greater capacity to absorb the loss of welfare that the economic reform entails without falling below a minimum level of consumption. Low-income people, on the other hand, cannot afford a substantial decline of their living standards because they would fall below the poverty thresh-

---

[22] Maybe people wanted the PECE to continue if it was considered a better policy than the available alternatives. Although no alternatives to PECE were discussed by policy makers or known by the public, it is still plausible that people compared the inflation rate under the PECE to the high inflation rate generated under the economic programs implemented in the mid-1980s. This comparison would have led them to support continuation of the PECE. I thank an anonymous referee for this suggestion.

old or they could be very close to starvation (Cortes and Rubalcava, 1991:85; Przeworski, 1991:174–178).[23]

On the other hand, we would expect low-income people to be more sensitive to changing economic conditions because the return of a 1% increase (decrease) in welfare, however defined, is higher for them than for any other income group. As Richard Brody has written regarding inflation, "rising food prices affect all of us, but those who spend a larger proportion of their income on food are more affected than those who spend less" (1991:96). Furthermore, previous research has found that people at the low end of the socioeconomic scale are the ones who are more affected by unemployment (Hibbs, 1987:60; Schlozman and Verba, 1979:35–43).[24]

Mexican public opinion data show that wealthier people supported the PECE more than did poor people. Net scores on the effectiveness of the PECE in reducing inflation show a consistently negative sign for low-income groups and a positive sign for high-income groups, with middle-income groups falling in between (Table 5.5). There did not seem to be a trend over time in people's answers. Beginning with our first observation (June 1989), low-income Mexicans showed the lowest levels of approval, high-income Mexicans the highest. In 1993, however, when annual inflation fell to single digits for the first time, low-income Mexicans' opinion on the PECE showed a significant improvement (as reflected in positive net scores).

A similar finding appears regarding support for the continuation of the PECE. The lower the income, the higher the chances of opposing its continuation. This class-based support seems to have its origin in different perceptions of the effectiveness of the PECE: the higher a person's income, the greater the probability that he or she believed that the PECE was reducing inflation. The lower class tended to be more pessimistic about the PECE's effectiveness. Although the consumer price index shows that inflation has been somewhat higher for the goods consumed by the low-income group, this does not explain the difference of opinion among the

---

[23] Additionally, it could be argued that some of Salinas's policies, such as privatization of public enterprises and reduction of public spending, are closer to high-income people's positions than to low-income people's positions on what the role of the state should be. However, this hypothesis still needs to be tested.

[24] In our July 1993 poll, low-income people were 8% more likely to know people who had lost their jobs than were high-income people. Among those with a job, low-income people were also 8% more likely to fear losing it than were high-income people.

three main income groups.[25] Rather, this difference may be due to the fact that enduring the costs of economic reform is harder for low-income people than for high-income people, which in turn leads them to believe that they are the ones who are paying the costs of economic reform. It may even be the case that, before the economic crisis started, people who are now in the low-income stratum belonged to a higher income stratum (Nordhaus, 1991:39).

The Zedillo Years, 1994–1997

During Zedillo's first year in office the Mexican economy experienced its worst recession since the 1929 crisis. GDP declined by 6%, unemployment increased 60%, the peso lost half its value vis-à-vis the dollar, and inflation rose from 7% in 1994 to 52% in 1995. What was the Mexican public's response to this abrupt deterioration of the economy? Was the Salinas government to be blamed? After all, in recent decades it has become common for any new administration to blame the previous one for poor economic performance or for generating an economic crisis that the new government has had to deal with. The last year of the Echeverría administration (1970–1976) and the López Portillo administration (1976–1982) witnessed severe economic crisis; the incoming governments blamed their predecessors for the economic crisis they inherited. The same pattern developed in the first year of Ernesto Zedillo's government. His administration blamed the Salinas government for the crisis that erupted in December 1994. Unlike Salinas, who had held the main economic post in the cabinet before becoming the Partido Revolucionario Institucional's (PRI's) presidential candidate, the last post held by Zedillo in the cabinet was that of minister of education (1991–1993). His government at least could argue that President Salinas and his minister of the treasury, Pedro Aspe, were responsible for the economic crisis generated in their last year in government. Did Mexicans exonerate the new Zedillo government from responsibility for the economic crisis?

---

[25] From November 1987 (before the implementation of the PES) to December 1993, the general consumer national price index rose 289%. The same index calculated for the low-income group rose 311% (287% and 289% for the middle- and high-income groups, respectively). In the first year of implementation of the PES, prices increased at almost a similar pace for all income groups. It was under the Salinas administration that the price index rose a little faster for the low-income group.

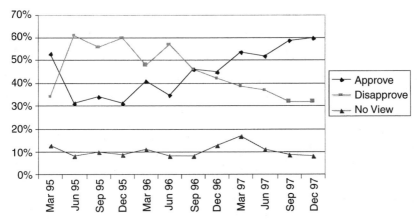

Figure 5.2 Opinions of President Zedillo, March 1995–December 1997.

The short answer is no. Zedillo's approval rates in his first year in office were among the lowest recorded in Mexican history.[26] After a short honeymoon period,[27] Zedillo's approval rate dipped to 31%, while disapproval reached 61% (Figure 5.2). Trust in his presidency declined abruptly after the first quarter from 55 to 24% and stayed at that level for almost a year,[28] while almost 70% thought his government's handling of the economy was bad (Table 5.7). As with the Salinas government, a bad economy meant lower approval rates for the president and his government.

Why did an exonerating position not work for the Zedillo government? After all, there were many pronouncements from high officials of the Zedillo administration blaming the previous government for the economic crisis. The most likely explanation is that Salinas and Zedillo were members

---

[26] The polling data I use for the 1995–1997 period are drawn from the national polls carried out quarterly by the *Reforma* newspaper. Rafael Giménez kindly shared these data with me.

[27] It is not clear if this brief honeymoon period was due to the fact that the public initially exonerated Zedillo or to the fact that the effects of the economic crisis were not felt until the second quarter of 1995: in the first quarter of 1995 the GDP fell 0.4% in comparison with the 1994 first quarter GDP, while the GDP in the second quarter (1995) fell 9.2% (Banco de México, 1997:9–10).

[28] The question reads as follows: "Considering the measures Ernesto Zedillo has taken as president, do you think those measures have led citizens to trust or not to trust him?" In the first quarter of 1995, 55% of people trusted him, indicating that Zedillo was still enjoying his honeymoon period. That figure dropped to 24%, 29%, and 25%, respectively, in the three following quarters.

Table 5.7. *Evaluation of Zedillo Government's Handling of the Economy*

	Very Good/Good	Regular	Very Bad/Bad	Do Not Know
Mar 95	17	21	52	10
Jun 95	12	12	67	3
Sep 95	12	22	63	3
Dec 95	11	19	67	3
Mar 96	13	23	60	4
Jun 96	11	22	64	3
Sep 96	21	27	48	4
Dec 96	15	30	48	7
Mar 97	21	34	38	7
Jun 97	25	33	35	7
Sep 97	25	40	30	5
Dec 97	24	38	34	4

of the same party. Mexicans were unlikely to perceive the transition from the Salinas to the Zedillo government as a sharp break, as they might have had the country experienced an alternation of power or a regime change. Both Salinas and Zedillo were part of the establishment that had ruled Mexico since 1929. Even though Zedillo was not involved in economic policy issues in the last years of the Salinas government, he was a member of Salinas's cabinet for most of the administration. Many high-ranking officials of the Salinas administration kept key offices in the Zedillo administration. For instance, Jaime Serra, Salinas's minister of commerce, was named to the most powerful economic post, minister of the treasury.[29]

Once the economy began to improve, public support for Zedillo, his government, and the handling of the economy also began to grow. In 1996 and 1997, the economy grew 5.2% and 7%, respectively, while inflation fell to 16% in 1997.[30] By the end of 1997, presidential approval rates hovered around 60% and the percentage of people with a negative opinion of the Zedillo's government handling of the economy had been cut in half (see Figure 5.2 and Table 5.7).

Correlation analysis for the quarterly data available for the 1995–1997 period ($N = 12$) suggests that normal economic voting prevailed during

[29] Serra held this post for less than a month, as he was unable to manage the economic crisis that erupted in December 1994.
[30] Real wages, however, continued to decline (Bank of Mexico, 1998:248), and the 1997 GDP was barely at the same level as in 1994.

Table 5.8. *Correlation Analysis (Pearson's) of Presidential Approval and Selected Economic Indicators (N = 12)*

	Approval	Management of Economy	Inflation Reduction	Wage Improvement
Inflation	−.58[a]	−.59[a]	−.58[a]	−.58[a]
Unemployment	−.95[a]	−.87[a]	−.47	−.73[a]
Real wages	−.23	.31	−.67[a]	−.7[a]
Management of economy	.91[a]			
Inflation reduction	.48	.69[a]		
Wage improvement	.78[a]	.85[a]	.83[a]	

Notes:
Inflation is measured as the quarterly inflation rate.
Unemployment is the average of the monthly unemployment rate in each quarter.
Real wages are the average of the monthly real wages index in each quarter.
Management of the economy is the percentage of people who have a very good/good opinion of the Zedillo government's handling of the economy.
Inflation reduction is the percentage of people who think the government has had a lot/some success in fighting inflation.
Wage improvement is the percentage of people who think the government has had a lot/some success in improving wages.
[a] Statistically significant at the .05 level or below.

this period. Inflation and unemployment are negatively related to presidential approval. In consonance with our analysis of the Salinas years, unemployment is strongly associated with the evaluation of presidential performance and real wages are not statistically related to presidential approval (Table 5.8).

Correlation analysis also suggests that presidential approval is closely related to judgments of how well the economy is being handled by the government and to perceptions of wage improvement. Mexicans' perceptions of the economy under Zedillo were coherent: they associated good governmental management of the economy with inflation reduction and wage improvement. Their perceptions of the economy were also associated with hard economic indicators: when inflation and unemployment rose, they perceived the government's management of the economy as bad. In all these cases the evidence shows that Mexicans' attitudes are consistent with normal economic voting patterns.

The only hint of an intertemporal attitude comes – as in the Salinas period – in relation to real wages. Again, Mexicans may have believed that rising real wages would lead in the medium and long term to a deterioration of their purchasing power. This is suggested by the negative sign of the correlation coefficient relating real wages and expectations of a decline in the rate of inflation. Rising real wages were seen as leading to higher inflation levels. Mexicans may believe that firms will transfer the wage increase to the public by raising the prices of the goods they produce. Although not statistically significant, an increase in real wages also led to reduced governmental support, a result consistent with an intertemporal mindset.[31] The public interpreted rising real wages as a signal of bad times ahead and showed some inclination to turn against the president.

In sum, in the first three years of the Zedillo administration, the dynamics of presidential approval and public opinion of the economy were consistent in general with normal economic voting patterns. Even if the political context – a new administration inheriting an economic crisis – was conducive to acceptance of the government's self-exonerating arguments, the Mexican public did not buy them: they punished Zedillo when the economy deteriorated and rewarded him when the economy began to improve.

Conclusions

Unlike other countries considered in this volume, in Mexico support for the president followed a well-known pattern: when the economy improved, people supported the president; when conditions deteriorated, they turned against him. Rising inflation and unemployment were not seen as signs that better times were to come but rather as indicators that the economic policy was failing. In the period under analysis, price increases made people angry, substantially reducing presidential approval rates and eroding confidence in the success of the anti-inflation plan.

We've seen some indications, however, that rising real wages were interpreted intertemporally as bad news about future inflation. This response emerged most clearly under Zedillo. If citizens believe that the government is manipulating the economy, they will tend to discount pos-

[31] It is possible, however, that the pattern for the real wages data is due to a measurement problem. The data on real wages refer only to the manufacturing sector, whereas the survey data are derived from national samples. The possibility of a measurement problem is suggested by the negative sign in the correlation between an increase in real wages and the perception of improvement in real wages (–.7). Unlike the hard data on inflation, which are correctly correlated with public perceptions of the rate of inflation, the hard data on real wages are not correlated correctly with perceptions about them.

itive economic information. As a product of past experiences with populist policies, the Mexican public may have perceived that an increase in real wages predicted higher future inflation rates. This type of intertemporal judgment seriously undermines any effort to generate support for economic reform: good performance is associated with a dark future.

Even though there were good reasons to expect exonerating arguments to succeed at certain moments in Mexico, for the most part in the period under study, normal economic voting prevailed. Carlos Salinas de Gortari may have been responsible for the economic crisis that erupted during the first days of the Zedillo government, but Zedillo could not dissociate himself completely from the Salinas, since both belonged to the same party that governed Mexico for most of the twentieth century.

Economic conditions affected various social groups in different ways. The wealthy were more tolerant than the poor of deteriorating economic conditions, and they backed the anti-inflationary program known as the PECE. The poor were more likely to oppose the PECE. This finding confirms the idea that it is among the wealthy that the government finds support for economic reforms, confirming the hypothesis that an unequal distribution of income makes economic reforms "politically more palatable" (Przeworski, 1991:178).

Our analysis also highlights the importance of timing for the ability of governments to demand public support for economic reforms. Intertemporal arguments asking for patience, as well as self-exonerating accounts, are more likely to succeed when they are presented by new governments. Therefore, reforms will tend to to be introduced early in the term. Otherwise, negative retrospective evaluations will weigh heavily in people's assessment of the government's ability to implement the economic program successfully. Even if the government implementing an adjustment program is new, there is no guarantee that the people will not punish it because of the bad economic performance. A clean break with the previous government, as in Poland, seems necessary: Mexicans blamed the Salinas administration for the mismanagement of the economy, but the Zedillo government was still punished by public opinion.

The *consolidation* of economic reforms in Mexico suggests that building support for reforms can no longer be based on asking people to be patient until the economy improves. After several years of economic hardship, the public is likely to reward the government if the economy improves and to punish it if the economy does not improve. Unlike the initial stage of economic reforms, in the consolidation stage the government's room for maneuver to build support for its policies narrows, especially if the same party or the same government continues to be in power. Under such circumstances, governments have no choice but to spur economic growth. Otherwise, their public support will ebb.

References

Alduncin, Enrique. 1991. *Los Valores de los Mexicanos. Mexico en Tiempos de Cambio.* México: Fomento Cultural Banamex.

Alt, James. 1991. "Ambiguous Intervention: The Role of Government Action in Public Evaluation of the Economy." In Helmut Norpoth, Michael Lewis-Bect, and J. D. Lafay (eds.), *Economics and Politics. The Calculus of Support.* Ann Arbor: University of Michigan Press, pp. 239–263.

Aspe, Pedro. 1993. *El camino mexicano de la transformación económica.* México: Fondo de Cultura Económica.

Bank of Mexico. 1995. *The Mexican Economy. 1995.* Mexico: Banco de México.
1997. *Informe Anual 1996.* México: Banco de México.

Basañez, Miguel. 1995. "Public Opinion Research in Mexico." In Peter Smith (ed.), *Latin America in Comparative Perspective: New Approaches to Methods and Analysis.* Boulder, CO: Westview.

Bates, Robert H., and Anne O. Krueger. 1993. "Generalizations Arising from the Country Studies." In R. Bates and A. Krueger (eds.), *Economic and Political Interactions in Economic Policy Reform.* Oxford: Blackwell, pp. 445–472.

Brody, Richard A. 1991. *Assessing the President: The Media, Elite Opinion and Public Support.* Stanford, CA: Stanford University Press.

Buendía, Jorge. 1999. "The Unchanging Mexican Voter." Unpublished manuscript, Center for U.S.–Mexican Studies, University of California, San Diego.

Cortés, Fernando, and Rosa María Rubalcava. 1991. *Autoexplotación forzada y equidad por empobrecimiento.* México: El Colegio de México.
n.d. "Structural Change and Concentration: An Analysis of the Distribution of Household Income in Mexico, 1984–1989." Unpublished manuscript, Colegio de México.

Domínguez, Jorge. 1993. "La opinión pública en México frente a la crisis económica. La víspera de la elección presidencial de 1988." In Carlos Bazdresch (ed.), *México. Auge, crisis y ajuste.* México: Fondo de Cultura Económica, volume 1, pp. 194–211.

Haggard, Stephan, and Robert R. Kaufman. 1992. "Institutions and Economic Adjustment." In S. Haggard and R. Kaufman (eds.), *The Politics of Economic Adjustment.* Princeton: Princeton University Press, pp. 3–37.

Hibbs, Douglas. 1987. *The American Political Economy: Macroeconomics and Electoral Politics.* Cambridge, MA: Harvard University Press.

Hirschman, Albert. 1985. "Reflections on the Latin American Experience." In Leon N. Lindberg and Charles S. Maier (eds.), *The Politics of Inflation and Economic Stagnation.* Washington, DC: The Brookings Institution, pp. 53–77.

Katz, Jonathan N., and Gary King. 1999. "A Statistical Model for Multiparty Electoral Data." *American Political Science Review* 93(1): 1–14.

Kinder, Donald. 1993. "Coming to Grips with the Holy Ghost." In D. Kinder and T. Palfrey (eds.), *Experimental Foundations of Political Science*. Ann Arbor: University of Michigan Press, pp. 43–51.

Kinder, Donald, and L. Sanders. 1990. "Mimicking Political Debate with Survey Questions: The Case of White Affirmative Action for Blacks." *Social Cognition* 8(1): 73–103.

Lustig, Nora. 1992. *Mexico: The Remaking of an Economy*. Washington, DC: The Brookings Institution.

    1993. "El efecto social del ajuste." In Carlos Bazdresch (ed.), *México. Auge, crisis y ajuste*. México: Fondo de Cultura Económica, volume 3, pp. 201–238.

Nannestadt, Peter, and Martin Paldam. 1994. "The V-P Function: A Survey of the Literature on Vote and Popularity Functions After 25 Years." *Public Choice* 79: 213–245.

Nordhaus, William. 1991. "Comment to Fiorina." In A. Alesina and G. Carliner (eds.), *Politics and Economics in the Eighties*. Chicago: University of Chicago Press, pp. 38–40.

Peretz, Paul. 1983. *The Political Economy of Inflation in the United States*. Chicago: University of Chicago Press.

Presidencia de la República. 1989. "La política económica para 1989." *Comercio Exterior*, January 1989, pp. 66–73.

Przeworski, Adam. 1991. *Democracy and the Market*. New York: Cambridge University Press.

Quattrone, George A., and A. Tversky. 1993. "Contrasting Rational and Psychological Analyses of Political Choice." In D. Kinder and T. Palfrey (eds.), *Experimental Foundations of Political Science*. Ann Arbor: University of Michigan Press, pp. 159–184.

Remmer, Karen. 1993. "The Political Economy of Elections in Latin America, 1980–1991." *American Political Science Review* 87(2): 393–407.

Salinas de Gortari, Carlos. 1988. "Discurso de toma de posesión." *Comercio Exterior*, pp. 1137–1144.

Schlozman, Kay Lehman, and Sidney Verba. 1979. *Injury to Insult: Unemployment, Class and Political Response*. Cambridge, MA: Harvard University Press.

Text of the Economic Solidarity Pact. 1988. *Review of the Economic Situation of Mexico*. Mexico: BANAMEX, pp. 67–73.

Zaller, John. 1992. *The Nature and Origins of Mass Opinion*. Cambridge: Cambridge University Press.

6

Economic Reform and Public Opinion in Fujimori's Peru

Susan C. Stokes

On August 8, 1990, the finance minister of the newly installed Fujimori government announced price increases. Gasoline would go up more than 3,000%, kerosene almost 7,000%, bread more than 1,500%, and medicines, on average, 1,400%. The inflation rate in August, reflecting these increases, was 400%.

Any government would worry about the political fallout from increases of this magnitude. It was not a coincidence that tanks were stationed on streets in Lima on August 7, the day before the announcement. But the Fujimori government had particular reason to worry. The theme of the new president's campaign had been opposition to a price adjustment or *shock*; the shock was his first major action upon taking office.

If normally governments in democracies do in office more or less what they promised in campaigns (Klingemann, Hofferbert, and Budge, 1994), Peruvian politics at this juncture was anything but normal. And these were not normal times in other ways as well. A guerrilla movement threatened the state; the state, in response, threatened the security of many citizens. Between 1980 and 1990, 25,000 people died in the conflict. And the economy was simply out of control. In 1989 gross national product (GNP) had fallen by 10.4%, inflation was 2,775%, and the external debt was $19 billion, almost $1,000 per capita.

In these abnormal times, should we expect a *normal* response of public opinion to changes in the economy? Would people look for immediate

The author's research was supported by National Science Foundation Grant SBR-9617796. Todd Benson and Carlos Vargas provided research assistance. Alfredo Torres of Apoyo, S. A., provided survey data.

improvements, and, if improvement wasn't visible, would they turn against the government and its economic policies?

As noted in Chapter 1 of this volume, people living through pro-market reforms in new democracies, even in less chaotic circumstances than Peru's, might well observe the economy and make inferences about the government's merits in ways that defy the economic voting model. If they think that economic performance is not the direct result of government actions but, say, of foot dragging by the opposition in approving the government's program or of manipulation by special interests, they might support the government even when economic outcomes are bad. This is an *exonerating* or *antidotal* posture. Alternatively, if people regard economic downturns in the present as necessary if things are to improve in the future, when the economy goes down they may infer that this is the necessary downturn before things get better. Then they will become optimistic and support the government. This is an *intertemporal* posture. Or, if they think the economy as a whole has improved and will continue to but see themselves as being left behind, they may turn against the government even when times are good and they feel optimistic about overall economic performance in the future. This is a *distributional* posture.

A priori it was difficult to predict how public opinion in Peru would respond to changes in the economy under the Fujimori government's economic liberalization program. The rhetoric of some political elites hinted that improvement wouldn't be immediate. Political leaders offered people reasons not to turn against the government even when times were hard. Mario Vargas Llosa was the leading candidate for the presidency until Fujimori caught up with him in the final months leading up to the election in May 1990. Vargas Llosa's campaign called for reforms much like the ones his challenger ended up pursuing. Vargas Llosa's campaign slogan in 1990 was "Nos costará . . . pero juntos haremos el Gran Cambio": "It will cost us [hurt us, do us harm], but together we will make the Great Change." The message was that pro-market reforms would cause pain followed by gain; even the structure of the phrase, with a pain clause (nos costará) followed by the gain clause (haremos el Gran Cambio) is suggestive of an intertemporal trade-off.

Not intertemporal trade-offs but self-exoneration was Fujimori's preferred rhetorical stance. Rather than predict pain followed by gain, he blamed the former government of Alan García for ongoing hardship after the change of government. And he blamed Congress, controlled by the opposition, for the slow pace of improvement even once his reform program was in place.

What's more, there was good cause for many Peruvians to feel left behind by the successes of the neoliberal program and to display a distributional response to improvement. Despite sustained periods of economic growth, income distribution remained highly unequal in Peru during the Fujimori years, poverty increased, and social spending, although increasing in the 1990s, remained well below the Latin American average (see IDB, 1999; ECLA, 1999; Hunter and Brown, 1999).

Yet by some accounts, at least, the real story of the Fujimori government was one that came to power amid chaos and despair, turned the economy around, and was reelected (see, e.g., Domínguez, 1998). This would seem to be a case of a government that benefited from normal economic voting.

In sum, there are reasons why people's responses might have been – in the terms laid out in Chapter 1 – intertemporal, antidotal, distributional, or normal. I study the dynamics of public opinion to determine which (if any) response prevailed. My data cover Fujimori's first term and the first two years of his second term (1990–1997). They are restricted to Lima residents.

In the following section I describe the government's economic policies and their results, as well as some other key developments. Next, I analyze the impact of economic conditions on people's opinions of the economic program and on their optimism regarding the future of the economy. This is followed by a similar analysis of opinions of President Fujimori. Next, I explore class dynamics: were postures toward the program and the president the same across the class structure? In the penultimate section I test the hypothesis that the Fujimori government was the victim of its own success. I end with a discussion of the implications of my findings for the assessment of this important and controversial experience of neoliberal reforms in this new South American democracy.

Peru in the 1990s: The Neoliberal Revolution

The transformation of the Peruvian economy under the governments of Alberto Fujimori (1990–1995, 1995–2000) rivals the depth of transformation of the former socialist bloc. The Peruvian state withdrew from the economy. The ratio of public gross investment to gross domestic product (GDP) fell from 5.5% in 1986 to 2% in 1991 (Edwards, 1995:244). By mid-1995, 72 state-owned enterprises had been privatized, including agroindustries, telephones, airlines, mines, banks, oil, and electric utilities. Remaining state-owned enterprises were subjected to hard budget constraints (Gonzáles Olarte, 1993; Wise, 1997). The government encouraged foreign investment in newly privatized firms as in other sectors. At the same time that the state sloughed off employees through privatization, it fired or encouraged early retirement of one in four civil servants by 1993 (Kay, 1996). As the state withdrew from a direct role in production, it also opened the economy to international trade. The average tariff on imported goods fell from 64% in 1985 to 15% in 1992 (Edwards, 1995:126); export and nontariff barriers were similarly reduced. The Fujimori government also reduced spending and loosened macroeconomic controls. The fiscal deficit, which amounted to 10.7% of GDP in 1989, fell to 3.2% in 1991. The government liberalized the exchange rates and raised the interest rate. The real interest rate had been negative in the final years of the García government; it shot up to 654% in 1991 (IMF, 1993).

In a few eventful years, Peru was transformed from pariah to darling of the financial world. International financial institutions had regarded with skepticism the García government's (1985–1990) experiment with price and wage controls, incomes policy, and restrictions on repayment of the foreign debt. And they regarded as inevitable the economy's subsequent collapse: inflation, to give one indication, reached 2,777% in 1989. Less than a decade later, the Peruvian economy grew faster than any other in the world: 13% in 1994. Its stock market was the hottest in Latin America, with the value of shares traded trebling from 1992 to 1993 and doubling again in 1994 (Kay, 1996).

For many Peruvians the neoliberal revolution was less than an unambiguous good. Inflation abated, from 30% per month in May 1990 to 0.5% on average per month in 1997. But even as inflation fell and production grew, jobs were lost. An index of employment in medium-sized firms in Lima declined steadily during Fujimori's first term, from 97.3 in July 1990 to 74.7 in March 1995, one month before the president was reelected. The trend was later slowly reversed, but as of May 1997 the index remained 19 points below its 1989 level.[1] If more goods and services were being produced, they were produced by fewer workers with less secure jobs.

---

[1] Most workers who lost these jobs did not become unemployed in the sense common in the advanced industrial countries. With no unemployment insurance, they could scarcely afford to remain jobless. Instead they were likely to be partially absorbed into the informal

The wage story was also less glowing than we might expect given the overall performance of the economy. By March 1997, real wages had edged up a mere 11% with regard to their average monthly level seven years earlier, whereas overall production shot up by more than 50% in the same period.

The Economic Program in Public Opinion

The analysis throughout this chapter draws on surveys conducted by Apoyo, S. A., a respected polling firm (Apoyo, 1990–1997). As part of a broader survey, every month Apoyo asks a random sample of Lima residents "Do you approve or disapprove of the government's economic program?" (average $N = 540$). The proportion that approved, disapproved, or expressed no opinion in surveys conducted between September 1990 and November 1997 is displayed in Figure 6.1.

The figure suggests unstable support of the economic program, even despite the government's most dazzling achievement: price stability. Monthly inflation was 63% in July 1990, when Fujimori took office; it fell to 3% in May 1993 and never again rose above this level. Support for the program, in turn, was unstable but rising from 1993 until late 1995, when it began a sharp decline – even though prices remained stable and economic activity increased. Is this the normal retrospective response?

To find out, I modeled opinions (support, oppose, no opinion/don't know) of the government's economic program as a function of GDP, inflation, employment, and real wages. Economic data are from Peruvian government sources and are measured monthly, allowing me to estimate the lagged effect of changes in economic conditions on public opinion the following month.[2] Following Katz and King (1999), I treat the outcomes of monthly polls as compositional data. The Katz–King model meets the natural restrictions of the data, that proportions sum to 1 and that each proportion falls within the unit interval. The model works by transforming the restricted data to an unrestricted space, for which many distributions exist, via the additive logistic transformation. It generates probability distributions for the proportion of each response as a function of inde-

economy, that is, underemployed, working fewer than 36 hours per week, often in low-paying jobs.
[2] The one-month lag was appropriate given that Apoyo polls are conducted early in the month.

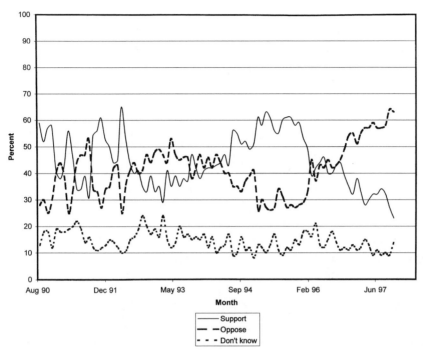

Figure 6.1 Opinions of the economic program, September 1990–November 1997.

pendent variables (for more details see Katz and King, 1999). Estimation results will now be described.

GDP

Anyone who approached the Lima data with a strong expectation of normal economic voting would find the effect of GDP on opinions perverse. When GDP rose, the proportion of respondents who opposed the program rose, relative both to the proportion of supporters and to people with no opinion. Both effects were statistically significant. Tables 6.1 and 6.2 presents seemingly unrelated regression estimates of opinions of the economic program as a function of economic states.

Figure 6.2 illustrates the effects more intuitively. It shows the expected proportion and the 95% confidence interval of people opposing the program when GDP was at its minimum, mean, maximum, and

165

Table 6.1. *Seemingly Unrelated Regression Estimate of Opinions of the Economic Program (Reference Variable OPPOSE) Monthly Data, 81 Observations*

	Coefficient	Std. Err.	z	p > z	[95% Conf. Interval]	
			SUPPORT			
GDP	−0.007	0.003	−2.133	0.033	−0.013	−0.001
Inflation	−0.031	0.018	−1.785	0.074	−0.066	0.003
Real wages	0.003	0.008	0.316	0.752	−0.014	0.019
Employment	0.022	0.010	2.090	0.037	0.001	0.042
Elect	0.611	0.127	4.801	0.000	0.361	0.860
Constant	−1.21	1.171	−1.033	0.302	−3.506	1.086
			NO OPINION			
GDP	−0.005	0.002	−2.153	0.031	−0.010	−0.000
Inflation	0.004	0.013	0.277	0.782	−0.023	0.030
Real wages	−0.013	0.006	−2.075	0.038	−0.026	−0.001
Employment	0.004	0.008	0.474	0.636	−0.012	0.019
Elect	0.160	0.097	1.655	0.098	−0.029	0.350
Constant	0.707	0.890	0.794	0.427	−1.038	2.452

Chi-square: SUPPORT 29.45, $p = 0.000$; NO OPINION 23.56, $p = 0.0003$.

intermediate levels.[3] In a hypothetical month in which GDP was at its minimum (index of 70) and all other economic variables were at their means, 36% of respondents would oppose the program; with GDP at its maximum (152), 49% would oppose the program.

Inflation

The effect of inflation was to increase the proportion of people opposing the program in relation both to supporters and to don't knows. To give a sense of the magnitude of the effect, a 5% increase in inflation from the mean of 3% to 8% was associated with a 4.5% decrease in support of the program. The anomaly here, from the vantage point of the economic

---

[3] GDP is an index; August 1990 = 100. Analysis includes observations from October 1990 through November 1997. I exclude September from the analysis because of its extraordinarily high lagged inflation rate (nearly 400%). Inflation, employment, and real wages are all lagged one month and held at their mean. A dummy for the preelection period (see later) is held at 0.

Table 6.2. *Seemingly Unrelated Regression Estimate of Opinions of the Economic Program (Reference Variable DON'T KNOW) Monthly Data, 81 Observations*

	Coefficient	Std. Err.	z	$p > z$	[95% Conf. Interval]	
			SUPPORT			
GDP	−0.002	0.003	−0.588	0.557	−0.007	0.004
Inflation	−0.035	0.015	−2.364	0.018	−0.064	−0.006
Real wages	0.016	0.007	2.243	0.025	0.002	0.030
Employment	0.018	0.009	2.050	0.040	0.001	0.035
Elect	0.451	0.107	4.197	0.000	0.240	0.661
Constant	−1.917	0.989	−1.939	0.053	−3.855	0.021
			OPPOSE			
GDP	0.005	0.002	2.153	0.031	0.000	0.010
Inflation	−0.004	0.013	−0.277	0.782	−0.030	0.023
Real wages	0.013	0.006	2.075	0.038	0.0007	0.259
Employment	−0.004	0.008	−0.474	0.636	−0.019	0.012
Elect	−0.160	0.097	−1.655	0.098	−0.350	0.030
Constant	−0.707	0.890	−0.794	0.427	−2.452	1.038

Chi-square: SUPPORT 41.45, p = 0.0000, OPPOSE 23.56, p = 0.0003.

voting paradigm, is that inflation drove people to uncertainty more powerfully than to opposition. (Hence note, in Tables 6.1 and 6.2, that the coefficient relating inflation to SUPPORT is negative both when the reference variable is OPPOSE and when it is NO OPINION, but only the second coefficient is significant by conventional standards.)

Real Wages

The impact of growing real wages was more in line with normal economic voting. When real wages rose, people became more certain about the economic program and supported it. But – and here's the anomaly – there was also a tendency, only slightly weaker and still significant, for people to move from don't know to opposition when wages expanded.[4] To put it differently, *falling* wages moved people from support *and opposition* to

---

[4] Hence, in the SURE model in Tables 6.1 and 6.2, the coefficient relating real wages to SUPPORT was 0.016 and to OPPOSE it was 0.013; both are statistically significant.

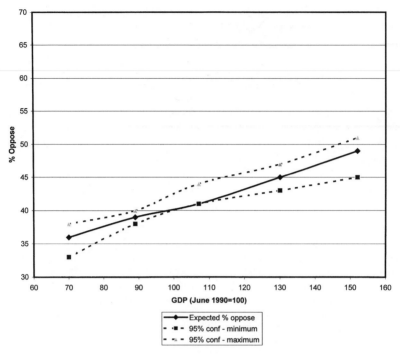

Figure 6.2 Expected proportion opposing the economic program, by GNP.

uncertainty but did not move them from support to opposition, as normal economic voting would lead us to expect.

Employment

Here Lima residents' response is as predicted under normal economic voting. When employment rose, both disapproval and uncertainty dissipated and support rose.

Figure 6.3 illustrates the effect of changes in employment levels on opinions of the economic program. It shows the expected values and 95% confidence interval of support for the program when the employment level is fixed at its minimum (index of 72), mean (81), and maximum (95). The expected proportion of respondents supporting the economic program rises from just over 40%, to 43%, to nearly 51% as employment rises. (All other economic variables are held at their means.)

168

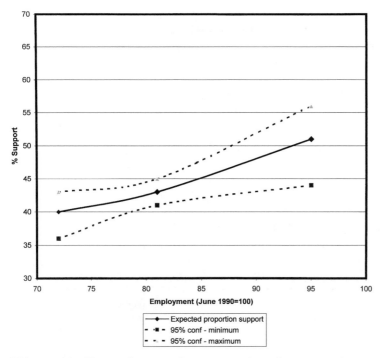

Figure 6.3 Expected proportion supporting the economic program, by employment.

To summarize, the effect of employment and real wages on opinions of Fujimori's economic program was consistent with normal economic voting, except that we see some movement of people from uncertainty to opposition when wages rose. Inflation seemed to make people unsure rather than to throw them into opposition, and GDP growth reduced support for the economic program.

To learn more about why these sometimes unorthodox reactions occur, I next explore the impact of changing economic states on people's views of how the economy would fare in the future. In 61 of the 89 months that our period covers, people were asked whether they expected the economy to improve, stay the same, or get worse in the future. SURE models appear in Table 6.3, which reports the effect of economic states on predictions about the future (WILL GET BETTER, STAY THE SAME, NO OPINION); the reference variable is WILL GET WORSE. Note that standard errors are large here; because of the small number of

169

Table 6.3. *Seemingly Unrelated Regression Estimates of Opinions of the Future Course of the Economy (Reference Variable WILL GET WORSE), Monthly Data, 55 Observations*

	Coefficient	Std. Err.	z	$p > z$	[95% Conf. Interval]	
ECONOMY WILL GET BETTER						
GDP	−0.006	0.006	−1.143	0.253	−0.017	0.004
Inflation	−0.129	0.073	−1.776	0.076	−0.271	0.013
Real wages	0.003	0.013	0.194	0.846	−0.023	0.029
Employment	−0.017	0.025	−0.689	0.491	−0.065	0.031
Elect	0.925	0.194	4.776	0.000	0.545	1.305
Constant	2.486	2.185	1.138	0.255	−1.80	6.768
ECONOMY WILL STAY THE SAME						
GDP	−0.003	0.003	−0.926	0.354	−0.009	0.003
Inflation	−0.029	0.039	−0.746	0.455	−0.105	0.047
Real wages	−0.006	0.007	−0.847	0.397	−0.020	0.008
Employment	0.0003	0.013	0.025	0.980	−0.026	0.026
Elect	0.365	0.104	514	0.000	0.1613	0.568
Constant	1.260	1.171	1.075	0.282	−1.036	3.555
NO OPINION						
GDP	−0.005	0.004	−1.293	0.196	−0.0132	0.003
Inflation	−0.042	0.054	−0.774	0.439	−0.147	0.064
Real wages	−0.011	0.010	−1.125	0.260	−0.030	0.008
Employment	−.0131	0.018	−0.717	0.474	−0.049	0.023
Elect	0.794	0.143	5.541	0.000	0.513	1.075
Constant	2.846	1.617	1.759	0.079	−0.324	6.016

Chi-square: BETTER 59.69, $p = 0.0000$, SAME 16.58, $p = 0.0054$, NO OPINION 46.62, $p = 0.0000$.

observations, we should nevertheless view as suggestive the effects that come close to achieving statistical significance.

GDP

When it rose, people tended to move from optimism to pessimism.

Inflation

When inflation rose, people tended to shift from uncertainty to pessimism and from optimism to uncertainty. Rising prices also increased the pro-

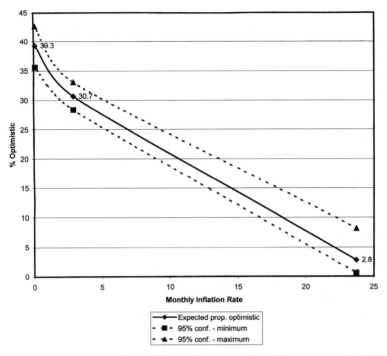

Figure 6.4 Expected proportion optimistic about the economy, by inflation.

portion of those expressing pessimism about the future in relation to optimism. The departure from economic voting is that, when prices rose, the shift from optimism to uncertainty was stronger than the shift from optimism to pessimism.

Figure 6.4 shows the predicted percentage of people who expect the economy to improve at the minimum, mean, and maximum inflation rates. In a hypothetical month with inflation at its lowest monthly rate (0.1%) and all other economic conditions at their means, 39% of respondents are optimistic. Optimists drops to under 3% when inflation is fixed at its maximum (23.7%).

Real Wages

Wage contraction did not significantly move people from optimism to pessimism, but it did move them significantly from optimism to uncertainty.

Employment

Employment had no significant effect on views of the future. Hence, although we saw that it did influence people's attitudes toward the economic program, they seemed to be reacting to it as a present state, rather than because of an effect it would have later.

We are now in a position to characterize Lima public opinion in the terms laid out in Chapter 1 of this volume. Table 6.4 reproduces Table 1.1, with the modification that I have inserted "uncertain" between "support" and "oppose" the economic program, and between "optimistic" and "pessimistic" about the economy. The effects, summarized in Table 6.4, are under conditions of economic deterioration.

People's responses to inflation and employment tended toward the normal, southeastern quadrant of the table, with the following caveats. Inflation created more uncertainty than opposition to the program. And the impact of falling employment – to increase opposition to the program – seemed to be unmediated by views of the future.

People's reaction to wages tends toward the center of Table 6.4. This is because declining wages had the monolithic effect of increasing uncertainty, both about the future of the economy and about the appropriateness of the economic program. When wages fell, both previous supporters and opponents of the program became uncertain.

GDP

GDP tended toward the northwestern, intertemporal quadrant. When economic activity declined, optimism increased. When GDP declined, the

Table 6.4. *Postures Toward Reform of Lima Residents*

Under deteriorating economic conditions, how do they react to reforms?				
		Support	Uncertain	Oppose
	Optimistic	*Intertemporal*		
What are their expectations about the		GDP		
future of the economy?	Uncertain		Wages	
				Normal
	Pessimistic	*Antidotal*		Inflation
				Employment

172

proportion of people supporting the program also increased, at the expense of both opposition and uncertainty. It was as though people believed that GDP had to fall if things were to improve later, and that rising GDP spelled bad news for the future (a further refinement, regarding growth, is introduced later).

Given Peruvians' recent experiences with growth and inflation, this reaction made sense. For most of the previous 20 years, GDP had fallen. Income per capita in 1996 was still below its 1970 level. The one sustained respite from recession and depression came early in the García administration: GDP growth in the 1986–1987 biennium was 16%. This growth spurt was followed in 1988–1990 by the worst bout of inflation of the century and one of the steepest declines in wages, income, and economic activity. People may have reacted to this experience by inferring that an overheated economy was a prelude to disaster.

Alternatively, they may have responded to overall growth rates, in the context of stagnant real wages and job loss, in distributional terms. They could see that the economy on the whole was growing: the stock market was purring, and more luxury cars appeared on the streets. Yet their own experience was of being left behind. Later I return to these alternative explanations.

Economic trends, and people's reactions to them, were not uniformly good news for the government. During Fujimori's first term the overall trend was for employment and inflation to fall, wages to rise but slowly, and GDP to rise. Even if people's responses had been as predicted by the economic voting literature, these trends might have made the government, facing reelection, nervous. Would good news on inflation and growth outweigh mixed news on wages and an unremitting loss of jobs? Given the departures from normal economic voting, the government had even more to worry about. Price stability would not help the government as much as might be expected, because it induced more uncertainty about the appropriateness of the program than support. And overall growth – the fact that the economy went from a deep recession to a 7% growth rate in 1994 – would only seem to create pessimism and opposition.

Sensing this dilemma, to help the president's chances of reelection the government began in late 1994 to pour money into public works and antipoverty programs (Kay, 1996; Roberts and Arce, 1998; Schady, 1998). At its height the level of spending was astounding. Shady reports that the government spent the equivalent of 0.5% of GDP on the FONDCODES antipoverty program alone. Although we might wish to distinguish conceptually between the Fujimori government's antipoverty programs and its economic liberalization efforts, people on the streets tended not to. Therefore we should expect the antipoverty program to increase the number of people who reported to pollsters that they approved of the government's "economic program." A person who was asked whether she approved of the government's economic program might consider both, say, a school-building project in her neighborhood and the price of kerosene and her unemployed neighbor.[5]

The preelection spending spree indeed boosted approval of the economic program. The effect is illustrated in Figure 6.5, a simulation of the proportion supporting the program (and the 95% confidence interval) during the spending spree and at other times. In a hypothetical month during the preelection spending spree, with all economic variables at their means, expected support for the program was 57%. In a hypothetical month falling outside of this period, expected support falls 14 points, to 43%.

Presidential Support

In addition to the economy, other matters of public concern were prominent in Peruvian politics, and in any setting we would expect people to use several criteria in formulating opinions of a president or a prime minister. Were opinions of Fujimori shaped by economic states at all? And if so, did people simply turn against the president when economic states deteriorated? The impact of economic factors on opinions of the president will now be considered.[6]

GDP

GDP did not have a significant impact on support for Fujimori. But to the extent that it had an effect, it was not in the direction anticipated

---

[5] One poll, conducted in March 1995, asked people who said they planned to vote for Fujimori in the following month's presidential election the reasons for their intended vote. In a closed-ended format, they were given the options (among others) of answering "because of his public works" or "because of the economic program or the economy" (see Stokes and Baughman, 1999). Poor people in particular tended to support public works but oppose the economic program, whereas a disproportionately large proportion of wealthy respondents cited the economy or economic policy.

[6] As earlier, this analysis excludes one lagged observations at the beginning of Fujimori's term, when inflation had an extreme value (62.7% in one month).

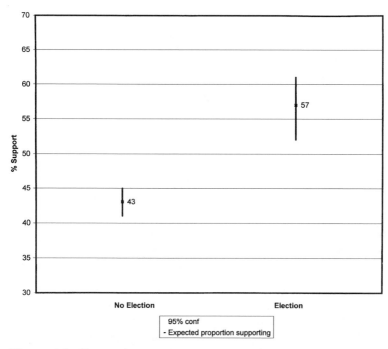

Figure 6.5 Expected proportion supporting the economic program, election versus nonelection period, and 95% confidence interval.

in the retrospective voting models. Economic growth shifted people from support to no opinion of the president and (weakly) from support to opposition.

Inflation

Inflation significantly shifted people from support to opposition of Fujimori. The effect is similar to that of inflation on opinions of the economic program and conforms with expectations from economic voting models.

Real Wages

Changes in real wages had no significant effect on opinions of the president.

175

Employment

As employment fell, people shifted from support to opposition of the president and from uncertainty to opposition. The effect is strong. As in the other countries studied in this book, unemployment had the simple, "normal" effect of undercutting support for the head of state and for pro-market reforms.

Coup d'Etat

The April 1992 coup d'etat, which at the time was responsible for a big surge in support for the president (from 52% to 82% in one month), over the longer term had a slightly positive effect on support of the president, increasing it in relation both to opposition and to uncertainty. Yet the effect fails to achieve statistical significance at conventional levels.

Preelection Spending Spree

During the period leading up to the election, people made their minds up about the president – NO OPINION fell – but SUPPORT and OPPOSE were both categories that absorbed significant numbers of the previously uncertain. Fortunately for Fujimori, the shift from uncertainty to support was stronger than the shift from uncertainty to opposition. It seems, then, that the preelection spending spree made people think of the economic program as successful and helped the president win, but other factors, such as the opposition's campaign against the government, kept the shift from being uniformly in Fujimori's favor. One concludes that the preelection spending spree and the government's campaign helped the president, but that his fear that he might face stiff opposition was not unfounded.

Time

Peruvian analysts make frequent mention of the "exhaustion" (*desgaste*) of the president, which, given the Latin American experience of dictatorship, is believed to have increased as the president tried to maneuver himself in the late 1990s toward running for a third term – a move of questionable constitutionality. Including a time-trend variable in the analysis shows that, with the passage of time, opposition increased at the expense of support. Not surprisingly, as time passed uncertainty declined in relation to both support for and opposition to the president.[7] The president was unknown when he came to office but was someone whom Limeños knew well by the late 1990s, and they indeed appeared to grow weary of him.

Class Dynamics

The Lima working classes were less enthusiastic than the rich about neoliberalism. The difference shows up in the fact that 75% of the rich but only 49% of the poor agreed that "the State should leave productive activity to the private sector" and that 72% of the rich but only 45% of the poor agreed that prices should be determined by free competition (see Table 6.5). As Carrión (1996) shows, working-class Peruvians were on the whole less in favor of a free market in 1994 than before Fujimori's neoliberal revolution began. The support gap for neoliberal programs between rich and poor is also apparent in Figure 6.6, which tracks the percentage supporting reforms among the richest and poorest groups in Apoyo's sample.[8] On average, 60% of the wealthiest respondents supported the economic program each month, whereas only 40% of the poorest supported it.

Estimations performed separately by social class reveal some differences in the dynamics of support across the class structure. The wealthiest respondents were relatively less sensitive than the poor to economic conditions in formulating views of the program. The exception is that the wealthy reacted more strongly than the poor against economic growth, opposing the program more, supporting it less, and expressing less uncertainty when the economy heated up. But inflation drove down support only slightly, and employment and wages had no effect.

---

[7] Time and employment were highly negatively correlated, creating a problem of multicollinearity when both were included on the right-hand side of estimation equations. The estimation reported here yielded better results when employment was excluded and a time-trend variable included.

[8] Apoyo publishes many results broken down by socioeconomic strata, which they label "A," "B," "C," and "D." A is the wealthiest stratum, and socioeconomic stratum declines through D, the poorest. The average proportion of respondents in each category was 10% (A), 23% (B), 35% (C), and 32% (D). Apoyo assigns respondents to socioeconomic strata according to their score on an index, which is calculated on the basis of the district in which they live, the quality of their housing, and the presence or absence in their home of various consumer goods (e.g., cars, electric appliances).

Table 6.5. *Opinions of the Market Economy by Social Class, March 1994 (Percentage Agreeing)*

Opinion	Wealthiest			Poorest
Private enterprise is good for the country	89%	87%	71%	59%
The state should leave productive activity to the private sector	75%	67%	56%	49%
The state should be small	69%	51%	43%	33%
Prices for most products should be determined by free competition	72%	66%	57%	45%
N =	85	120	169	140

Source: Apoyo, S.A., cited in Carrión (1996).

In contrast, at the bottom of the class structure, the poorest respondents' opinions of the program were more sensitive to economic states. They shifted away from support more noticeably than did the rich when prices rose. They shifted toward support when jobs were created. Yet their reaction to growth was more tempered than that of the rich. GDP growth did not change significantly the proportion of poor people supporting the program but did shift people from "don't know" to opposition. The effect of class was generally monotonic, with the second wealthiest group reacting like the wealthy to economic changes and the second poorest like the poorest.

It is interesting to note that the preelection spending spree drove up support at both extremes of the class structure, although the wealthy showed greater uncertainty (as well as support) during this period, the poor simply more support.

The effect of economic states on respondents at different places in the class structure is as we would expect. Job loss was concentrated in industrial and lower-end service sectors (public and private), affecting low-income more than high-income workers. It was the legions of people holding

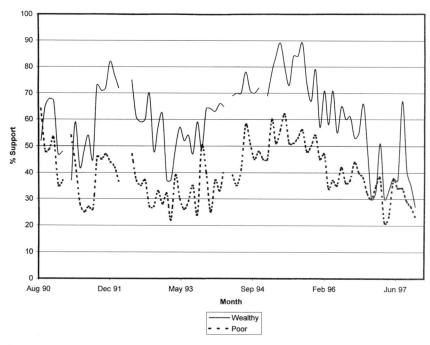

Figure 6.6 Support of the economic program by the wealthiest and poorest groups. July 1990–November 1997.

factory jobs and low-paying public-sector positions who found themselves out of work, many of them seeking refuge in the informal economy, where pay was even lower. Poor people's sensitivity to inflation should also not be surprising: households at the margin could see their very survival threatened by increases in the prices of bread, medicine, or cooking fuel.

In addition to their greater insulation from economic changes, the relative insensitivity of wealthy Limeños' opinions to economic ups and downs may reflect an ideologically driven certainty about the appropriateness of the neoliberal program. If the poor were more uncertain about the effects of the program, their opinions would have been more sensitive to outcomes, even if these outcomes affected them no more than they did the wealthy (see Harrington, 1993).

More surprising than the incongruence of job and inflation effects by class is the uniformity of the effect of economic growth, in particular that it was not an entirely welcome development among the poor. We are accustomed to thinking, since the pioneering work of Douglas Hibbs,

179

of the working class and its associated socialist and social democratic parties as favoring growth and tolerating some inflation, and the upper classes as favoring low inflation and low growth. When inflation is – or threatens to be – at the levels experienced in Peru, the antipathy toward it throughout the class structure is unsurprising. But why would the poor seem to oppose growth?

Earlier I noted that the adverse reaction of Limeños to economic growth was an intertemporal reaction: expansion foretold a dark future, specifically renewed inflation. But I wasn't able to reject the possibility that this response was instead distributional. As in Hirschman's tunnel effect, perhaps some people saw others moving ahead and, rather than optimistically believing that they would follow, resented being left behind.

By breaking down the Peruvian data by class, we can see that in fact both mindsets were present. I analyzed separately by class the impact of GDP on people's views of the future. At the top of the class structure, economic growth significantly increased the proportion of respondents that was pessimistic and decreased the proportion that was optimistic. At the bottom of the class structure, the effect was the reverse: growth tended to instill optimism and reduce pessimism (the effect was weaker).

The mindset of the wealthy, then, was intertemporal. Economic growth caused them to infer that the economy would take a turn for the worse in the future; they may have worried that inflation would return if the economy overheated. The mindset of the poor, in contrast, was distributional. Among the poor, growth induced optimism about overall economic performance. Their growing opposition to the economic program when the economy expanded therefore had to be on different grounds. I hypothesize that, like Hirschman's travelers in the tunnel, they saw people around them move ahead and thought that the overall economic picture would continue to brighten (recall that they were answering a question about overall economic performance, not their own or their family's). But they remained stuck, and rather than inferring that they too would soon move ahead, they believed that they would continue to be left behind by growth.

Note that the contrasting inferences about the future in response to current growth, with the rich becoming pessimistic and the poor optimistic, were not due to the insensitivity of the poor to future inflation, of which current growth might be an omen. We saw that, if anything, they were *more* sensitive to inflation than were the wealthy.

Paradox of Success?

The day after a person recovers from the flu she is likely to wake up pleased not to be sick. The pleasure may last for a few days. But eventually the absence of illness will not give her pleasure. By a similar logic, governments may become victims of their own success. They work on a pressing problem, it goes away, and for a period people give the government credit for having solved the problem; but soon people forget, and the absence of the problem will not enter their calculus of support.

Weyland (1999) presents evidence that Fujimori suffered just such an affliction. Weyland's major claim is that victory over the Shining Path insurgency did not sustain presidential support once the absence of a movement became the status quo. He extends his claim to inflation as well. Fujimori reduced inflation, but after a time price stability lost salience and stopped being a reason to support the government.

Do the Lima data support this interpretation? If so, the effect of inflation on support should be nonlinear. A decrease, say, from 20% to 19% monthly inflation should raise support more than a decrease from 5% to 4%.

I tested this proposition by dividing the sample between an early, high-inflation period (October 1990 to June 1993) and a later, low-inflation period (July 1993 to November 1997). In the early period inflation averaged 6.3%; it peaked at 23.7% in December 1990 after the government announced a second price adjustment.[9] In the second period it dropped from 3% to 1.8% in July 1993, never again to reach 3%. Separate compositional transformation analyses by periods show that, when inflation was high, people were in fact *less* sensitive to it than when it was low. Furthermore, in the period of low inflation, people's posture toward inflation was normal: price increases turned them against the economic program. In the period of high inflation, if price increases had any effect, it was exonerative (antidotal): it turned people from opponents to supporters of the program.[10]

---

[9] The finance minister, Juan Carlos Hurtado Miller, appeared on television in mid-December to announce the new prices. He ended his appearance, grim-faced, by wishing his audience a merry Christmas, much to the derision of many viewers.

[10] People's response to inflation was antidotal rather than intertemporal because when it increased in the high-inflation period, people did not become optimistic but pessimistic. This response is consistent with their reasoning that not the government's actions but other factors cause inflation; there is no inherent reason to believe that things will improve, but the government's actions are appropriate.

It seems that the reverse of the paradox of success is at work. Rather than turning their attention away from a problem once it was solved, people were willing to exonerate the government for mixed results while it grappled with a problem, and then expected the government to continue to produce good results once the problem had been solved.

Discussion: Neoliberalism, Neopopulism, and the Strategy of State Power

Several findings are salient. In formulating opinions of the president and his economic program, people paid attention to economic conditions. But they did not always react to conditions as the economic voting literature would lead us to expect. People did not always react to deterioration in the present by turning against the government. Sometimes they appeared not to blame the government for bad economic results. Sometimes they appeared to connect the government's actions with bad results, but thought that things had to be bad if they were to get better. By extension, sometimes they observed good results and seemed to infer that these were portents of dark times ahead. Or they resented being left behind in the midst of expansion.

The strategic implication for governments is not that they should foster bad economic results (in some cases bad results simply had the expected effect of driving down the popularity of the government and its programs) but instead that bad results may be tolerated when the government is visibly grappling with difficult problems. Another implication is that, even when results are good, if some large segments of the electorate can't be sure that they are sharing fairly in the benefits, or soon will, governments can expect their support to ebb. If politicians believe that "it will cost us, but together we will make the Great Change," then they must persuade voters that the costs will be fairly shared among "us" and that the Great Change will be not only for a lucky few.

Another salient finding is the preponderance of uncertainty in Limeños' reactions to the economy in transformation. In some surveys a full quarter of respondents could produce no opinion of either the president or his economic program, and the average percentage of "don't knows" was 11% about the president and 14% about the program. Limeños reacted to many economic changes not by turning against the government or turning in support, but simply by throwing up their hands in doubt. When prices rose, the economic voting literature tells us that people will turn from support of the government's program to opposition, but in Lima more of them turned from support to uncertainty. When wages fall, the economic voting literature tells us that people will move from support to opposition, but in Lima they moved from both support and opposition to uncertainty. And when wages fall, the economic voting literature implies that people become pessimistic about the future, but in Lima they moved from optimism to uncertainty, not to pessimism.

It may be tempting to explain the high levels of uncertainty and its preponderant role in people's reactions in terms of an ill-educated and therefore ill-informed population. But this explanation is too facile. The average percentage of people each month without an opinion about the economic program was smaller among the two wealthiest and presumably best-educated strata (10% and 11%, respectively) than among the two poorest and least-educated (13% and 17%, respectively), but the differences were not large. The gap in uncertainty about the president between rich and poor was only 3%. Peruvians are relatively well educated by South American standards. Of the poorest Peruvians, 90% have a first-grade education and 60% have a fifth-grade education, and in Lima the education rates are much higher (IDB, 1999). And it is difficult to be ignorant of states of the economy when monthly inflation rates are in double digits, employment falls to 70% of its level a few years earlier, or GDP rises 7% in one year.

A more plausible explanation is that Peruvians knew themselves to be in a whole new economic world in the 1990s, and were not sure what the present foretold about the future, or who was responsible for the changes happening around them, or whether what was good for the well-heeled was good for them. The shared suspicion of the authors in this volume is that uncertainty plays a larger role in perceptions of the economy and calculi of political support in the advanced industrial economies as well, but has been ignored.[11] But in the countries we have studied, it is no surprise that uncertainty about the economy is endemic.

What does this story tell us more broadly about the logic of state power under neoliberalism in Latin America? It tells us something of relevance to debates about the connection between populism and neoliberal economics. A revisionist perspective has appeared of late that claims that we

---

[11] A reason why it is ignored is that up to now we have lacked good statistical tools to study it. We hope that the Katz–King model will encourage scholars to reconsider nonopinion responses.

were wrong to think of neoliberalism and populism as antithetical. They display, instead, some "underlying affinities" (Weyland, 1996) and respond to a single logic. Neoliberals dismantle the state and marshall a sustained assault on those privileged by the prior statist model, such as labor unions and the domestically oriented bourgeoisie. Populists (neopopulists) draw political sustenance from an alliance of the disorganized underclasses and the middle class. Both neoliberalism and neopopulism oppose organizations; both are individualistic; both appeal to the masses directly, without the intervention of traditional parties or interest organizations. Alberto Fujimori is held up as the leading specimen of the new species of neoliberal populists; Kay (1996) coined the term *Fujipopulism*, which entails *both* "the retreat of the state from the economy, the expansion of control of private (mainly foreign) capital, and the elimination of many governmental redistributive and allocative functions that favor the working classes" *and* mass political support (56). And Roberts (1995:83) writes that the emergence of a new populism in contemporary Latin America "demonstrates that populism can adapt to the neoliberal era and that it is not defined by fiscal profligacy."

The lesson of the Fujimori era in Peru is not so much that populism and neoliberalism have come under a "single logic" in contemporary Latin America, but that they are in uneasy coexistence with one another. When, with elections looming, Fujimori used income from privatization to build schools and clinics, he may have been acting the populist but he was also acting as elected leaders do everywhere. If Fujimori managed to be both a neoliberal and a politician who won the votes of the lower classes, this feat was not carried off via conversion of the masses to neoliberalism. Formulations such as that of Roberts and Arce (1998:225), that "the lower class vote . . . became congruent with a neoliberal project," are misleading if they suggest anything other than that the lower classes voted for a neoliberal for reasons other than his neoliberalism.[12]

To square the circle of neoliberalism and democratic elections, Fujimori used the time-tested strategy of showering employment and public works on critical constituencies at critical moments in the electoral cycle. Contemporary scholars of neoliberal-populism, among others, offer much evidence on this point. In important studies, for example, Kay

[12] Roberts's earlier formulation, that Fujimori demonstrates how "populist economic measures . . . can be incorporated into an overarching neoliberal project" (1995:107), is more accurate.

184

demonstrates that the Peruvian government financed its preelection spending spree with cash raised through the sale of state-owned firms and improved tax receipts. In turn Roberts and Arce (1998) observe that working-class voters defected from the government by voting heavily against its proposed constitution in the 1993 referendum, and did so because of "anxiety over the rollback of the state's social responsibilities under the new economic model" (230). The government then busied itself "buying back" (233) working-class voters with targeted social spending and poverty-reduction programs.

In sum, neoliberalism and populism (read: redistribution to lower classes to mobilize political support) do indeed coexist in contemporary Latin America. But, far from sharing a single logic, state rule requires a back-and-forth movement between neoliberalism and compensation for its unpopular effects.

References

Apoyo, S. A. 1990–1997. *Informe de Opinión*. Lima: Apoyo, S. A.
Carrión, Julio. 1996. "La opinión pública bajo el primer gobierno de Fujimori: de identidades a intereses?" In Fernando Tuesta Soldevilla (ed.), *Los Enigmas del Poder: Fujimori, 1990–1996*. Lima: Fundación Friedrich Ebert.
Domínguez, Jorge I. 1998. "Free Politics and Free Markets in Latin America." *Journal of Democracy* 9(4): 70–84.
Economic Commission on Latin America (ECLA). 1999. *Panorama Social en América Latina 1998*. Santiago, Chile: ECLA.
Edwards, Sebastian. 1995. *Crisis and Reform in Latin America*. New York: Oxford University Press and the World Bank.
Gonzáles Olarte, Efraín. 1993. "Peru's Economic Program Under Fujimori." *Journal of Interamerican Studies and World Affairs* 2: 51–80.
Harrington, Joseph E., Jr. 1993. "The Impact of Reelection Pressures on the Fulfillment of Campaign Promises." *Games and Economic Behavior* 5: 71–97.
Hunter, Wendy, and David Brown. 1999. "Democracy and Social Spending in Latin America, 1980–1992." Paper presented at the 57th annual meeting of the Midwest Political Science Association, Chicago, April 15–17.
Inter-American Development Bank (IDB). 1999. *Facing Up to Inequality in Latin America*. Washington, DC: Inter-American Development Bank.
International Monetary Fund (IMF). 1993. *International Financial Statistics*. Washington, DC: IMF.
Katz, Jonathan N., and Gary King. 1999. "A Statistical Model for Multiparty Electoral Data." *American Political Science Review* 93(1): 15–32.
Kay, Bruce. 1996. "'Fujipopulism' and the Liberal State in Peru, 1990–1995." *Journal of Interamerican Studies and World Affairs* 38(4): 55–98.

Klingemann, Hans-Dieter, Richard I. Hofferbert, and Ian Budge. 1994. *Parties, Policies, and Democracy*. Boulder, CO: Westview Press.

Roberts, Kenneth M. 1995. "Neoliberalism and the Transformation of Populism in Latin America: The Peruvian Case." *World Politics* 48: 82–116.

Roberts, Kenneth M., and Moisés Arce. 1998. "Neoliberalism and Lower-Class Voting Behavior in Peru." *Comparative Political Studies* 31(2): 217–246.

Schady, Norbert. 1998. "Seeking Votes: The Political Economy of Expenditures by the Peruvian Social Fund (FONCODES), 1991–1995." Unpublished manuscript, Princeton University.

Stokes, Susan C., and John R. Baughman. 1999. "From Policy Change to Preference Change? Neoliberalism and Public Opinion in Latin America." Paper presented at the 57th annual meeting of the Midwest Political Science Association, Chicago, April 15–17.

Weyland, Kurt. 1996. "Neopopulism and Neoliberalism in Latin America: Unexpected Affinities." *Studies in Comparative International Development* 31(3): 3–31.

    1999. "A Paradox of Success? Determinants of Political Support for president Fujimori." Paper presented at the annual meeting of the Midwest Political Science Association, Chicago, April 15–17.

7

Public Opinion, Presidential Popularity, and Economic Reform in Argentina, 1989–1996

Fabián Echegaray and Carlos Elordi

On a sticky morning in late May 1989, Argentines woke up to news of food riots and looting spreading across the country. For a society socialized in the easy assumption of food opulence, even if moderated by the burden of continuous economic impoverishment, the shock could not have been greater. By noon, rumors of spontaneous bouts of social turmoil and collective violence reached closer and closer to the major avenues and neighborhoods of the capital city and greater Buenos Aires, adding to the *porteños'* concern with food shortages. By afternoon, stores in the northern and southern regions of the metropolitan area closed their doors, and television news was filled with scenes of owners shuttering their shops and protecting them at gunpoint, along with images of desperate neighbors in their rush to markets to buy and store up whatever food was available.

These images of a radical social and economic collapse, however, were not the only ones to shape citizens' sense of what had suddenly taken place in their country. As Argentine television broadcast the events in detail, it also showed pictures of the security forces oscillating between brutal repression that killed several dozen people and a laissez-faire attitude that permitted looters to bring home their booty. The national media then presented the ironic, almost pathetic appeal of elected officials to appease the looters and to ask the police to restore public order. Even worse for the democrats ruling the country, as the day ended news leaked to the media that the military had insisted that, as a condition for putting down riots, they would be granted full exoneration for their role during the past dictatorship, during which they accumulated one of the worst records of human rights abuses on the continent.

To most Argentines, these events proved that after years of recession and raging prices their country had hit bottom. Hyperinflation was accompanied by mass revolt as social violence spread across the nation. The restoration of public order and the stabilization of the economy soon crystallized as the top priorities in public opinion.[1] And, as would become clearer in retrospect, the public began to demand a reassertion of public authority through effective control of politics and economics.

A few days later, the declaration of a state of siege preceded the antic-ipated resignation of the president, speeding the transfer of power to Carlos Menem, the newly elected chief of state. In response to the dis-turbances and economic collapse, the incumbent and incoming govern-ments agreed to a transfer of power in July rather than December.

The financial collapse of Argentina in June and July 1989 had impli-cations beyond the economy and would shape people's future reactions to public events not in the economic sphere alone. The economy did career into complete disorder, with consumer price increases reach-ing 114.5% in June and 196.6% in July.[2] But equally true was that the country's political leader, Raúl Alfonsín (1983–1989), was an "exhausted president, without any authority,"[3] and he left the country closer to ungovernability and statelessness than at any time since the nineteenth century (O'Donnell 1989).

The collapse at the end of the Alfonsín government demonstrated how both economic efficacy and political leadership matter for the survival of governments, and for popular support of its leaders and policies. This lesson would not pass unnoticed by the incoming government of Carlos Menem. The ungovernability of the final weeks of the Alfonsín presidency would soon shape Menem's reforms of the economy and the opinion of the masses, giving him the opportunity to turn circumstantial approval into lasting political support.

It is essential to keep this backdrop in mind in interpreting the dynam-ics of public opinion in light of the far-reaching changes that the Menem administration introduced. These included a series of attempts at eco-nomic stabilization and structural reform, the most successful and lasting of them known as the Convertibility plan.

The Argentine experience suggests that no single pattern of mass response may ensue when a new government embarks on economic reform. Certainly the bulk of the electorate sent a clear message of protest

---

[1] Mora y Araujo (1991); Zuleta Puceiro (1993).
[2] Source: Instituto Nacional de Estadísticas y Censo.
[3] *El Cronista Comercial*, cited in Smith (1991:37).

against the Alfonsín government when they voted his party out of power. As analysts and pollsters acknowledged, Alfonsín's Radical Party (UCR) was sanctioned by voters for its failings in economic management.[4] But there was more to the election outcomes than classic economic voting. Even though the popular perception by mid-1989 was that the country was hitting rock bottom and every new day was a new financial hell for Argentines, this did not necessarily mean that they identified the new president as a wiser or safer option for the future. After all, 4 out of 10 voters had chosen to support the incumbent party in the presidential election of May. This support could scarcely have derived from any personal magnetism of the UCR candidate, Eduardo Angeloz.[5] In turn, the survival of Menem's government after the initiation of its painful stabilization program was comprehensible in terms of the public's patience and willingness to believe intertemporal promises.[6] Later, when Menem ran for reelection, people seemed willing to use the vote to promote the long-term welfare of the nation rather than their own pocketbooks.[7] We develop each of these points later in this chapter. Suffice it to say that people were willing to make some sacrifices in order to gain economic stability and that they supported the new government despite deterioration of the economic situation, a deterioration reflected in several economic indicators.

In this chapter we study the dynamics of public opinion in response to economic change during the first six years of Menem's presidency. We believe that this is a critical period, one that can shed light on the dynamics of changes in public opinion during times of economic reform, thus extending the scope of the studies conducted in this field so far.[8] We test several hypotheses regarding the linkage between the economy, approval of the president, and the neoliberal economic program implemented in Argentina from 1989 until 1996. We analyze these linkages within the framework of the economic voting literature. We also test other alternative hypotheses, such as those suggested by Stokes in Chapter 1 of this book.

---

[4] Catterberg and Braun (1989).

[5] Mainwaring (1995).

[6] For a definition of intertemporal politics see Stokes (1996). See also Chapter 1 of this volume.

[7] "Argentina: Back to Work." *The Economist*, May 20, 1995: 42.

[8] While theories that explain presidential popularity are common among American scholars, most of these theories have not been tested under different political institutions or across other cultures. For a few exceptions see Lewis-Beck (1988) and Anderson (1995).

We first present a brief description of Menem's government and its main economic policies. We focus only on these policies, leaving aside other important areas, such as foreign policy, internal security, and social policies, which might also have had some impact on the popularity of the president. Next, we analyze public opinion regarding the president and support for his economic program, using public opinion data collected each month during an 80-month period between 1989 and 1996. In this section, we relate public opinion regarding the president and support for the economic program to three economic indicators: inflation, real wages, and the level of unemployment.

Our analysis was conducted using the method developed by Katz and King (1999) for the analysis of compositional data. This method allows us to estimate the impact of economic indicators on the proportion of respondents that favored, opposed, or had no opinions about the president and his economic plan.[9] We estimate two basic models: one for support of the economic program and another for opinions about the president.

Economic Reform in Argentina

Carlos Menem was elected president in May 1989 with 47% of the valid votes in the first competitive elections held under fully democratic conditions since the early 1970s. Menem defeated the candidate of the incumbent UCR by a margin of 11%. Such a difference in the final tally clearly demonstrated the degree to which the Alfonsín government had left expectations unfulfilled and revealed how rapidly the electorate had learned to sanction the government. Argentines acted as a "god of vengeance" in a situation that not only showed terrible results in the economic sphere but also erosion of democratic authority.

Menem came from the ranks of the Peronist Party, traditionally oriented toward inflated budgets and big government. His support came (among others) from the same marginal sectors that participated in the looting and rioting. Having mobilized support on the basis of populist promises and alliances with trade unions and the military, Menem seemed the least probable leader to implement stability, either economically or politically. And yet, taking office five months ahead of schedule, Menem reacted in the least Peronist way that anyone might have predicted.

---

[9] For a brief description of the methodology used across this book see Chapter 1 of this volume. See also Katz and King (1999).

The same week that he took the oath as the second president in the new democratic period, Menem launched a series of economic reforms that revealed a new alliance, struck with the top multinational groups of the country and right-to-center forces. It came as a surprise to see a Peronist president pushing forward an economic orthodoxy more stringent than the one practiced by his predecessors. One foreign newspaper captured this amazement with the headline, "Pinch Me, I Must Be Dreaming!"[10]

Menem did not waste either time or momentum. He chose dramatic words for a radical policy shift: the time had come for Argentines to face "a tough, costly and severe adjustment." To succeed, Menem convoked his fellow citizens for a new cycle of financial heroism, cautioning the public to prepare for "surgery without anesthesia."[11]

These dramatic words served to prepare the public for the first fiscal shock program. Born out of Menem's 11-hour alliance with the oldest multinational corporation of Argentine origin (Bunge y Born, or BB), whose local vice president was appointed economic minister,[12] the BB plan encompassed a number of shock policies designed to stabilize the macro-economy. The plan established a freeze on government-controlled prices after a 200–650% hike and a 170% currency devaluation. An agreement on prices was reached with the leading 350 private companies. Tax breaks and other public incentives to private capital were suspended. The government cut spending on social welfare programs and imposed a 25% cut in the public payroll.[13] For citizens living on wages, pensions, or income from small business activities, who had seen their savings vanish in the wake of devaluations and hyperinflation in the first two quarters of 1989, the shock was more bad news. It was bad news as well for import-export businesses, for firms with sales to the domestic market, and for those with state contracts. Nevertheless, many reacted in support of the new plan, which represented a slight improvement compared to recent times. For

---

[10] *The Economist.*

[11] Cited in Smith (1991), 53.

[12] Bunge y Born's local vice president, Miguel Roig, was hand-picked by Menem and Jorge Born, the head of the Argentine multinational, and was responsible for laying down the grounds of the BB plan. One week after taking office, Roig died of a heart attack and was immediately replaced by Néstor Rapanelli, another Bunge y Born executive, thus consummating the alliance between the multinational firm and the Menem government.

[13] Argentina, Ministerio de Economía (1989), "Principales medidas económicas del 9 de Julio de 1989," web site of the Argentine Economic Ministry.

example, inflation, a critical measure of success or failure in restoring control, fell from 196.6% in July 1989 to 5.6% in October 1989.

To explain these measures, Menem spoke to his countrymen in plain words. The task was as simple as it was immense: to "pulverize the crisis." The country had hit rock bottom; the crisis was "terminal."[14] The government's strategy vis-à-vis the general public was to celebrate the harshness of the adjustment. Political and economic survival was the objective of everyone; in the context of the search for survival, people would deem legitimate any authoritative action aimed at reversing the status quo.

Observers consistently point out two effects created by the crisis. At the level of private perceptions, Menem's clear-cut interpretation of events generated a consensus that something needed to be done. Equally important, the presidential strategy established an individual rationale for tolerating the idea that a time for painful sacrifices had to come first, before one could anticipate real economic improvement.[15]

This crisis mindset had several implications. First, it created a situation conducive to proactive initiatives and bold manifestations of political will. The image of the previous government as being swallowed up by the crisis led people to favor powerful governmental rule; once order was reestablished, they would find ways to accommodate to the new situation. For those hit hard by the inflation and economic slump prior to the 1989 elections, wage freezes, price hikes, and cuts in social spending meant that the government was taking charge following a mandate to rule. Hence, measures that may not have implied good news for the pocketbook in the short run were still saluted in light of the degree of psychological security they provided. The government was doing something.

Elaborating on these feelings, Palermo and Torre (1994) speak of a disposition to conform to whatever action represents an "escape from the present." The conviction that the past was hell and that any alternative could only be better induced toleration for the economic reforms. Bolder government actions were better than timid programs or no actions at all. An inflation bout smaller than the price peak record of July 1989 meant progress. Given the mindset that bold decision making was good in itself, Menem's government also took the opportunity to construct a rationale for the nature of actions that was in line with common sense. If the choice

---

[14] For impressionistic recollections of this climate, see "Menem's Miracle," *Time International*, July 13, 1992.

[15] Ibid.

of acting boldly was Menem's own, the choices his officials were making merely reflected the options left by the previous administration. Menem had campaigned and won votes on the promise of a *salariazo* (a dramatic increase of wages) and a *revolución productiva* (productive revolution); he justified the imposition of a wage freeze and fiscal austerity policies the day after taking office by claiming that these were the only choices that Alfonsín had left open to him. Self-exonerating arguments were at work even before Menem took office, arguments that matched people's version of recent economic events. This gave some additional leeway to the new incumbent, much as it has in other polities undergoing similar processes of stabilization (e.g., Peru, Poland).[16]

In relation to the public assessment of policies, this situation meant tolerance for a soft authoritarianism in public policy, as well as a moderation of criticisms about the foundations and appropriateness of economic decisions. Menem's unwillingness to retreat from neoliberalism and austerity in response to protest gave the impression that he was willing to let his electoral coalition break up. The public, instead, regarded this intolerance and indifference as a display of leadership.

Menem's bold rhetoric and his eventual success in breaking inflation should not lead us to forget the erratic movements of his economic policies in the first two years. Between December 1989 and April 1991, the exchange market was controlled, then split in two, then liberalized, then indirectly regulated; similarly, taxes paid by exporters were first increased, then programmed to be gradually phased out, then raised again, and ultimately slowly eliminated. Other examples abound. Yet, these oscillations were different from the stop-and-go policies of the Alfonsín term; they represented different routes within a single path: privatizations, economic opening, a movement toward a free-market society (Acuña 1995).

Whether because of the appeal of the president's speeches, the image effect of sustained endorsement of the president and his policy by key power holders inside and outside the country, or the material and symbolic benefits these measures provided to specific groups of citizens, a majority of the public saw Menem's policies as more good than bad. Content as well as format was critical in maintaining political capital. The president not only announced drastic measures but also carefully drafted

---

[16] See the series of articles published in the October 1996 edition of the *Comparative Political Studies Journal*.

each stage at which such announcements took place so as to convey a sense of intense activity. To the mass public that had witnessed Alfonsín's stop-and-go policies over five years, such a bold demonstration of political will transmitted a sense of psychological security. The government was in command, even if its actions did not have the best effect immediately or even produced some negative results in the short run.[17]

The gambit of promising tougher times in the short run and good times in the near future paid off in 1989: popular support for the president and his economic policy soared. The ruling Peronists increased their share of seats in the legislature in 1991. This was more than a honeymoon. Observers attributed these successes to the positive reception of the government's boldness and audacity. Others went so far as to suggest that this involved a learning process among voters, their discovery of the limits of policy making, and wrote of the emergence of "responsible" voters.[18]

Menem's initial economic plan struck a responsive chord among citizens and businessmen. In spite of its social costs, optimism soared. As inflation rates went down throughout the second half of 1989, perceptions of the future at the personal and national levels remained optimistic.[19] By October 1989, in a poll conducted by the firm of Sofres-Ibope of 400 residents of the federal capital, 55.5% agreed that "the general economic situation will be better," against only 8.9% who were pessimistic.

This early, bouyant optimism soon subsided. Divisions in the economic team appeared in November 1989. These divisions eroded the confidence of markets that price stability would be sustained, causing public optimism to recede. Still, in November 1989, 47.1% foresaw a promising future; yet, two months later, as Minister of Economy Néstor Rapanelli resigned and the alliance between the government and the Bunge y Born corporation collapsed, only 34% were optimistic about the economy (Table 7.1).

By January 1990, the public faced a government already unsuccessful in its first attempt to maintain price stability, one that had gone through three ministers of finance in less than six months. Panic seemed to return to markets and voters once again.

---

[17] This was recognized by many observers, even those committed to the Alfonsín government, such as Enrique Zuleta Puceiro (personal interview, May 1995). Other students of public opinion interviewed, such as the Peronist pollster Hugo Haime and the academic Juan Carlos Torre, emphasized the leadership factor as well.

[18] See "Menem's Miracle," *Time International*, July 13, 1992.

[19] Zuleta Puceiro (1993).

Table 7.1. *Sociotropic Views of the Economic Future: Optimism and Pessimism*

Would You Say That the General Situation of the Country in the Near Future Will ...	February 1989	October 1989	November 1989	January 1990	March 1990
Be better off	20.9%	55.5%	47.1%	34.0%	29.6%
Not change	34.1	25.9	27.9	34.2	31.9
Be worse off	30.6	8.9	13.1	23.2	32.9
Can't say/No opinion	14.3	9.8	11.9	8.6	5.6
	100.0%	100.0%	100.0%	100.0%	100.0%

Source: Sofres-Ibope; Capital Federal (*n* = 400). Data from surveys carried out by Sofres-Ibope, 1989–1990.

Table 7.2. *Public Concerns – List of Priorities (Multiple Responses Allowed)*

Which of the Following Would You Say Are Important Problems These Days?	For the Country	For Yourself/ Your Family
Inflation	48.1%	67.1%
Unemployment	44.0%	16.2%
Instability	43.2%	51.6%
Low wages	40.8%	46.2%
Economic stagnation	21.5%	16.5%
Can't say/No opinion/No answer	1.5%	1.3%

Source: Sofres-Ibope; Capital Federal (*n* = 400) – January 1990.

Optimism ebbed as prices again rose in late 1989. By January 1990, 67% of the people interviewed by pollsters in the city of Buenos Aires identified inflation as the most important problem for them and their families. The second most frequently mentioned problem was general instability (51%) and, in third place, low wages (46.2%). Recession and unemployment were still low on the list of public concerns, a situation that was bound to change as the government proved successful in controlling prices and making the economic process predictable a few years later (Table 7.2).

Despite signs that the electorate would not be satisfied with stability alone, but that further grievances (against low wages and unemployment) were around the corner, the Menem government did not let up on its austerity program or shift to distributional populism. Quite the opposite: the government persevered on a neoliberal path and deepened its commitment to structural adjustment.

Once again in 1990, Menem made a dramatic plea to shore up support for a framework of austerity and liberalization. As his new finance minister, Erman González, was sworn in, Menem used emotional pleas to mobilize support: we are making a gamble, he declared, "for all or nothing" ("a todo o nada") . . . we're all, absolutely everyone, embarked on an airplane, and on this airplane – for God's sake – there are no parachutes!"[20] Minister González chose to side with a radical version of free-market policies rather than drawing back from them. In a series of big shocks and small adjustments that lasted from December 1989 to March 1990, González sped up economic liberalization by freeing prices and exchange rates, authorizing bank deposits in U.S. dollars, lifting export taxes, and – most stunningly – freezing bank deposits over the equivalent of US$500, which were then converted into long-term state debt.

The devaluation, in a market with prices fully tied to the fate of the U.S. dollar, combined with a hike in interest rates and the unexpected freeze in financial assets, was a terrible cocktail, one that conditioned the economic situation of the following months. Prices skyrocketed by 95.5% in March 1990 and the economy fell into recession, with gross domestic product (GDP) declining by almost 3% in the first quarter of 1990. Still, the official message was relentlessly intertemporal, as in Menem's diagnosis in March 1990: "we are ill but improving" ("estamos mal, pero vamos bien").[21] Recession was the only cure for hyperinflation, a malady that Argentines suffered three times in the span of a year. The government continued to offer intertemporal reasoning to keep public support from eroding at a rapid pace.

Menem relied not on intertemporal rhetoric alone, however, but also on a rhetoric of self-exoneration. Facing growing dissent from unions, Peronist legislators, and the Radical opposition – but sensing that support would be forthcoming from leaders in commerce – Menem sought to rewind politics back to the chaotic days of July 1989, emphasizing Alfonsín's fault for the sorry state of the economy. At the same time, Menem exploited public frustration with Congress, an institution that he portrayed as an obstacle to progress. He criticized key economic and media sectors as well as Congress for delaying the passage of measures critical to the progress of the plan (e.g., liberalization of labor markets, restriction of the right to strike). Even if this strategy failed to slow the decline of

[20] Menem speech, *La Nación*, December 19, 1989:1,16.
[21] Menem speech, *Clarín*, March 5, 1990:1.

support for Menem's program, it at least might dampen the appeal of any alternative leadership. In April 1990, Menem chose the inaugural session of Congress to put things bluntly. He pronounced, "I have the certainty that we are on the right path," and warned that the only other option for the country was a return to the past, "to a system that drove us to the depths of hyperinflation and, worse still, to the depths of national hyper-frustration, to hyper-poverty . . . and to economic and cultural hyper-backwardness."[22]

The message struck a responsive chord among the public and shifted approval ratings up, both for the president and for the economic plan. One can observe this process through the results of a series of surveys conducted by the Argentine firm SOCMER. Menem's job performance index,[23] for example, switched from a net difference of –6 points to a net difference of +21 in April 1990. In May this index rose to +45 points! The economic program followed a similar path: from a net disadvantage of –47 points in March to an advantage of +24 points two months later. People's optimism about the future course of the economy, the variable most closely reflecting the spirit of Menem's core message, increased as well: from –3 points in March to +15 points in May.[24]

Hope may have fed on the emotionalism of Menem's words. More likely, people were responding to the persistence of the general policy orientation established by the Menem government, despite the harsh results. Menem's insistence on the application of a "bitter pill" policy, even in the face of mounting resistance, revealed to some a quality of capable leadership, providing psychological comfort.[25] And the new status quo contained some promise of a bearable future, in contrast to the dire experience of the recent past. After all, an average quarterly inflation rate of 109% in the second quarter of 1990 was good news compared to 235% in the second quarter of 1989.

Intertemporal reasoning, the idea of recovery after painful treatment, was the major asset the government had to offer to a disgruntled electorate. So was the sour memory of the final months of the prior government, led by the party now in opposition. Both intertemporal and

[22] Latin American Regional Reports/Southern Cone, 1990.
[23] This index is the difference between those who approved of and those who disapproved of Menem's job.
[24] SOCMERC data, valid only for the Buenos Aires metropolitan area (average $N = 350$).
[25] On the notion of psychological security linked to presidential leadership see Sigelman (1990).

exonerating arguments had some real power. The government suggested a manner of reasoning, a framing of events, such that current suffering was considered the guarantee of a brighter future (known generations ago), while the hardships such suffering imposed were considered the direct result of the hyperinflation legacy and the policy swings that characterized the previous Radical administration.

From the second quarter of 1990 on, Menem had only equanimity to offer as recession persisted and inflation did not recede as rapidly as expected. All key statistics of growth were negative: GDP per capita fell more than 3%, average real wages plunged by 20%, and unemployment rates rose to 15% of the economically active population.[26] And consumer prices soared: between March 1989 and March 1990, the consumer price index (CPI) rose more than 20,000%. The radical nature of this stagnation amid high inflation did not help to keep popular expectations high. The government made real progress toward the privatization of state-owned enterprises and received hearty endorsements of its economic program from abroad, but neither produced much mass optimism. By the end of 1990, approval ratings were very low once again and political confidence vanished, not least because of corruption scandals that touched some of the president's family members. And in the absence of positive results, and with mounting opposition both in the streets and in the barracks, the response of markets was a "market coup": a massive run on the currency.[27]

The government responded with another devaluation, less than 50%, to reduce some of the economic pressures and allow some competitiveness for local products, moves that might help reactivate the economy and bring in external resources. The cost was González's resignation and the government's adoption of a strategy of stabilization without recession in the medium term.

Throughout the period of early reforms the government faced pressure from traditional Peronist constituencies, especially labor unions. In 1990, the union leaders who had fervently backed Menem during the presidential campaign cried betrayal and mobilized against government. But they did so halfheartedly, and labor was afflicted by several internal divisions. Furthermore, Menem did not hesitate to resort to the Peronist culture of

[26] *Clarín Económico*, 1990.
[27] This referred to the financial sector's opposition to government policies, forcing the economic authorities to implement drastic changes such as a devaluation.

loyalty and the threat of outlawing strikes. He also wrested control of social welfare programs from the unions to keep quarreling leaders in check. Like the unions, the military was restive. Nationalistic officers expressed unhappiness with the move toward reduction of the state apparatus and spending cuts that affected their role in the economy and their living standards. In late 1990, a faction of the military rebelled against the government. Menem's prompt action, which suffocated the rebellion, burnished his image as a man of action and solved a pending problem. From then on the military would be under civilian control, deactivated as a destabilizing element.

The Launching of the Cavallo Plan

After 18 months in office and with inflation still raging, Menem opted for a renewed effort to deepen the government's commitment to combat financial instability and recession. As in previous months, and – again – different from his predecessor, he did not switch plans but further accelerated the reforms contained in his original blueprint. With an eye on the first legislative elections in the third quarter of 1991, Menem appointed Minister of Foreign Relations Domingo Cavallo as the new minister of economy. He charged Cavallo with the task of putting into place a more effective and comprehensive scheme to bring the economy under control and make prosperity possible.

In March 1991, Cavallo launched an ambitious program that would accentuate the neoliberal policies applied by his predecessors, with the addition of an innovative plan designed to halt inflation. Beginning April 1, 1991, the Argentine peso would be freely convertible into dollars and there would be no further emission of currency unless it was backed by gold or foreign currency. These measures represented a watershed; and, as usual, they were accompanied by dramatic rhetoric. The press echoed the government's words: "we are burning our ships" – meaning that after the decision was made, there was no way back.[28] Concomitantly, the government would continue with the privatization process started in 1989 and accelerate the deregulation of the economy. Other measures included budget cuts and a massive reduction of public-sector employment.[29]

---

[28] *Ambito Financiero*, April 2, 1991.
[29] For a detailed account of the Cavallo Plan see Argentina, Ministerio de Economía: "El Plan de Convertibilidad" (April 1991), web site of the Argentine Economic Ministry.

After the swearing in of Domingo Cavallo as Menem's fourth minister of economy in January 1991, and particularly after his formal launching of the Convertibility Plan in April, policies as well as outcomes would take a far more cogent and homogeneous path. Currency revaluation, deregulation, state downsizing, and privatization would be the basic pillars of the government's action. As a result of the Convertibility Plan, the country's inflation fell dramatically and definitively; real wage rates stabilized, and the economy began to grow. As in no other time in recent political history of Argentina, confidence in the economy was supported not by short-term effects but by lasting macroeconomic achievements. Beginning on April 1, 1991, the local currency became freely convertible into dollars. Moreover, the Congress enacted a law prohibiting the Central Bank from printing money to cover budget deficits without the required backup in gold or foreign currency. Legal deregulation of business and financial investments followed, which reduced some of the bureaucracy and red tape that prevented commercial initiatives and competition. Austerity and fiscal balance were furthered by personnel reductions in the bureaucracy and in state-owned enterprises, as well as by an aggressive policy against tax evasion. The legal sanctioning of these measures, or their strong enactment through unchallenged presidential decrees, plus the actual transfer to private hands of major state-owned companies,[30] exerted a powerful impact in restoring confidence among key economic agents, both domestic and foreign.

The effect of the Cavallo Plan was to end inflation. Inflation went down from 11% in March 1991 to just 0.6% in December of that year; since then, for the following 51 months, it never exceeded 1% except on nine occasions, with the highest peak of 3% in January 1992.[31] Real wages and purchasing power also stabilized, but with a slight downward trend. In March 1991 real wages stood at 76% of their 1985 level and fell to 68% by 1995.[32] Yet, some of this reversal was neutralized by episodic deflation, which occurred 10 times during the period under analysis. Also, different from previous attempts to stabilize the economy, price stability and a halt in the real-wage free fall came without the deep recession that seemed

[30] Involving major "sacred cows" such as the telephone company, the national flag air carrier, water and power utilities, highways and road tolls, railways and the metropolitan subway, and the gas and oil companies.
[31] INDEC.
[32] FIEL, *Indicadores de Coyuntura*, various issues.

Table 7.3. *Ranking of Major Individual Concerns*
(Multiple Responses Allowed)

	1990	1995
Inflation	67.1%	—
Unemployment	16.2%	86.4%
Economic stability/instability	51.6%	50.9%
Low wages	46.2%	63.7%

Note: The January 1990 survey involved 400 respondents in the capital city by Equas/Zuleta Puceiro & Asocs. The January 1995 survey involved 800 respondents in the capital city and Greater Buenos Aires by CEOP/Clarín.

necessary in 1990. The economy grew 8.9% in 1991, 8.7% in 1992, 6% in 1993, and 7% in 1994. Hence appeared the "Argentine Miracle," capable of successes where most other troubled-ridden countries had failed, in bringing stability to the economy without sacrificing growth. Not until the Mexican crisis unfolded in 1995, bringing with it a loss of confidence among investors, did the economy again contract, with plummeting rates of economic activity of −4.4% in 1995 and −3.2% during the first quarter of 1996.[33]

Despite the mixed economic results of Menem's early years and the return of recession in the mid-1990s, in people's perceptions Argentina had experienced a sharp break with the past in the way policy was being implemented. And just as sharp a break occurred in people's perceptions of the key economic challenges the country faced. Public opinion data reveal these breaks. Whereas price stability was a primordial concern in the earlier days of 1990, rising unemployment and, to a lesser extent, stagnant wages would become the new causes of concern during Menem's second term (1995–1999). In early 1990, a survey of 400 people in the capital posed a question about individuals' economic concerns. Respondents overwhelmingly listed inflation. A similar question in a survey of 800 residents of the capital and Greater Buenos Aires in 1995 found unemployment as the number one problem, with economic stability as a second-level concern. Inflation was not even mentioned by respondents (Table 7.3).

[33] The Economic Intelligence Unit, *Country Report*, 2(3), 1996.

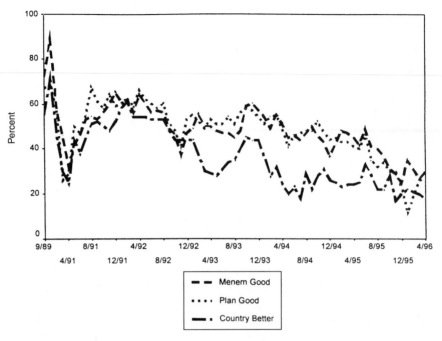

Figure 7.1 Popularity of the president, approval of the economic plan, and situation of the country, 1989–1996.

This pattern of responses made sense in light of the sudden jump in unemployment from 6% in 1991 to 16.4% in 1995,[34] whereas annual inflation fell in the same period from 84% to 1.6%.[35]

The Convertibility or Cavallo Plan was clearly an immediate success in ending inflation and gave an immediate boost to the president's popularity (Figure 7.1).

The proportion of people who thought that Menem was doing a good job almost doubled in the ensuing months, climbing from 32% in April 1991 to 65% by the end of the year. This performance seemed to be backed by success in halting inflation, up to then an enduring problem. In Figure 7.2 we observe that after mid-1991 inflation was flat and close to zero.

How did the public cope with the transformation of the Argentine economy during these years? How did the public react to a Peronist pres-

[34] FIDE *Coyuntura y Desarrollo* (1996). [35] Ibid.

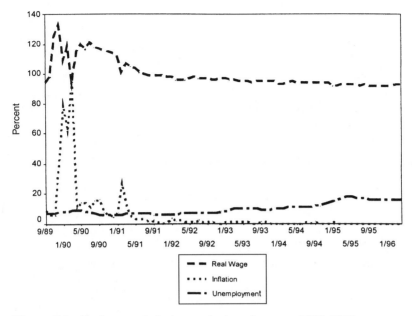

Figure 7.2 Real wages, inflation, and unemployment, 1989–1996.

ident who started his tenure in office by dismantling the state apparatus that his Peronist predecessors helped to build? Did Argentines' response to fluctuations in the economy follow the patterns predicted by normal retrospective economic voting models, or did they accept the government's intertemporal terms: sacrifice now in exchange for a brighter future?

Up to now, our description has suggested that the government tried to frame its discourse in intertemporal and exonerating terms. What evidence do we have that the public accepted the logic proposed by the government? In the following section, we present data suggesting that in Argentina the public's response to the performance of the economy cannot be explained by normal economic voting models alone. Empirical analysis suggests an alternative hypothesis to explain the dynamics of people's opinions in a context of economic transformation.

Support for the Economic Program

Between July 1989 and April 1996, respondents in the city of Buenos Aires and in the Greater Buenos Aires area were asked 83 times whether they thought that the program implemented by the government was "Very Good," "Good," "Fair," or "Bad."[36] The biweekly and monthly studies were conducted by Mora y Araujo, Noguera & Asociados, with an average of 350 respondents. As one can observe in Table 7.4, inflation played an important part in determining levels of support for economic reforms in the Menem era, just as the fight against inflation played a key role in the government's discourse. People's reaction to rising prices was straight-forward. Responding in a typical economic voting fashion, with every upsurge in the inflation rate, public opinion shifted from approval to dis-approval of the plan. With inflation, opinion also shifted from disapproval to uncertainty.

The effect of unemployment on the opinion of the Menem economic reform program was also consistent with normal economic voting models. Unemployment eroded the popularity of the plan and increased uncer-tainty about it.

Normal economic voting models do not, however, prepare us for Argentines' responses to changes in real wages. Whereas according to normal economic voting postures one would expect rising real wages to have a positive impact on the support of the economic program, the analy-sis in Table 7.4 reveals just the opposite effect. An increase in real wages is associated with a shift from approval of the program to disapproval. (Rising real wages also reduce uncertainty about the program, again in comparison with disapproval, but the effect is not statistically significant.) The impact of real wages on opinions of the economic program are thus suggestive of an intertemporal posture: people observe rising real wages, infer that the economy will deteriorate in the future (perhaps because inflation will rise), and turn against the program.

To give a sense of the impact of unemployment and real wages on approval of the plan, we simulated some quantities of interest. These simulations provide a more meaningful interpretation of the coefficients shown in Table 7.4 and make explicit the levels of confidence associated with our results.[37]

---

[36] Answers to questions were structured on a 4-point scale to evaluate approval of the eco-nomic plan/policy, the president's job, and prospective views of the economy. Additional questions explored retrospective views and approval of the minister's job. The authors would like to thank Manuel Mora y Araujo and Felipe Noguera for making these data available.

[37] Quantities of interest were simulated using Clarify. See Michael Tomz, Jason Wittenberg, and Gary King, CLARIFY: Software for Interpreting and Presenting Statistical Results,

Table 7.4. *Seemingly Unrelated Regression Estimates of Opinions of the Economic Program, as a Function of Economic Variables (Monthly Data, 83 Observations), with "Disapprove" as the Base Category*

Variable	Coeff.	Std. Err.	Z	$P > |z|$	[95% Conf. Interval]	
			Approve of Plan			
Inflation	−0.122	0.036	−3.428	0.001	−0.193	−0.052
Real wage	−0.035	0.006	−6.068	0.000	−0.047	−0.024
Unemployment	−0.125	0.016	−7.807	0.000	−0.156	−0.093
Constant	4.769	0.663	7.195	0.000	3.470	6.068
			Don't Know			
Inflation	0.146	0.057	−2.531	0.011	−0.258	−0.033
Real wage	−0.004	0.009	−0.436	0.662	−0.022	0.0142
Unemployment	0.030	0.026	1.151	0.250	−0.021	0.0799
Constant	−1.967	1.065	−1.847	0.065	−4.056	0.1208

Regarding the impact of unemployment on approval of the plan, an increase in the unemployment rate from 5% to 15%, holding other variables at their mean levels, is associated with about a 20% decrease in support for the program. Figure 7.3 gives a graphical representation of this effect, with confidence intervals. The decline in approval of the plan shows dramatically the political trouble economic reform programs may run into when they have a negative impact on the labor market.

The impact of real wages on opinions of the program, however, was startling and contrary to conventional wisdom. When the real-wage index went from 100 to 120, all else equal, approval of the plan *declined* by about 15%. Figure 7.4 illustrates this relationship.

How can one explain these results? As Stokes suggests in Chapter 1 of this book, we have to assume that the way people translate changes in the economic environment into public support within the context of neoliberal reforms may be quite different from the process that takes place under normal conditions. In this context, a logical explanation is offered by either

Version 1.2, (Cambridge, MA: Harvard University, September 16, 1998) *http://gking.harvard.edu/*. See also Gary King, Michael Tomz, and Jason Wittenberg, "Making the Most of Statistical Analyses: Improving Interpretation and Presentation," paper prepared for presentation at the Annual Meetings of the American Political Science Association, Boston, August 1998.

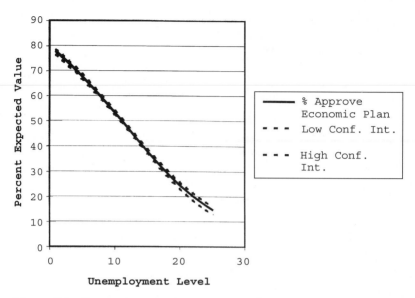

Figure 7.3 Expected proportion supporting the economic program, by unemployment (holding real wages and inflation at their mean).

intertemporal or exonerating postures. Unlike the *populist myopia explanation* that envisions an impoverished mass public in developing countries pressing shortsightedly for immediate benefits, the intertemporal logic suggests that citizens may accept short-term sacrifices in exchange for an improvement in the near future. Alternatively, Stokes suggests, even if people think current sacrifice doesn't bode well for the future, they may continue to support the government through hard times if they think that a "well intentioned government does not control the economy" (1996:508).

To adjudicate between intertemporal and exonerating explanations of Argentine public opinion, we would have to estimate the effect of changes in real wages on optimism about the future course of the economy. Although we have some poll results on optimism, we unfortunately do not have enough data points to generate such estimates. We note, however, that optimism prevailed during about the first two-thirds of the period for which we have collected data. Optimism receded and was replaced by pessimism in the last 30 months for which measurs are available. Of the 61 months after the launching of the Cavallo Plan, the first 30 were characterized by optimism. Optimism reached its apex in early 1992, when

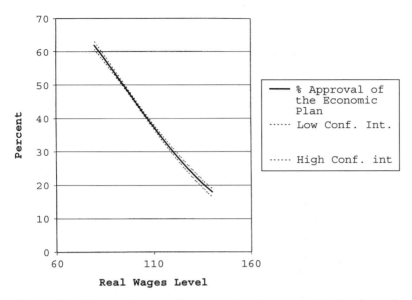

Figure 7.4 Expected proportion supporting the economic plan, by real wages (holding unemployment and inflation at their mean level).

the difference between positive and negative assessments of the future was 51%.[38] Nevertheless, from early 1994 on, the trend changed to more or less permanent pessimism, except for four isolated months when pessimism was briefly surpassed, with the gap between pessimistic and optimistic responses reaching a peak of 27% in December 1995[39] (see Table 7.5). This shift from optimism to pessimism also coincides with a general trend toward lower real wages over this period, as shown in Figure 7.2.

Putting together these two facts – the decline over time of wages and of optimism – we speculate that people's apparent tolerance for low real wages was connected not to an intertemporal calculus but to the fatalistic view that times would continue to be hard but that no better alternative to the Menem government's reform program existed. This interpretation is also consistent with the fact that, even though stagnant real wages did not reduce support for the government, still – as reflected in various poll results cited earlier – people did consider low real wages to be a serious

[38] SOCMERC database.   [39] SOCMERC database.

Table 7.5. *Economic Sentiment Across Time*

	April 1991 to August 1992	September 1992 to March 1994	April 1994 to April 1996
Economic sentiment	+33.3%	+19.8%	−9.6%

Note: Economic sentiment measures the average difference in the period selected, between aggregate responses signaling that the national economic situation would get better versus those indicating that it would get worse. A figure preceded by a positive sign represents the difference favorable to an atmosphere of optimism; when preceded by a negative sign, it points out a difference that reveals pessimism as predominant. The question read: "How would you say the country's economic situation will get a year from now . . . Will get better, the same, or worse?"

problem. Their posture was, in this sense, exonerative. Hence, even though low wages may have been a cause for concern among the public, this concern did not always translate into a demand for a change in government or in government policy.

Opposition to the plan, in turn, was based on concrete economic frustrations, mainly the government's repeated inability to control inflation once and for all during the first 18 months. However, the fact that the inflation rate remained almost flat after the implementation of the Cavallo Plan explains why the public would keep an eye on other factors, such as real wages, to have a clue about future changes in price levels.

Support for the President

Contrary to what we expected, the fate of the president did not follow the same path as his economic program. According to the economic voting literature, the public is more likely to approve of the president if unemployment and inflation are kept low. One might expect the public to hold the government responsible for the economy because candidates typically run in part on the state of the economy. Incumbents presiding over growth take credit for their achievement; when the economy performs badly, people tend to place the blame on incumbents. If people react in terms of normal economic voting to fluctuations in the economy, one expects inflation and unemployment to have a negative effect on the level of approval of the president. On the other hand, one can expect rising real wages to have a positive effect on the rating of the president. In Table 7.6 we analyze the impact of economic variables on the popularity of the president during his first six years in office. We have monthly measures of the proportion of people who answered the question "Would it be good or bad for the country if Carlos Menem . . . plays an important political role in the next couple of years?". People could answer by saying that it would be "Very Good," "Good," "Not So Good (Fair)," or "Bad." These categories were collapsed as follows: "Very Good" and "Good" responses were collapsed into one category, and "Not So Good" and "Bad" responses were collapsed into another category. The analysis also includes a "Don't Know" category, which in our model is assumed to be measuring uncertainty about the impact of the plan and the president's performance. We analyze the impact of three economic variables – level of unemployment, inflation, and real wages – on aggregate answers to this question. As before, we modeled the president's popularity using the method for the analysis of compositional data.

Neither inflation nor real wages had a significant impact on the approval of the president. The absence of significant effects may reflect the vagueness of the question, which did not specify whether Menem's future role would be as president. It is clear, however, that the president's image was tarnished by high unemployment (Table 7.6).

The analysis presented in Table 7.6 shows that the impact of unemployment was quasi-normal. Rising unemployment reduced support for Menem. Unemployment induced negative views of the president. In addition, rising unemployment increased uncertainty about Menem at the expense of disapproval.

Table 7.6. *Compositional Data Analysis Estimates of Opinions of the President, as a Function of Economic Variables (Monthly Data, 83 Observations), with "Menem Bad" as the Base Category*

Variable	Coeff.	Std. Err.	Z	$P > \|z\|$	[95% Conf. Interval]	
			Menem Good			
Inflation	−0.010	0.031	−0.312	0.755	−0.071	0.051
Real wages	−0.003	0.005	−0.511	0.610	−0.012	0.007
Unemployment	−0.076	0.014	−5.449	0.000	−0.103	−0.049
Constant	1.123	0.572	1.964	0.050	0.0024	2.245
			Don't Know			
Inflation	−0.054	0.047	−1.146	0.252	−0.146	0.038
Real wages	−0.009	0.008	−1.193	0.233	−0.024	0.006
Unemployment	0.070	0.021	3.316	0.001	0.029	0.111
Constant	−2.201	0.866	−2.540	0.011	−3.899	−0.503

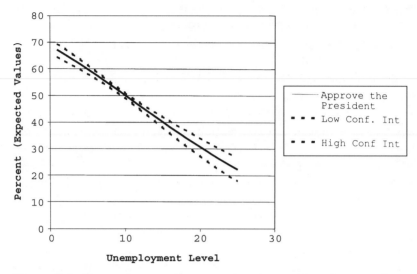

Figure 7.5 Expected proportion supporting the president, by unemployment (holding real wages and inflation at their mean).

To give a more intuitive sense of the effect, in Figure 7.5 we simulate the impact of unemployment on the popularity of the president, holding inflation and real wages at their mean level.

Unemployment has a deep impact on the popularity of the president. When unemployment rose from 5% to 15% – a level that was surpassed during Menem's first term – the proportion of the public saying that Menem was either good or very good plunged from 60% to 40%. It will come as little surprise that Argentine presidents, like many elsewhere, who preside over high levels of unemployment should be nervous about their own jobs!

To most observers, the background picture to these changes was straightforward: while economic reforms were successful in stabilizing the economy, some of their side effects were negative, especially the growing level of unemployment that followed the implementation of the Cavallo Plan. This was the single most damaging factor in determining the president's popularity.

As the presidential elections of 1995 approached, the Menem government became interested in underlining its achievements and promoting the belief that the worst finally was past. The earlier rhetoric, centered on the need to swallow the bitter pill, slowly vanished from authorities' lips.

Instead, Menem and his officials emphasized both the transformation of the society and its visible consequences of stability and individual cases of opulence and financial success. To most voters, these statements might have conveyed a clear and new message: the time for sacrifice was about to end, and the moment to reap at least some of the rewards had arrived.

Argentines reelected President Menem in May 1995 with 49% of the votes, 2% more than he was able to gather six years earlier. To most local observers, this reflected a noncontroversial choice for the success obtained at the economy level,[40] despite the galloping recession and skyrocketing jobless rates of mid-1995. Their view was that, overall, voters behaved retrospectively and looked at the future through conservative lenses.[41] Our discussion suggests a different interpretation: voters followed their leaders rather than their pocketbook experience alone.[42] They embraced an exonerative logic for as long as it took before a new economic context crystallized; even if many voters were not entirely convinced of that logic, the dramatic memory of hyperinflation easily helped to persuade them.[43]

Behind these endorsements of intertemporality and exoneration, political support for the plan and the president in Argentina reflected the extent to which authority and leadership became major considerations to be factored in. The leverage exerted on voters by the president's commanding voice on economic decisions throughout these years was acknowledged even by opponents.[44]

Yet, as the message from the top shifted, partly backed up by people's experiences of economic change, so did public expectations. Normal economic voting crystallized as a suitable criterion for determining one's posture toward the government. Public opinion data reveal this rise

---

[40] *Clarín*, May 14, 1995:3; *Clarín*, May 16, 1995:18.

[41] Of course, Menem and Cavallo did not miss the chance to underscore that the options faced by Argentines were between "choosing to go back to 1989 with opportunists and demagogues, or to follow the path of this great and prosperous Argentina" (*La Nación*, May 10, 1995:13).

[42] For additional evidence, see Echegaray (1996).

[43] Blaming the Radicals was not sufficient in 1995. Rather interestingly, survey data reveal that the economic depression of 1995 that followed the Mexican peso crisis was attributed to external agents by about 44% of respondents, whereas another 30% blamed both external and government-related factors. What stands out clearly was the government's ability to place blame on extranational forces (or share it substantially) and thus survive politically.

[44] Personal interview with Frepaso/Radical pollster Enrique Zuleta Puceiro, May 1995.

of the normal retrospective economic posture: six months after having reelected the president in a landslide, a bold majority dismissed the economic policy as wrong (in the face of low inflation but burgeoning unemployment and recession) and disapproved of the president's job performance[45] (see Figure 7.1).

Conclusion

In May 1996, Argentines approached the 150th month of democracy skeptical of the way economic policy was justified and skeptical of their president. But, unlike in earlier times, their skepticism was not accompanied by fears of looters ransacking their property or of the military extorting the civil authorities. Nor was their skepticism accompanied by second thoughts about the appropriateness of democracy. Pessimism prevailed in May 1996 once again, as in July 1989, and eyebrows were raised even more a few weeks later when Minister Cavallo was removed from office in what, under many circumstances, would have been a signal that another wave of instability was around the corner. As it turned out, the basic elements of the economic order remained untouched: prices remained stable, real wages did not budge, high unemployment endured, and GDP grew timidly once again.

Intertemporal politics, which leaders and public embraced in the 1989–1991 period, faded away slowly in the post-1994 years. But that occurred only because, earlier and for about two years, Argentines were persuaded that the "bitter pill" entailed both cost and benefit, and a majority of them chose this path, as inflation remained a latent or actual threat and the president succeeded in communicating this message rationally and emotionally with equal effectiveness. Following such a route required not only individual will but political leadership capable of proposing such a path and sustaining consistency in the face of adverse conditions. The introduction of the economic stabilization plan in April 1991 divided the waters in the way people linked economic conditions and political judgments of the government plan and the head of state. This occurred particularly once the new program proved its efficiency by taming prices and yielding steady and spectacular levels of growth that were unknown to previous generations.

[45] See also the survey conducted by Estudio Graciela Römer & Asociados in the federal capital and Greater Buenos Aires with a sample of 510 respondents.

Argentina

The Argentine experience between 1989 and 1996 teaches us that dramatic events tied to macroeconomic conditions, as well as political leadership, are critical to understanding tolerance of hardships. The embracing of intertemporal politics and the acceptance of exonerating arguments operate as rational shortcuts for reducing the individual dissonance between current conditions and future expectations, as well as for sustaining political support.

References

Acuña, Carlos. 1995. "Politics and Economics in the Argentina of the Nineties." In C. William Smith, Carlos H. Acuña, and Eduardo A. Gamarra (eds.), *Democracy, Markets, and Structural Reform in Latin America*. New Brunswick, NJ: North-South Center/Transaction.

Ambito Financiero. 1989. "Entendamos: el país entró en la era de los golpes de mercado en lugar de los antiguos golpes de estado que hacían los militares." December 15.

Anderson, Christopher. 1995. *Blaming the Government: Citizens and the Economy in Five European Democracies*. Armonk, NY: M. E. Sharpe.

Catterberg, Edgardo, and María Braun. 1989. "Las Elecciones Presidenciales Argentinas del 14 de Mayo de 1989: la Ruta a la Normalidad." *Desarrollo Económico* 115: 361–374.

Clarín. 1990. "Voy a terminar con la patria financiera, dijo Menem." January 16.

Clarín Económico. 1990. "El Ajuste del Fondo." July 15.

Echegaray, Fabián. 1996. "The Determinants of Electoral Choice in Latin America, 1982–1995." Ph.D. dissertation, University of Connecticut.

Katz, Jonathan N., and Gary King. 1999. "A Statistical Model for Multi-Party Electoral Data." *American Political Science Review* 93(1): 15–32.

Lewis-Beck, Michael. 1980. "Economic Conditions and Executive Popularity: The French Experience." *American Journal of Political Science* 24: 306–323.

Mainwaring, Scott. 1995. "Democracy in Brazil and the Southern Cone: Achievements and Problems." *Journal of Interamerican Studies and World Affairs* 1: 113–179.

Mora y Araujo, Manuel. 1991. *Ensayo y Error*. Buenos Aires: Sudamericana.

O'Donnell, Guillermo. 1989. "Argentina . . . Otra Vez." *Novos Estudos* 23: 1–14.

Palermo, Vicente, and Juan C. Torre. 1994. "A la sombra de la hiperinflación: La política de reformas estructurales en Argentina." Manuscript, Instituto Torcuate Di Tella, Buenos Aires.

Sigelman, Leo. 1990. "Answering the 1,000,000-Person Question: The Measurement and Meaning of Presidential Popularity." *Research in Micropolitics* 3: 209–225.

Smith, William C. 1991. "State, Market and Neoliberalism in Post-Transition Argentina: The Menem Experiment." *Journal of Inter-American and World Affairs* 33(4): 45–82.

Sofres-Ibope, 1989–1990. Public opinion surveys, Buenos Aires.

Stimson, James. 1976. "Public Support for American Presidents." *Public Opinion Quarterly* 40: 1–12.

Stokes, Susan. 1996. "Public Opinion and Market Reforms: The Limits of Economic Voting." *Comparative Political Studies* 29: 499–519.

Zuleta Puceiro, Enrique. 1993. "Economic Culture and Political Attitudes Under Hyperinflationary Conditions." Unpublished manuscript, University of Buenos Aires.

Author Index

Author Index

Subject Index

accountability, 2, 35
Alfonsín, Raúl, 188, 189, 193
Angeloz, Eduardo, 189
antidotal calculus of support, *see*
  exonerative calculi of support
Argentina, 10, 12n, 23, 187ff
  exonerative calculi of support in, 23,
    198, 203, 206ff
  intertemporal calculi of support in,
    14, 26, 197, 203, 206ff
  normal economic voting, 205ff

Balcerowicz, Leszek, 21
Balcerowicz Plan, 21, 106, 108, 112,
  124
blame, *see* exonerative calculi of
  support
Bolivia, 10
Born, Jorge, 191n
Borrell, José, 45n
Brazil, 112n
Bunge y Born, 191, 194

Calvo-Sotelo, Leopoldo, 40, 44,
  53
campaign messages, *see* prospective
  voting
Cavallo, Domingo, 199–200
Cavallo Plan, 199n, 200ff
Centro de Investigaciones Sociológicas
  (CIS, Spain), 48–49

Centro de Investigaciones y Docencia
  Económica (CIDE, Mexico),
  141n
Chiapas uprising (Mexico), 135, 142
Christlich Demokratische Union
  (CDU, Germany), 21, 79
Christlich Soziale Union (CSU,
  Germany), 21, 79
coalition governments
  in Germany, 21
  in Spain, 19
Collor Plan, 112n
Colosio, Luis Donaldo, 135, 142
Columbia school of electoral
  studies, 4
compositional data, 25, 91
Convertibility Plan, 200ff
Costa Rica, 10
Czechoslovakia, 14, 104

De la Madrid, Miguel, 22, 133, 139
democracy, definition, 23
Deutsche Bundesbank, 90
distributional calculi of support (*see
  also* entries for individual
  countries), 17, 18, 106

East Germany, *see* Germany
Echeverría, Luis, 152
egocentrism (in voting and public
  opinion), 5ff

Subject Index

Treuhandanstalt (THA), 82, 83, 92

uncertainty, statistical analysis of, 24–25
unemployment, and calculi of support (*see also* entries for individual countries), 27, 39
  in Argentina, 204ff
  in Germany, 84, 92–93
  in Mexico, 134, 144–146
  in Peru, 163–164, 168
  in Poland, 104, 114, 117ff
  in Spain, 44, 47, 49, 71
UNICEF, 121
Unión de Centro Democrático (UCD, Spain), 20, 38ff
Unión Cívica Radical (UCR, Argentina), 189, 190, 197, 198

United States, 9
  electoral studies of, 4–6, 145

Vargas Llosa, Mario, 161
Venezuela, 10

wages, real (*see also* entries for individual countries), 15, 26
  in Argentina, 200ff
  in Germany, 80, 82
  in Mexico, 156
  in Peru, 165ff
  in Poland, 26
  in Spain, 45, 48
Walesa, Lech, 105
Washington consensus, 12

Zedillo, Ernesto, 22, 132–133, 135, 152ff